T0321036

Environment, Inequality and Collective Action

Efficiency is the hallmark of environmental economics. Economists are concerned with the environment primarily because it challenges the efficiency of competitive markets, yet limited attention has been paid to distributional issues.

The essays in this volume identify and address the main issues in the inequality–environment relationship, issues such as: does increasing economic inequality lead to better or worse environmental quality? Which individual or social features play a role in determining the differentiated impact of changes in the environment? What impact does economic inequality or social segmentation have on collective action? How important is the complex economic and social institution in which the inequality–environment relationship takes place?

This book will prove essential to economists with an interest in the environment and will be useful to readers with a more general environmental studies background.

Marcello Basili is Associate Professor of Microeconomics and Environmental Political Economics at the University of Siena, Italy. **Maurizio Franzini** is Full Professor of Economic Policy at the University of Rome 'La Sapienza', Italy. **Alessandro Vercelli** is Full Professor of Economic Policy and Environmental Economics at the University of Siena, Italy.

Routledge Siena Studies in Political Economy

The Siena Summer School hosts lectures by distinguished scholars on topics characterized by a lively research activity. The lectures collected in this series offer a clear account of the alternative research paths that characterize a certain field. Different publishers printed former workshops of the school. They include:

Macroeconomics: A Survey of Research Strategies
Edited by Alessandro Vercelli and Nicola Dimitri
Oxford University Press, 1992

International Problems of Economics Interdependence
Edited by Massimo Di Matteo, Mario Baldassarri and Robert Mundell
Macmillan, 1994

Ethics, Rationality and Economic Behaviour
Edited by Francesco Farina, Frank Hahn and Steffano Vannucci
Clarendon Press

Available from Routledge:

The Politics of Economics and Power
Edited by Samuel Bowles, Maurizio Franzini and Ugo Pagano

The Evolution of Economic Diversity
Edited by Antonio Nicita and Ugo Pagano

Cycles, Growth and Structural Change
Edited by Lionello Punzo

General Equilibrium
Edited by Fabio Petri and Frank Hahn

Cognitive Processes and Economic Behaviour
Edited by Nicola Dimitri, Marcello Basili and Itzhak Gilboa

Environment, Inequality and Collective Action
Edited by Marcello Basili, Maurizio Franzini and Alessandro Vercelli

Environment, Inequality and Collective Action

**Edited by Marcello Basili,
Maurizio Franzini and
Alessandro Vercelli**

LONDON AND NEW YORK

First published 2006
by Routledge
2 Park Square, Milton Park, Abingdon, Oxon OX14 4RN

Simultaneously published in the USA and Canada
by Routledge
270 Madison Ave, New York, NY 10016

Routledge is an imprint of the Taylor & Francis Group

Typeset in Baskerville by
HWA Text and Data Management, Tunbridge Wells
Printed and bound in Great Britain by
Antony Rowe Ltd, Chippenham, Wiltshire

British Library Cataloguing in Publication Data
A catalogue record for this book is available from the British Library

Library of Congress Cataloging in Publication Data
A catalog record for this book has been requested

ISBN10: 0–415–34234–1
ISBN13: 9–78–0–415–34234–6

Contents

Figures

Tables

Contributors

Jean-Marie Baland is Professor of Economics at the Faculty of Economics, Facultés Universitaires Notre-Dame de la Paix, Namur.

Stefano Bartolini has taken up the Chair of Comparative Politics at the University of Bologna, Italy, and was part-time Professor for the period October–December 2004 in the Department of Political and Social Sciences of the European University Institute.

Marcello Basili is Professor of Microeconomics and Environmental Political Economics at the University of Siena, Italy.

Simone Borghesi is Assistant Professor in the Department of Quantitative Methods and Economic Theory at the University of Pescara, Italy, where he teaches development economics.

Daniel W. Bromley is Anderson-Bascom Professor of Applied Economics at the University of Wisconsin-Madison, USA.

Juan-Camilo Cardenas is Professor at the Faculty of Economics – CEDE, the University of Los Andes, Colombia.

Graciela Chichilnisky holds the UNESCO Chair of Mathematics and Economics and is a Professor of Statistics at Columbia University, New York. She is Director of Columbia's Center for Risk Management (CCRM) and created Columbia's Program on Information and Resources (PIR).

Sylvie Faucheux is Professor of Economics and Director of C3ED: Center of Economics and Ethics for Environment and Development at the Institute for Development, the University of Versailles Saint-Quentin-en-Yvelines.

Maurizio Franzini is Professor of Economic Policy at the University of Rome 'La Sapienza', Italy, and is the Director of Criss, a Network on the Economics of the Welfare State.

Anil Markandya is Professor of Economics at the Department of Economics and International Development, the University of Bath, UK.

Martin O'Connor is Professor of Economics at the Université de Versailles St-Quentin-en-Yvelines in France and the Scientific Director of the IACA (Incertitudes, Analyse, Concertations) research unit at the Centre d'Economie et d'Ethique pour l'Environnement et le Développement (C3ED).

Charles Perrings is Professor of Environmental Economics at Arizona State University, and President of the International Society for Ecological Economics.

E. Somanathan is Associate Professor at the Planning Unit, the Indian Statistical Institute, Delhi, New Delhi.

Alessandro Vercelli is Professor of Economic Policy and Environmental Economics at the University of Siena, Italy.

Abbreviations

BSP	Blue Sky Program
CBA	cost–benefit analysis
CBD	Convention on Biological Diversity
CDIAC	Carbon Dioxide Information Analysis Center
CFC	chlorofluorocarbon
CO_2	carbon dioxide
CPR	Common Property Resource
DENS	population density
E-capacities	Ellsberg capacities
EKC	environmental Kuznets curve
FAO	Food and Agriculture Organization of the United States
FE	fixed-effect
GASP	growth as substitution process
GATT	General Agreement on Tariffs and Trade
GDP	gross domestic product
GEF	global environmental facility
GEO	global environmental organization
GMO	genetically modified organism
IMF	International Monetary Fund
IND	industry value added as share of GDP
IPCC	Intergovernmental Panel on Climate Change
IUCN	The World Conservation Union
LSDV	least-squares dummy variable
MPCR	marginal per capita ratio between the public good and the private alternative
MPE	marginal propensity to emit
NAFTA	North American Free Trade Agreement
NATO	North Atlantic Treaty Organization
OECD	Organization for Economic Co-operation and Development
OLS	ordinary least squares
ORNL	US Oak Ridge National Laboratory
PM_{10}	particulate matter (less than 10 microns in diameter)
PP	precaution principle

PPP	purchasing power parity
QOV	quasi-option value
R & D	research and development
RE	random effect
SEC	Securities Exchange Commission
SO$_2$	sulphur dioxide
SSE	small-scale enterprise
UNCTAD	United Nations Conference on Trade and Development
UNDP	United Nations Development Programme
UNEP	United Nations Environment Programme
UNESCO	United Nations Educational, Scientific and Cultural Organization
VOC	volatile organic compound
WCED	World Commission on Environment and Development
WEO	World Environmental Organization
WIPO	World Intellectual Property Organization
WTO	World Trade Organization

Introduction

Marcello Basili, Maurizio Franzini and
Alessandro Vercelli

Efficiency has been the hallmark of environmental economics. Indeed, a large number of economists became concerned with the environment only when they realized that it led competitive markets to allocate goods and services in ways that were not consistent with Pareto optimality. On the other hand, the search for the most cost-effective forms of state interventions to correct such failures was itself largely conditioned by the efficiency requirement, in order to make the costs of the required corrections as low as possible. Efficiency is unquestionably of utmost importance. However, the very limited attention paid to distributional issues is not to be reckoned in positive terms. One of its implications is that not much progress has been made in the attempt to connect social and environmental sustainability as advocated as early as 1987 by the well-known Bruntland's report. This is not to say that distributional issues have been totally ignored by environmental economists. But contributions to this field of studies have, until recently, been few and rather limited in scope.

The problem of how a change in environmental quality affects the well-being of rich and poor people has been one of the most frequently addressed. In their classical and deservedly well-known book, Baumol and Oates (1988) dealt with this problem in a framework where environmental changes are seen essentially as a pure public good and therefore the decisive element is the income elasticity of the willingness to pay for the environment – i.e. whether environment is a luxury good. Other authors made important contributions to this issue, in particular Pearce (1980) and Chichilnisky and Heal (1994). But the problem of the distributional effects of changes in environmental quality is still unsettled (OECD 2004).

This is so partly because it is not entirely satisfactory to view environmental changes as a pure public good to which everybody may have the same access. Under such a hypothesis there are no distributional differences in the physical enjoyment of the good and problems arise only because preferences or willingness to pay may differ across individuals or social groups. In fact, most environmental changes are not pure public goods and, therefore, may have a widely differentiated 'physical' impact on individuals, which depends not only on income but also on other discriminatory attributes (geographical location, age, ethnicity and so on).

The problem of the distributional impact of environmental policies has also engendered much debate. One of the first studies to address this problem was published by the Organization for Economic Co-operation and Development (OECD) (1994). But several other studies (in particular on the distributional impact of taxation, tradable permits programmes and also on the provision of some environmental services) have ensued (OECD 2003). In this case the crucial question was to establish whether those policies were regressive, that is whether the costs of employing economic instruments were borne more by poor or rich people. Account was taken of both direct and indirect costs, the latter consisting in any increase in output and other prices caused by the environmental policy adopted. Also with respect to this problem, no shared consensus has been reached (OECD 2004), even though we know better which are the crucial issues to be clarified at both the empirical and theoretical level.

The questions of how people in different income brackets are affected by environmental quality changes and how the costs of environmental policies are distributed are important. They deserve continuing efforts, perhaps in a broader setting than the one that has been dominant so far. In particular, the recurrent assumption that environment is a pure public good should be abandoned in favour of alternative, more realistic, hypotheses. There are, however, many other important aspects and dimensions of the relationship between the environment on the one hand and inequality and disparities on the other which may span in both directions. Recently some work has been done in this vein (Boyce 2002).

One very important question, especially in the perspective of linking social and environmental sustainability, is whether increasing economic inequality leads to better or worse environmental quality. Another important issue is to understand which individual or social features, besides income and other economic variables, play a role in determining the differentiated impact of changes in the environment.

Given the indispensable role of collective action in environmental matters – at a global level but most importantly at local level – one very interesting issue is whether, *ceteris paribus*, economic inequality or more generally social segmentation makes collective action easier or more difficult.

Finally, the relationship between inequality and the environment cannot be fully understood independently of the complex set of economic and social institutions in which such interaction takes place.

These four broad issues correspond to the four parts into which this volume is divided, each of them consisting of three essays. This is not to say, however, that the content of each essay refers strictly to the issue signalled by the title of the part it belongs to.

How does economic inequality impact on the quality of the environment? This is a very complex question that admits no simple answer, also because very different indices can be used to measure both the environmental quality and economic inequality.

An important element in this respect is the environmental impact of the typical consumption habits of rich people vis-à-vis those of poor people. For example, if income is redistributed from the rich to the poor, the resulting change depends on the impact on the environment of the consumption foregone by the rich with respect to the increased consumption of the poor. Not much is known on the environment-degrading implications of the two patterns of consumption.

In the chapter included in the first part of this volume, Alessandro Vercelli looks at the empirical evidence worldwide in the post-World War II period to see how inequality developed between and within OECD countries in the time-frame observed, on the one hand, and how this relates to most indices of environmental deterioration, on the other. From his analysis he draws conclusions also on the sustainability of the globalization process which characterised the Washington consensus period.

In his chapter, Simone Borghesi analyses the link between environmental degradation, economic growth and income inequality within the framework of the environmental Kuznets curve literature. In particular he sets out to understand how inequality relates to carbon dioxide emissions and to the link between the latter and economic growth. He shows that the results depend heavily on the specification that one chooses and argues that, in this context, the fixed-effect model is more appropriate than the pooled ordinary least square model that has been used in the literature on this subject.

Environmental degradation, income inequality and economic growth can be linked through many different routes. One of them is explored by Stefano Bartolini, who starts from the assumption that the growth process generates extensive negative externalities which reduce the capacity of the social and natural environment to supply free goods. Therefore individuals, in keeping with their income, have to rely increasingly on private goods to counter the negative effects of a decline in social and natural capital on their well-being or their productive capacity. This generates an increase in output which feeds back into the negative externalities, giving rise to a self-reinforcing mechanism whereby growth generates negative externalities and negative externalities generate growth.

As already noted, it is of utmost importance to understand which features are at work in determining a differentiated impact of changes in the environment both at the individual and social level. The role that power and wealth play in determining the distribution of environmental costs has been demonstrated in an empirical analysis by Boyce (2003). In particular, wealth and power support lobbying activities that may have a great effect in this respect. Moreover, rich people may protect themselves, also individually, in effective and welfare-enhancing ways against some forms of environmental degradation.

But attention should not be focused on economic inequality only. It is important to understand which other attributes make for disparities in the enjoyment of the environment.

In the second part of the volume, Sylvie Faucheux and Martin O'Connor go into this problem by making use of the very general notion of ecological distribution, which refers to the different access that people have to the benefits warranted by natural resources and the environment and to their differential exposure to the danger and harms from degraded environmental conditions. Disparities may be due to several circumstances (spatial ecological distribution) and one may wonder whether monetary compensation of any kind could be the right solution for this kind of inequality.

In relation to inequalities due to income and to poverty, Anil Markandya looks at the double direction nexus between poverty and the environment. He argues that there is no clear evidence, or a convincing theoretical basis, that poor people are more damaging to the environment than rich people, as the environmental Kuznets curve would have it. On the contrary, he maintains that poor people suffer more from environmental degradation. This is at variance with the more conventional view, stemming from the Baumol-Oates approach. Indeed, the settings of the two approaches are very different.

E. Somanathan draws a comprehensive picture of the factors that may explain a differential response to environmental degradation. In particular, he argues that when an environmental problem is not mitigated, this is because the affected persons do not know it is happening, cannot locate the cause or do not have the resources to abate it, if they are the originators of the problem, or do not have the political power to influence policy to stop it, if they are not the originators. He draws from his analysis interesting implications for the existence (more precisely, non-existence) of the 'Environmental Kuznets Curve'.

The third part of the volume refers to collective action, which is all too important in coming to grips with environmental problems. A weak propensity to give course to collective action may be a factor making for a more serious exposure to environmental deterioration. The elements that may induce people to cooperate are numerous and extremely diversified. One issue long debated since Olson's seminal work (Olson 1965) has been whether inequality is an obstacle or, on the contrary, a facilitating factor in the development of collective action. Olson himself argued in favour of a positive effect of inequality on collective action essentially because the prospect of appropriating a larger share of benefits may prompt people to cooperate more. Other scholars have disputed this view (Sandler 1992).

Jean-Marie Baland presents an overview of the literature dealing with the impact of inequality on 'collective action' and takes issue with Olson's approach to the problem. He argues that there are many more relevant variables than he considered. On this basis Baland finds that the Olsonian conclusion does not hold under several conditions. In particular, it fails when production technology is not convex, or when contributions are not perfect substitutes.

Juan-Camilo Cardenas provides an overview of his experimental work with rural communities in Colombia. Behavioural experiments like this are typically performed in university laboratories, not in the field. Cardenas designs an experiment concerning the exploitation of a common resource which is set in the real life of the people involved. The results point to a negative impact of inequality on collective action – wealth distance among members of the experimental groups studied inhibits cooperation. From his experiment it comes out that not poverty or wealth but social homogeneity is the relevant variable.

Collective action is important also with respect to biodiversity. As Charles Perrings points out, biodiversity can be seen as a public good, and as such open to the risk of free riding. However the fact that biodiversity conservation is both a local (the capacity of the local system to deliver a particular ecological service) and a global (the global gene pool) phenomenon makes the problem much more complicated. The question is whether a more decentralized solution than the creation of large protected areas would not be a better response to the problems posed today by biodiversity to local communities. The answer depends to a large extent on the easiness of collective action at the local level.

The last part of the volume presents three chapters that deal with important institutional problems, which arise in connection with disparities and the environment.

Institutions are a broad concept; they include formalized norms, conventions, working rules and property relations. Usually a distinction is drawn between state property, private property and common property. A large body of literature has argued that only private property fosters efficiency (Alchian and Demsetz 1973, Demsetz 1967, and Furubotn and Pejovich 1972). This should concern us because most natural resources, both at the national and international level, are common property. Indeed, many other variables may play a role, particularly the country's development stage. The conclusion that private property is necessary for efficiency has been challenged by several authors and the more specific point that efficient institutions, including the appropriate property regime, may be the result of an evolutionary process has gained wide audience.

Daniel Bromley gives a contribution to this critical approach. He believes that a high investment level may be the result of the property regime but also the reverse may hold – the property regime is affected by the investments made. Causality may run in the opposite direction, weakening the presumption that private property is always a necessary institutional pre-condition for efficiency. Bromley also states that economists need a new way of thinking about alternative property regimes – especially what we like to call 'the commons'. In this respect he argues in favour of a shift towards an evolutionary model of institutional change, which he would frame in the logic of 'volitional pragmatism'.

Graciela Chichilnisky holds that poverty has the remarkable implication, among many others, of making it difficult to establish private property rights on environmental resources. The persistence of common property has deep consequences on the efficiency features of commercial trade between the rich North – where private property prevails also with respect to these resources – and the poor South, largely characterized by common property. One relevant implication of this approach is that to relieve poverty is also to promote efficiency, by making the establishing of private property much easier.

In the last chapter of the volume, Marcello Basili and Maurizio Franzini analyse the Precautionary Principle from an institutional point of view. They start by asking how to make it consistent with rational behaviour in the face of radical uncertainty or ignorance. In their interpretation particular emphasis is put on ambiguity aversion. Then they argue that the implementation of the principle involves deep agency problems mainly because the benefits of precaution are very unevenly distributed. With the aim of understanding some of the problems involved, they present a Principal–Agent model, where the Principal but not the Agent abides by the Precautionary Principle.

References

Alchian, A.A. and Demsetz, H. (1973) 'The property rights paradigm', *Journal of Economic History*, 13: 16–27.

Baumol, W. and Oates, W. (1988) *The Theory of Environmental Policy*, Cambridge: Cambridge University Press.

Boyce, J.K. (2002), *The Political Economy of the Environment*, Northampton: Edward Elgar.

Boyce, J.K. (2003) *Inequality and Environmental Protection*, PERI Working Paper No. 52, Amherst, MA: University of Massachusetts.

Chichilnisky, G. and Heal G. (1994) 'Who should abate carbon emissions? An international viewpoint', *Economic Letters*, 44: 443–9.

Demsetz, H. (1967) 'Towards a theory of property rights', *The American Economic Review*, 57: 347–59.

Furubotn, E. and Pejovich, S. (1972) 'Property rights and economic theories: a survey of recent literature', *Journal of Economic Literature*, 10: 1137–62.

OECD (1994) *The Distributive Effects of Economic Instruments for Environmental Policy*, Paris: OECD.

OECD (2003) *Social Issues in the Provision and Pricing of Water Services*. Paris: OECD.

OECD (2004) *Environment and Distributional Issues: Analysis, Evidence and Policy Implications*, Paris: OECD.

Olson, M. (1965) *The Logic of Collective Action*, Cambridge, MA: Harvard University Press.

Pearce, D.W. (1980) 'The social incidence of environmental costs and benefits', *Progress in Resource Management and Environmental Planning*, 2: 63–87.

Sandler, T. (1992) *Collective Action: Theory and Applications*, Ann Arbor, MI: University of Michigan Press.

Part I

Inequality, growth and the environment

1 Globalization and sustainable development[1]

Alessandro Vercelli

Introduction

The debate on the economic and social implications of globalization has attracted increasing attention from public opinion and the mass media. Scientific research has managed to clarify a few specific questions raised in this debate but the light shed on global issues and their policy implications is still too faint. This is disappointing but not surprising, as global issues are awfully complex. In order to delve into them we need the convergent effort of different specializations belonging to different disciplines (as diverse as economics, sociology, law, and so on). Unfortunately the success of modern science is based on a growing division of intellectual labour that makes it increasingly difficult to coordinate the knowledge and empirical evidence necessary to tackle global issues. However science cannot seclude itself in ivory towers and abdicate from its social responsibilities ignoring issues that are vital for the future of mankind. Therefore science must struggle to overcome its existing limitations in order to clarify them and their policy implications.

According to this spirit, in this chapter we wish to pose the question of whether the globalization process as observed after World War II can be considered sustainable, that is, compatible with the requirements of sustainable development. The contribution that we are able to offer is just a conceptual framework that aims to synthesize some of the results obtained by scientific research in different fields of economics, whilst drawing on a few valuable insights from other disciplines, in order to clarify the main issues and stimulate further research.

To this end we have first to define the two keywords of our analysis – globalization and sustainable development. By globalization we simply mean the progressive integration of world markets induced by the liberalization of international trade in goods, services and productive factors.[2] Although the process has had a long gestation period,[3] we can give it a fairly accurate birth date – the third decade of the nineteenth century, when the prices of goods traded on national markets began to converge towards a single price due to the influence of international trading (see O'Rourke and Williamson 2000, and Lindert and Williamson 2001). In fact, given that a fundamental characteristic of a competitive market is a single price for a traded good, it is impossible to speak of a truly unified international market without a consolidated tendency of local prices to converge towards this single price. It was then that the liberalist economic theories of Adam Smith and the other classical economists of the end of the eighteenth century began to shape the markets through systematic policies of lower protective tariffs in the UK, and then in the other principal industrialized countries. Free trade progressed until World War I, after which a phase of protectionism lasting three decades set in.

Globalization did not bounce back until after World War II but from then on it has continued uninterruptedly up to the present time. The following analysis will focus on the most recent phase, which can be divided into two periods. The first can be called the 'Bretton Woods period', lasting from the end of World War II to the end of the 1960s. In that period international markets were regulated by the organizations set up during the peace conference of the same name, which also established their underlying behavioural rules. After the collapse of the Bretton Woods monetary system in 1971,[4] a new international economic order emerged, based on floating exchange rates, radical policy changes at the International Monetary Fund (IMF) and World Bank and a new organization instituted in 1995 with the task of systematically liberalizing international commerce – the World Trade Organization (WTO).[5]

After defining and giving a time-frame to the globalization process, we now have to introduce and discuss the concept of sustainable development.[6] We will adopt, as is customary, the now-famous definition introduced in 1987 by the so-called Brundtland Report, 'Development is sustainable if it satisfies present-day needs without compromising the capacity of future generations to satisfy their needs' (WCED 1987: 43). This definition gained instant popularity and soon became a crucial reference in the debate on the limits to economic growth and development. Attention was first focused on the environmental equilibrium of the biosphere, ignoring almost completely the social aspects whose crucial importance, however, have recently become increasingly recognized. In fact the rationale underlying sustainable development 'implies a commitment to social equity between generations which for consistency's sake must be extended to equity within each generation' (*ibidem*).

The *inter*-generational condition of sustainability is meant to guarantee that the freedom of choice of future generations is not compromised by myopic decisions of the preceding generations.[7] Henceforth we call this criterion of sustainability *environmental*, given that the real freedom of future generations will depend to a large degree on the state of the natural environment they inherit. In practical terms, this means that the indices of environmental deterioration should not worsen any further with time, as this would jeopardise the ecological equilibrium of the biosphere. Of course this minimal requirement of environmental sustainability is not sufficient if the current state of the biosphere lies beyond the threshold of ecological stability.

The *intra*-generational condition of sustainability is meant to guarantee equal opportunities to all participants in market competition. This prerequisite is met only when there is sufficient initial equality of opportunities among competitors, i.e. equal access to all significant economic options.[8] Henceforth we call this criterion of sustainability *social*, given that it depends to a large degree on indices such as the magnitude of income inequality and the incidence of poverty. The criterion of social sustainability should be evaluated in relation not only to economic indices but also other indices measuring the actual degree of individual freedom of choice. A significant example is poverty, which reduces access to economic opportunities. An extreme consequence of poverty, apart from the dire possibilities of death and diseases, is malnutrition that seriously reduces the psychophysical efficiency of the victim whose access to economic opportunities is therefore severely limited (there are still about 800 million people in the world suffering from under-nourishment; see, e.g., Lomborg 2001: 61). In practical terms, this means that these indices of social sustainability must not worsen any further with time. Of course, also in this case, the minimal requirement of social sustainability is not enough if the current indices lie beyond the threshold of social stability.

The two prerequisites of sustainable development that we have just defined are founded on principles of equity, freedom and equal opportunities, which are not necessarily in contrast with the more prosaic, yet vital, economic objectives. On the contrary, it may be argued that equal access to economic opportunities is a fundamental condition of efficiency. It is the only way reasonably to guarantee that the 'winners' of the continually renewed 'economic competition' taking place in the market are actually the best participants, those capable of adding the maximum value to society.[9] Thus there is no basic conflict between ethics and economics as far as long-term sustainable development is concerned. This conflict emerges when the time-period for economic decisions becomes confined to the short term, jeopardizing the long-term requirements of sustainable development (see 'Outlines of a causal analysis' below).

We intend now to evaluate the sustainability of post-war globalization by analysing the empirical correlations between globalization and each of the two prerequisites of sustainability.

Inequality, poverty and globalization

The empirical evidence examined by economic historians shows a precise long-term correlation between the process of globalization and inequality both between countries and within each country (see Figure 1.1).

Starting in the third decade of the nineteenth century, income inequality between countries showed a tendency to grow as the process of globalization spread and took root.[10] The same is true, albeit to a lesser degree, of income inequality within countries. The most relevant exception is the prolonged period of de-globalization which took place between the two world wars that was a period of marked de-globalization because of a widespread resurgence of protectionist, if not autarkic as in fascist Italy, policies in Europe and elsewhere.

The basic explanation is straightforward. The process of globalization tends to increase the growth rate of countries participating in it actively (see e.g. Dollar and Kraay 2001, Frankel and Romer 1999, and Table 1.1).

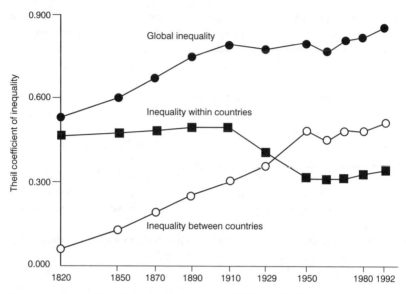

Figure 1.1   Inequality of individual incomes: 1820–1992 (Source: Bourguignon and Morrison, 1999)

Table 1.1 Orientation towards international exchanges and growth of income, 1963–1992

Orientation towards international trade	*Average rates of growth of per capita GDP in developing countries*		
	1963–1973	*1973–1985*	*1980–1992*
Strongly open	6.9	5.9	6.4
Moderately open	4.9	1.6	2.3
Moderately protectionist	4.0	1.7	−0.2
Strongly protectionist	1.6	−0.1	−0.4

Since demographic growth changes more slowly and mainly because of exogenous reasons, the growth rate of per capita incomes increases (as in the UK and in the USA: see Figure 1.2).

This tends to augment inequality because the diffusion of increases in sectoral and personal incomes is uneven and takes time.[11]

However, in the Bretton Woods period, following the systematic adoption of social security measures inspired by the principles of the welfare state, the net effect on disposable income in many countries was a moderate reduction in inequality.[12] Vice versa, inequality began to grow again since the early 1980s in most OECD countries (see Table 1.2), including the UK (see Figure 1.3) and the USA (see Figure 1.4) (see Burniaux *et al.* 1999, Brandolini 2002, Forster and Pellizzari 2000, and Forster and Pearson 2002). This was partly due to a great

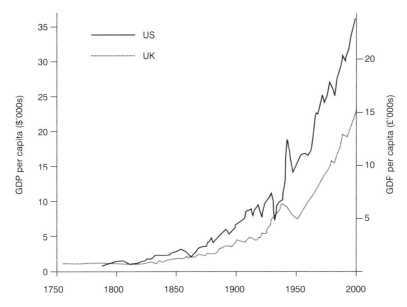

Figure 1.2 Evolution of per-capita income (Source: Lomborg, 2001)

Table 1.2 Variations in income inequality

	1975–1985	*1985–1995*
Austria	0	+
Belgium		+
Canada	+	0
Czech	– –	+
Denmark		+
Finland	–	+
France	–	+
Germany	–	+
Greece	–	
Hungary	+	+
Ireland	–	
Italy	– –	+
Japan	0	+
Korea	+	+
Netherlands	0	+
New Zealand		+
Norway	–	+
Poland	0	+
Sweden	–	+
Switzerland		+

Notes
+ moderate increase 2–7%; 0 no variation –2–+2 %; – moderate
reduction 2–7%; – – reduction 7–15%.

Source: OECD

Figure 1.3 Inequality in the UK, 1939–1996 (Source: Brandolini, 2002)

increase in higher-level incomes (see Table 1.3) and the fact that redistribution policies have not succeeded in completely compensating for the trend of growing inequality (see Figure 1.5).

The implications of globalization for the sustainability of development can be assessed more precisely on the basis of a research stream that has examined the available empirical evidence through rigorous econometric analyses. It began with the publication in 1955 by Kuznets of an article suggesting the existence of an inverted U, that is first rising and then falling, empirical relationship between per capita income and inequality (see Figure 1.6). If this relationship, which has been called 'Kuznets curve', were generally valid, the process of globalization would eventually become sustainable from a social point of view, at least in the long term (see, e.g., Lomborg 2001).

Kuznets recognized that his hypothesis, while compatible with the data examined, had yet to be fully confirmed and expressed the desire that it be corroborated by further research.[13] The theoretical plausibility of the Kuznets hypothesis is based on the structural characteristics of development. The process of economic development typically entails a progressive concentration of population in urban centres where the distribution of income and economic opportunities is generally less equal than in rural areas. The process of territorial and sectoral penetration of development requires time and thus creates temporary income gaps even when there is a prospect of a homogeneous result. Nonetheless,

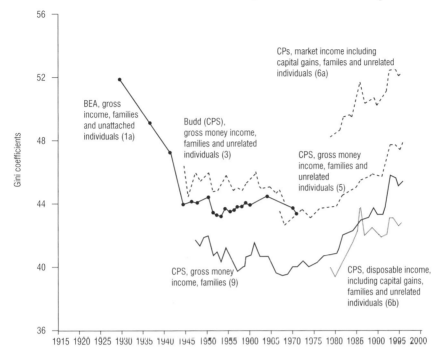

Figure 1.4 Inequality in the USA, 1929–1996 (Source: Brandolini, 2002)

the development process creates a 'growing pressure of political and legal decisions affecting higher-level incomes' (Kuznets 1955: 9) which manifests itself in increasingly effective re-distribution measures such as a progressive income tax.

Later studies seemed to initially confirm the Kuznets hypothesis (see Ahluwalia 1976, and Robinson 1976), but empirical support for it has steadily weakened since the 1980s. This evolution can easily be explained in the light of the data examined above, keeping in mind the existence of a temporal delay of a few years between a new empirical trend and the availability of data documenting it.[14] The hypothesis proposed by Kuznets and the first studies corroborating it found support in the attenuation of inequality occurring between the two world wars and continuing in different forms during the Bretton Woods period. However, since the 1980s econometric studies have progressively weakened empirical support for the original hypothesis as new data have increasingly reflected the widespread rise in inequality mentioned above.

Some people object that in order to evaluate the social effects of globalization we should concentrate on poverty, which has progressively diminished in recent years, rather than inequality.[15] It is doubtful, however, whether poverty has actually diminished – the answer depends on the precise definition of the period, the measure adopted and the geographical area under consideration (see Figure 1.7). In any case, there are still 1.2 billion people in the world who earn less than one dollar a day and almost 3 billion people who live on less than two dollars a day,

Table 1.3 Income shares (quintiles: 1985–1995)

	Lowest	*Average*	*Highest*
Austria	=	=	=
Belgium	=	– – –	+++
Canada	=	=	=
Denmark	+	=	–
Finland	=	– – –	+++
France	=	–	+
Germany	–	=	+
Greece	=	=	=
Hungary	+	=	=
Ireland	+	=	=
Italy	– – –	–	+++
Japan	–	=	+
Mexico	=	– – –	+++
Netherlands	–	=	+
Norway	–	–	+++
Sweden	–	=	+
Turkey	–	– – –	+++
UK	–	–	+
USA	=	–	+

Notes
+++ increase > 1.5%; + increase between 0.5 E 1.5%; = change between –0.5 E +0.5%;
– reduction between 0.5 E 1.5%; – – – reduction > 1.5%

Source: OECD

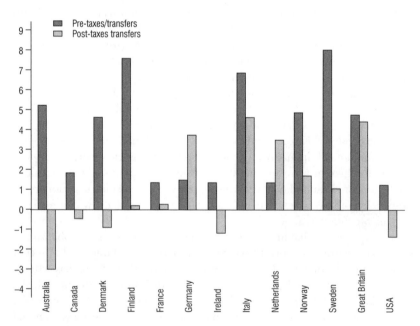

Figure 1.5 Rates of change of poverty (1985–1995) (Source: OECD)

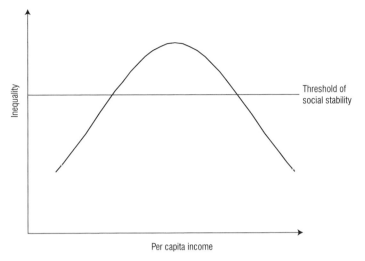

Figure 1.6 Kuznets curve

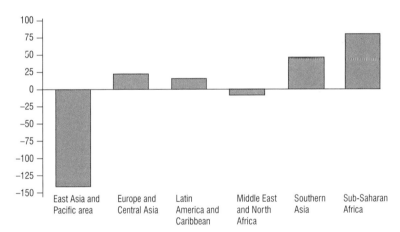

Figure 1.7 Poverty in the world (variations 1987 1998)

thereby compromising what we could call the 'social stability' of the process of globalization. However some authors claim that the percentage of poor people has decreased in the Third World from 28 per cent in 1987 to 24 per cent in 1998 and that these data would be compatible with sustainable development (see, e.g., Lomborg 2001: 72). This assertion seems to ignore the existence of a threshold of social stability below which the social fabric tends to disintegrate and the 'social contract' binding citizens to their institutions tends to deteriorate.

Social stability depends not only on the percentage but also on the absolute number of the poor. We note, moreover, that poverty is not only unacceptable from an ethical but also from an economic standpoint as it causes an enormous waste of potential resources which tends to worsen as the social protection net falters. In the last 20 years there has been a widespread weakening of the social protection net due to the dismantling of the welfare state, the privatization of education and health services and the systematic search for more flexibility in the labour market which has reduced the access of the less affluent classes to many fundamental economic opportunities. Different empirical studies have confirmed that high levels of poverty and inequality have negative effects on economic growth (see Alesina and Perotti 1996, and Benhabib and Rustichini 1996). We can therefore conclude this first part of the analysis by noting that the trends of the globalization process in the last two decades cannot be considered fully compatible with the social condition of sustainable development.

Environmental deterioration and globalization

We may now raise the question whether in the post-war period the trends of globalization were compatible with the environmental condition of sustainability. The question is difficult to answer as we do not have sufficiently long and comprehensive historical series on global environmental quality to make reliable statistical correlations.[16]

We must settle for an analysis of statistical correlations between per capita income and some specific indices of environmental deterioration for which we have adequate historical series. At the beginning of the 1990s some researchers observed that the curves corresponding to these correlations typically go up and then down (see Figure 1.8) exactly like the Kuznets curve (one of the first authors to notice this alleged empirical trend was Panayotou 1993).

Two main explanations for this behaviour have been put forward. It has been observed that in the first phase of industrial development the production structure undergoes radical changes, gradually reducing the percentage of the domestic product produced by agriculture and increasing that of heavy industry (steel, chemicals, etc.), which is much more polluting. There is a subsequent shift of production and labour to light industry and services which are less polluting and consume less energy, improving the aggregate indices of environmental stress. Furthermore, while in the first phase of industrial development environmental quality is seen as a luxury, in the second and even more so in the post-industrial phase environmental quality is considered crucial in improving the overall quality of life. The final users of goods and services exert growing pressure on their suppliers to enhance the environmental quality of productive processes and goods. Voters simultaneously exert growing pressure on their political representatives to reinforce environmental policies. Due to the changes in the productive structure and preferences of economic agents, it seems reasonable to assume that a per-capita income threshold exists above which the indices of environmental deterioration tend to decrease. If this hypothesis were verified the forthcoming message would be optimistic: the process of globalization, which as we have seen accelerates per capita income growth, eventually tends to reduce environmental deterioration, at least in the long term.

Further econometric research done along the lines of what has been called the 'Kuznets environmental curve' initially supported the hypothesis that most

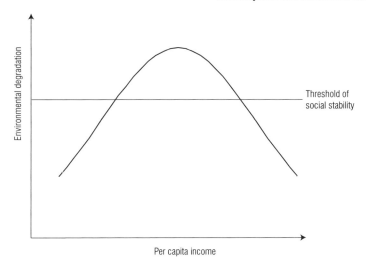

Figure 1.8 Environmental Kuznets curve

significant indices of environmental deterioration were characterized by a behaviour of this type (see Shafik 1994), while later research raised serious doubts about its validity (see Grossman 1995, and Cole *et al.* 1997). The hypothesis was only corroborated for some indices regarding problems whose effects are local, such as access to sewerage and drinking water, or the concentration in the atmosphere of sulphur dioxide (SO_2) (see Figure 1.9) or suspended particles (see Figure 1.10), but not for indices of environmental problems whose effects are global or could be transferred elsewhere, such as solid urban waste treatment or carbon dioxide emissions.

Even in cases where the data were compatible with the virtuous inversion of the Kuznets environmental curve, it is not clear whether in developing countries the hoped-for turning point will come before the threshold of ecological stability is crossed.[17] We must therefore conclude that the empirical evidence available does not corroborate the hypothesis that the recent globalization process has brought about a general improvement in the environmental sustainability of development. Furthermore, some indices show a particularly worrisome N-shaped curve – after an improvement in the 1980s and early 1990s, the trend has recently switched again towards deterioration (this is the case, e.g., of coliform bacteria; see Figure 1.11).[18]

While lacking sufficiently long and reliable historical series regarding global environmental deterioration, we can concentrate on some logical prerequisites of sustainable development, based on analytical considerations, which can direct economic and environmental policies towards reinforcing sustainable development. In particular, it may be demonstrated that the maximum sustainable growth rate of per capita income can be positive only if the intensity of environmental deterioration decreases at a rate higher than the population growth rate.[19] We can essentially count on two factors to respect this crucial condition of sustainable

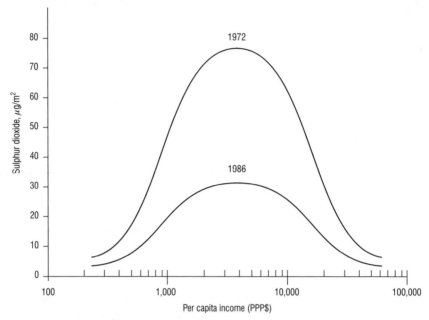

Figure 1.9   Environmental Kuznets curve (sulphur dioxide) (Source: World Bank, 1992; Shafik, 1994)

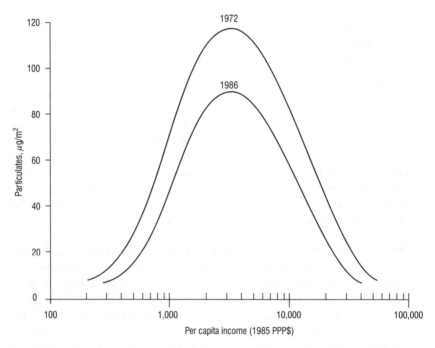

Figure 1.10   Environmental Kuznets curve (particulates) (Source: World Bank, 1992; Shafik 1994)

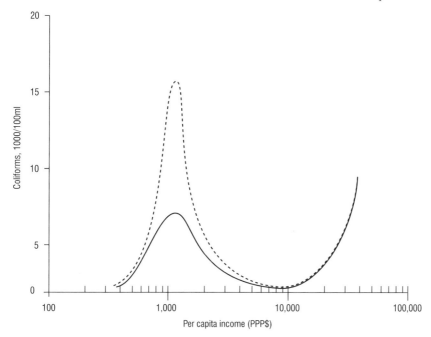

Figure 1.11 Environmental Kuznets curve (coliform bacteria) (Source: Shafik, 1994)

economic growth: (i) that technological progress be orientated towards a growing environmental compatibility of products and productive processes; (ii) that consumer preferences privilege products and services linked to better environmental quality.

These two processes have been at work for some time, but they are by nature rather slow to the point that they rarely manage to compensate for the effects of demographic growth. It is therefore necessary to speed them up with suitable environmental policy measures. This is particularly true for developing countries with higher demographic growth rates and fewer possibilities of reducing environmental deterioration.[20]

Summing up, the process of globalization has had an ambiguous influence on the environmental prerequisite of sustainability. From a technological point of view it favoured the transfer to developing countries of 'clean' technologies created by more advanced countries but also of toxic and radioactive waste and more polluting obsolete technologies rejected in developed countries. Regarding the cultural impact on preferences and behaviour of developing countries, the process of globalization has led to a deceleration of demographic growth and heightened environmental awareness, but has also fuelled consumerism with its attendant woes of pollution and waste of natural resources.

Outlines of a causal analysis

The analysis provided so far has tried to reconstruct the evolution of empirical correlations between globalization and sustainable development in the post-war period. With respect to the social condition of sustainability, the Bretton Woods phase managed to come close to sustainability as a result of the narrowing of the inequality gap between countries and within them.[21] The phase which has taken over in the last two decades (i.e. in the so-called Washington Consensus period) has instead distanced itself again from sustainability to the extent that the previous trend has been reversed.

As for the environmental condition of sustainability, neither of the two periods has completely passed the test of sustainability. The systematic adoption since the 1970s of increasingly rigorous environmental policies has led to the improvement of some significant environmental indices. We have seen, however, that not all of them have improved. Furthermore, most recent data show a worrying slowdown, and in some cases an inversion, of the trend towards better environmental quality.

As is well known, the existence of a statistical correlation between two variables does not necessarily imply a causal relationship between them (on the prerequisites of economic causality, see, e.g., Vercelli 1991, 1992 and 2001a). Thus we need analysis in greater depth to ground the causal inferences on consolidated theoretical foundations and to identify precise effect-generating mechanisms. What follows is a tentative first step in this direction.

The most convincing argument supporting globalization is based on the fundamental theorems of welfare economics which demonstrate how, with an initial distribution of resources and under rigid (indeed not very realistic) conditions,[22] a perfectly competitive market determines an optimal allocation of resources corresponding to maximum social welfare (see, e.g., Varian 2002). We could assert that the *raison d'être* of globalization is to unify local markets into a single competitive market in order to allocate world resources in such a way as to maximize the well-being of the global community. If this is the goal, however, the process of post-war globalization has shown some basic failures. The application of this argument to global markets requires free movement across countries of goods and services as well as productive factors. Looking at the recent globalization process from this point of view, we can identify some significant anomalies.

First of all, regarding goods and services, developed countries have continued to maintain heavy protectionist measures in sectors such as agriculture and textiles in which developing countries have more exporting potential. A United Nations report published in 1994 stated that 'industrialized countries, violating the principles of free trade, dump costs estimated at US$ 50 billion a year on developing countries – a figure almost equal to the overall flow of foreign aid' (quoted in Chomsky 1999: 140). In addition, developed countries often react to spontaneous increases in imports from developing countries with new tariffs by calling on, often surreptitiously, anti-dumping laws (see Stiglitz 2002).

Second, as far as productive factors are concerned, labour has undergone growing restrictions of movement in the last 20 years, while both theory and experience demonstrate that migratory movements are a formidable 'last-resort' instrument for equalizing incomes across countries. Obviously the preceding considerations do not exonerate us from doing everything in our power to bring development to countries with high emigration flows so as to offer effective alternatives to emigration. This is the only acceptable way for a civilized country to stem immigration flows. Moreover unjustified administrative or police restrictions would end up putting a constraint on the economic growth of the countries enforcing them.

The movements of capital, on the other hand, have been almost completely liberalized without discriminating between speculative and entrepreneurial flows. This has produced a few benefits, such as an increase in foreign direct investment in developing countries, but has given rise to serious problems such as accentuated financial instability (the structural nature of recent financial instability is stressed, e.g., in Vercelli 2000). The sharp increase in flows of speculative capital ('hot money') in an era of floating exchange rates has contributed to destabilizing economies at the first hint of a crisis and made it more difficult to control them. The flows of 'hot money' shifting very rapidly from one country to another have increased tremendously since the 1970s, jeopardizing the effectiveness of any type of economic policy. As summarized by Chomsky (1999: 29), 'in 1971, 90 per cent of international financial transactions concerned the real economy – either commercial or long-term investments   and 10 per cent were speculative. In 1990, the percentages were turned upside down … with daily flows frequently higher than the entire reserves in foreign currency of the seven major industrial powers'. In addition, 'of the US$ 1300 billion which feed daily global transactions, only a small part is linked to movements of productive capital, from savings of a country that are transformed into investments in another country. Developed countries move annually only US$ 200 billion dollars in investments into developing countries. Thus the majority of transactions are not correlated to desirable movements of productive capital from developed countries to underdeveloped countries' (Tobin 1999).

Moreover, recent econometric studies show that in a structurally imperfect international market like ours without international regulatory institutions enforcing effective controls, contrary to pure theory, the capital flows tend to move from poor countries towards rich ones (this empirical trend was called the 'Lucas paradox' by the author who emphasized it: see Lucas 1990).

The growing difficulty of the globalization process in complying with the requisites of sustainability is clearly linked to these structural anomalies. They also depend on the evolution of economic and environmental policies. Indeed, the sustainability of development in the last 20 years has been jeopardized in many countries by excessive faith in unfettered markets, causing a weakening in the social protection net and re-distribution policies. The weakening of the welfare state, the progressive privatization of education and health services, the reduction of progressive taxation and the systematic increase in flexibility of labour relations have led to greater internal inequalities, while protectionism towards developing countries, reduction in international aid and the restriction of migratory labour flows have led to greater income inequality between countries. By the same token, progress made in the 1980s and early 1990s regarding environmental sustainability is being undermined in many countries by weakening environmental policies. The difficulty of implementing the Kyoto agreements signed in 1997 is just one of the relevant examples.

Regarding the philosophy of regulation in international markets, the present one has a far different influence on markets with respect to what took place in the period following the Bretton Woods agreements. The latter were conceived in an era in which the limitations of the market economy, as witnessed in the Great Depression of the 1930s, were still deeply impressed in the collective memory. Thus an apparatus of institutions and regulations was set up to control international markets for the prevention, or at least attenuation, of market 'failures'.

This regulatory apparatus was based on the following main institutional principles: (i) a system of fixed exchange rates to stabilize expectations of international operators; (ii) the General Agreement on Tariffs and Trade (GATT) rounds, an international negotiating table aimed at the progressive liberalization of the exchange of goods, services and productive factors; (iii) the IMF, with the task of preventing, through anti-cyclical financial interventions, local deficits of aggregate demand to spread deflationist impulses into other economies; (iv) the World Bank, with the task of financing structural interventions to eliminate poverty. This regulatory structure did to some extent succeed in mitigating problems linked to poverty and inequality by promoting a certain degree of compliance with the social condition of sustainability. The same cannot be said of the environmental condition of sustainability, mainly because of a still very low public awareness of environmental issues.

The recent re-definition of the system of international markets has significantly altered the regulatory system and thus its impact on sustainable development. The new regulatory system of international markets in place since the early 1980s, commonly called the 'Washington consensus', can be summarized in the following way: (i) a system of flexible exchange rates which deregulated the currency market and set off a process of systematic deregulation of markets; (ii) the creation in 1995 of the WTO so as to complete the liberalization of the exchange of goods, services and capital by increasing its penetration in all possible directions; (iii) the concession of financial support from the IMF to countries in difficulty subject to their adoption of structural measures aimed at deregulating and privatizing national markets and their implementation of monetary and budgetary austerity measures; (iv) a *de facto* subordination of structural interventions of the World Bank to previous approval from the IMF, aimed to verify compliance with its policy directives in the recipient countries.

Within the new regulatory system it is possible to identify many causal mechanisms that may explain the recent worsening of the social condition of sustainability. In particular the WTO has often interpreted constraints on trade introduced by local laws or international agreements, even those with genuine social or environmental purposes, as non-tariff barriers incompatible with free trade and forced their elimination (a significant list of well-documented examples can be found in Wallach and Sforza 1999). This same organization has also extended the range of its authority to questionable sectors such as the defence of intellectual property rights (TRIP agreement) which entails a considerable re-distribution of wealth from countries using patents (usually poor) to (usually rich) countries which register most patents (see Legrain 2002, and Tisdell 2001). The low transparency of decision-making and the real difficulty of guaranteeing the active participation of member countries, especially developing ones, has at times led to biased rulings (see Wallach and Sforza 1999, Esty 2001, and Francioni 2002).

In particular, in the last 20 years the IMF has progressively modified its original (broadly speaking 'Keynesian') philosophy of intervention to a position favouring privatization and deregulation. It has also often recommended restrictive budget policies in situations where there was a lack of aggregate demand.[23] In many cases this has led to significant increases in structural unemployment as well as to the suspension of monetary transfers aimed at supporting low-income families and environmental protection. The goal of monetary stability has generally overridden the original key-objective of full employment.

Thus far we have considered a few relevant macro-economic aspects of sustainability. Now we turn briefly to a few equally important micro-economic aspects. The economy as a whole can be sustainable only if it is based on a network of sustainable enterprises. Empirical research suggests that the longest-lasting and, if we focus on medium to long-term performance averages, most profitable businesses are those with a longer-term decision-making horizon that at the same time pay closer attention to the interests of all stakeholders.[24] This is also confirmed by the recently introduced indices which synthesize the stock market performance of the most sustainable companies. These indices generally do better than the general ones, as can be seen from a comparison between the *Dow Jones Sustainability Group Index* and the general Dow Jones index (see Figure 1.12). The recent globalization process has jeopardized businesses' social responsibility and thus their sustainability in the medium/long term. The growing territorial dispersion of productive processes has made it more difficult to ensure active participation and control of the stakeholders. There has also been a progressive shortening of the time horizon of decision-making in markets unified by the Internet and deregulation and showing an increasing degree of imitation. This has induced many enterprises to focus on impressive short-term results even at the expense of their sustainability in the long term.[25]

To sum up, the new regulatory system of national and international markets that has emerged and consolidated in the last 20 years has weakened the social sustainability of development and is starting to jeopardize even the environmental sustainability of development. The empirical correlations identified above seem to be fairly supported, albeit inconclusively, by precise causal mechanisms, some of which have been touched on. Analysis of the data at our disposal does not justify either catastrophic pessimism or quietist optimism. The process of globalization since 1820 has led to an extraordinary increase in per capita incomes and world population but has tended to increase inequalities between countries and to a lesser degree within each country. Social and environmental policies have

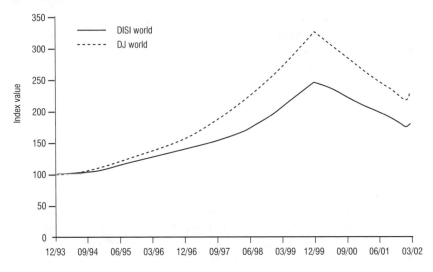

Figure 1.12 Dow Jones Indices (Source: www.sustainability-index.com) (Note: the values of the indices (Total Returns) have been normalized to 100 (December 1993))

been enacted to attenuate these problems by consolidating the sustainability of world development. These problems persist, however, and their solution entails more vigorous and far-sighted policy interventions.

Concluding remarks

The problems we have heretofore analysed are often presented, especially in the mass media, in terms of a simplistic confrontation between the case for or against globalization. In light of the preceding analysis, we can say that this simplistic dichotomy is highly misleading. The above-mentioned social and environmental problems depend partially on an incomplete and distorted process of globalization (e.g. protectionist barriers put up by rich countries towards poor countries and unjustified obstacles to labour migration) and partially on the growing weakness of regulations in international markets (leading, e.g., to huge and sudden uncontrolled flows of hot money and systematic elimination of the environmental and social constraints on international transactions).

For these two sets of reasons, the recent process of globalization cannot be considered completely sustainable, although it can be made so with the right structural interventions. If we wish to accomplish steady and long-lasting world development, it would be irrational to give up the potential benefits of globalization provided that its distortions are corrected and the proper active regulations are firmly established.

To this end local and international institutions must collaborate in order to continue the elimination of the remaining protectionist measures, giving priority to complete liberalization of imports from industrialized countries. It is instead reasonable to concede a more gradual elimination of the protective barriers raised by developing countries to the extent that they are strictly aimed to protect new or recent industries and to encourage the formation and consolidation of legal and administrative institutions to guarantee the smooth functioning of the market. The further opening up of international trade, however, must not relax the restrictions on economic transactions introduced in single countries, often in accordance with international agreements, to foster genuine social and environmental protection. Such limitations should actually be progressively reinforced to push competition towards higher standards of quality. In particular, ethical-environmental certification and reporting are a promising way to promote competition at higher ethical and environmental standards so as to orientate choices towards sustainable development.

In addition, the structural interventions of the World Bank and single states to reduce inequality, poverty and malnutrition should be supported without the imposition of external abstract conditions which do not consider institutional and cultural differences and exclude the active participation of the resident population. This should also hold for structural re-equilibrium programmes, including those promoted and financed by the IMF and the World Bank.

Finally, labour mobility should be freed of all unjustified cross-border limitations to allow it to play its crucial role of 'last resort' equalization of incomes and economic opportunities. Capital flows, on the other hand, cannot be left in the current state of anarchy. This has led to sudden large flows of hot money and intolerable levels of financial instability, encouraging financial laxity and crimes with the complicity of insufficient transparency in international transactions, due partly to the (feebly opposed) growing role of the offshore centres. Therefore, the debate on controls over speculative capital flows must be given serious consideration. For example, in the recent debate on the desirability of introducing the so-called Tobin tax, interesting ideas emerged that deserve serious consideration (see, e.g., Tobin 1999).

From a microeconomic point of view, it is necessary to promote greater social responsibility in businesses by perfecting *corporate regulations* to avoid conflicts of interests and the distorted use of private information (e.g., 'insider trading'), and encourage more far-sighted decision-making and greater attention to all stakeholders. Financial intermediaries should be encouraged to channel saving flows towards the enterprises that are more socially responsible and compatible with sustainable development, both through ethical investment funds and an in-depth analysis of environmental and reputation risks. The interventions suggested above should use the full potential of competitive markets without underestimating their limits requiring active regulation. Regulatory measures regarding markets are like medical treatments – the right ones must be prescribed in minimum doses to avoid side-effects; it would be senseless, however, to reject them systematically in the belief that the human body is always capable of taking care of itself.

Economic theory and experience confirm that without suitable regulation, markets are not able to resolve the social and environmental problems affecting sustainable development. This is true for global as well as local markets. This stems from the fact that environmental and social externalities are particularly widespread and significant. In addition the markets are incomplete, and this is true in particular of the future markets which are directly involved in the issue of long-term sustainable development. Finally, underlying the unstable interaction between the biosphere and world economic development are irreversible processes and radical uncertainty (see, e.g., Vercelli 1998a).

In the light of the preceding analysis, we must commit ourselves to building a new regulatory structure of international markets – a lightweight, efficient, open and democratically managed apparatus with the active participation of all countries to allow individuals of present and future generations to satisfy their needs and have access to fundamental economic opportunities. In particular, it is necessary to enact distribution policies on incomes and to guarantee access to resources and economic opportunities (see Bowles and Gintis 1998, and Dasgupta *et al.* 1997).

We conclude by observing that the interventions outlined above will only be truly effective if civil society becomes fully aware of the importance of the environmental and social conditions which can guarantee sustainable development. The educational and research system plays a fundamental part in reaching this goal. In particular scientific research can and must make a crucial contribution towards understanding problems and their causes, selecting mechanisms of intervention as well as encouraging far-sighted decision-making processes, inspired by the fundamental principles of solidarity, fairness and civil cohabitation.

Notes

1   This chapter is based on the text of the inaugural lecture of the 762nd Academic year of the University of Siena (Vercelli 2002). The author wishes to thank Simone Borghesi, Maria Carmen Siniscalchi, Massimiliano Ugolini and Davide Vercelli for their invaluable comments and support.

2   Other technological, social, cultural and institutional aspects of globalization have been stressed in recent debates. Due to limited space, we will deal with these aspects only insofar as they affect the globalization of markets.

3   The process of globalization originated long ago. Major milestones include the explorations of the sixteenth century, which unified the world from the point of view of physical accessibility, and the industrial revolution at the end of the eighteenth century which drove market expansion around the globe.

4   The Bretton Woods system started disintegrating at the end of the 1960s as a result of rising inflation in industrialized countries. It collapsed after the suspension of the convertibility of the dollar by President Nixon in 1971. A transition period lasting about 10 years followed until a new system of regulating international markets emerged.

5   Some authors call 'Washington Consensus' the regulatory system of the world economy which has emerged in the past 20 years (see, e.g., Chomsky 1999, and Stiglitz 2002).

6   In this work development refers to the expansion of freedom of individuals and society. This process depends not only on durable growth of economic indices, above all per capita income, but also of health as well as other social and cultural indices (see Sen 1999).

7   The crucial importance of this condition has been emphasized in Chichilnisky (1997) and Vercelli (1998b).

8   This does not imply either an absolute equality of distribution or a rejection of reasonable merit-based distribution criteria based on the results of individual efforts, as long as market competition is not distorted by an unequal access to economic opportunities.

9   This point was emphasized by Adam Smith and other founding fathers of 'classical' liberalism and was further clarified by the founders of the neoclassical school, Marshall, Walras and Pareto (see Vercelli 2004). In more rigorous terms, one can argue that the Pareto optimum associated

with a less equal initial distribution of opportunities is sub-optimal (see Borghesi and Vercelli 2003).

10 Not all economists agree that inequality among countries has increased in recent years, partially due to different data and methods of measurement. Nonetheless, as the thoughtful classification of inequality measures suggested by Wade (2001) clarifies, the increase in inequality is quite evident from all the most widespread measures used excluding those which weight countries with their population and simultaneously measure incomes in terms of purchasing power parity. However, even in the latter case, more sophisticated recent analyses seem to confirm a trend towards a progressive increase in inequality since the 1970s in many OECD countries (see Milanovic 2002, and Brandolini 2002).

11 An acceleration in development initially increases profits in the most dynamic sectors and only later affects, and not always to the same degree, wages and employment in the same sectors. The diffusion of these increases in other sectors requires more time and is often incomplete. The same is true for territorial diffusion of development from the most dynamic poles to other geographical areas.

12 Another significant example is that of the two world wars, when the spirit of cooperation and solidarity in the face of wartime troubles favoured vigorous re-distribution policies (Sen 1999: 54). A similar phenomenon occurred under the New Deal policies adopted by the USA and other industrialized countries to combat the drastic effects of the Great Depression. The almost continuous succession of these periods, together with the de-globalization process from 1915– 45 (see *retro*), interrupted for a long interval (1915–70) the increase in inequality that began with the globalization process set off in the 1820s.

13 Kuznets observes at the end of his article: 'in winding up my work, I am painfully aware of the scarce reliability of the information I have presented. This study consists of possibly five per cent empirical information and 95 per cent speculation, part of which boils down to pure wishful thinking' (Kuznets 1955: 26).

14 Kuznets himself observed that '... the recognition that each generalization tends to reflect a limited synthesis of historical experience forces us to evaluate each theory, past or present, on the basis of its empirical value and consequential limits of application – a precept that should naturally be applied to all excessively simplified generalizations contained in this article' (1955: 28).

15 The comparison of different ways of measuring poverty raises methodological problems that cannot be covered here due to lack of space (see Brandolini 2002). The data used here is from the World Bank.

16 Indices of this nature have been proposed lately. They are, however, controversial and only available for the most recent years (an example is the *Environmental Sustainability Index* published by the *World Economic Forum*.) Therefore they do not currently allow for an identification of significant medium-/long-term trends.

17 Given the non-linearity of the interaction between environmental and economic variables, there may be a threshold above which irreversible destabilizing processes may be set off (see Daily and Ehrlich 1992).

18 Among the indexes showing this trend we note those of some water pollutants such as coliform bacteria, mercury, arsenic and nickel. For a broader analysis see Borghesi (2001).

19 From the identity: $D' = y_p' + d_y' + P'$, where D' indicates the growth rate of global environmental deterioration, y_p' the per-capita income growth rate, d_y' the growth rate of the intensity of environmental deterioration and P' the population growth rate, assuming $D' \leq 0$ to guarantee the sustainability of development, we obtain: $\max y_p' = - (d_y' + P')$ (see Borghesi-Vercelli, 2003, p. 12).

20 The reasons are well expounded in the publications on the Kuznets environmental curve cited above.

21 We must point out, however, that even in this period the speed of reduction in inequality and poverty was insufficient to safeguard 'social stability'.

22 We have to emphasize amongst other conditions: a sufficient thickness of markets, lack of transaction costs, lack of information asymmetries, absence of externalities (including

environmental and social ones), perfect competition and dynamic and structural stability. These conditions are rarely found in real markets (Vercelli 2001b)

23   These policies are based on the conviction that unfettered markets are able to auto-regulate themselves and resolve any sort of economic problem in the best possible way. Economic theory from Adam Smith onwards has always disputed this position, stressing the nature and significance of the limitations of markets as well as the necessity to regulate them to avoid their 'failures'. Theory and historical experience have also shown the important repercussions of state failures. It is therefore necessary to keep in mind both aspects of the dilemma without forgetting that failure on the part of public authorities can be linked to processes of regulation as well as of deregulation. A recent example of the latter phenomenon is the privatization process in Russia in the 1990s (see Stiglitz 2002).

24   The stakeholders are all the subjects directly interested in the activity of a corporation. They include shareholders as well as employees, clients, suppliers and all those who live in the territories where the corporation is active. See Schmidheiny and Zorraquin (1996) and Turner (2001).

25   This point has been treated in some more detail in Vercelli (2001b).

References

Ahluwalia, M. (1976) 'Income distribution and development', *American Economic Review*, 66(5): 128–35.

Alesina, A. and Perotti, R. (1996) 'Income distribution, political instability and investment', *European Economic Review*, 81 (5): 1170–89.

Benhabib, J. and Rustichini, A. (1996) 'Social conflict and growth', *Journal of Economic Growth*, 1(1): 129–46.

Borghesi, S. (2001) 'The environmental Kuznets curve: a critical survey', in M. Franzini and A. Nicita (eds), *Economic Institutions and Environmental Policy*, Aldershot: Ashgate.

Borghesi, S. and Vercelli, A. (2003) 'Sustainable globalisation', *Ecological Economics*, 44(1): 77–98.

Bourguignon, F. and Morrisson, C. (1999) *The Size Distribution of Income Among World Citizens: 1820–1990*, Washington, DC: Manuscript, The World Bank..

Bowles, S. and Gintis, H. (1998) *Recasting Egalitarianism. New rules for Communities, States and Markets*, London: Verso.

Brandolini, A. (2002) 'A bird's-eye view of long-run changes in income inequality', Paper presented at the IEA World Conference in Lisbon.

Burniaux, J.M., Dang, T.T., Fore, D., Forster, M., Mira D'Ercole, M. and Oxley, H. (1999) 'Income distribution and poverty in selected OECD Countries', *OECD Economic Studies*, 29: 55–94.

Chichilnisky, G. (1997) 'What is sustainable development?', *Land Economics*, 73(4): 467–91.

Chomsky, N. (1999) *Sulla nostra pelle: Mercato globale o movimento globale?*, Milan: Marco Tropea Editore.

Cole, M.A., Rayner, A.J. and Bates, J.M. (1997) 'The environmental Kuznets curve: an empirical analysis', *Environment and Development Economics*, 2: 401–16.

Daily, G.C. and Ehrlich, P.R. (1992) 'Population, sustainability and Earth's carrying capacity', *Bioscience*, 42: 761–71.

Dasgupta, P., Mäler, K. and Vercelli, A. (1997) *The Economics of Transnational Commons*, Oxford: Oxford University Press.

Dollar, D. and Kraay, A. (2001) 'Growth is good for the poor', *World Bank Working Paper* No 2587, Washington, DC: Development Research Group, The World Bank.

Esty, D. (2001), 'Bridging the trade-environment divide', *Journal of Economic Perspectives*, 15: 113–30.

Forster, F. and Pellizzari, M. (2000) 'Trends and driving factors in income distribution and poverty in the OECD area', *OECD Labour Market and Social Policy Occasional Papers* No. 42, Paris: OECD.

Forster, M. and Pearson, M. (2002) 'Income distribution and poverty in the OECD area: trends and driving forces', *OECD Economic Studies*, 34: 7–39.

Francioni, F. (ed.) (2002) *Environment, Human Rights and International Trade*, Oxford and Portland, OR: Hart Publishing.

Frankel, J.A. and Romer, D. (1999) 'Does trade cause growth?', *American Economic Review*, 89: 379–99.

Grossman, G.M. (1995) 'Pollution and growth: what do we know?', in I. Goldin and L.A. Winters (eds), *The Economics of Sustainable Development*, Cambridge: Cambridge University Press.

Kuznets, S. (1955) 'Economic growth and income inequality', *American Economic Review*, 45: 1–28.

Legrain, Ph. (2002) *Open World: The Truth about Globalisation*, London: Abacus.

Lindert, P.H. and Williamson, J.G. (2001) 'Does globalization make the world more unequal?', *NBER Working Paper* No 8228, forthcoming in M.D. Bordo, A.M. Taylor and J.G. Williamson (eds), *Globalization in Historical Perspectives*, Chicago, IL: University of Chicago Press.

Lomborg, B. (2001) *The Skeptical Environmentalist: Measuring the Real State of the World*, Cambridge: Cambridge University Press.

Lucas, R. (1990) 'Why doesn't capital flow from rich to poor countries?', *American Economic Review*, 80: 92–6.

Milanovic, B. (2002) 'True world income distribution, 1988 and 1993: first calculation based on household surveys alone', *Economic Journal*, 112: 51–92.

O'Rourke, K.H. and Williamson, J.G. (2000) 'When did globalization begin?', *NBER Working Paper* 7632, Cambridge, MA: NBER.

Panayotou, T. (1993) 'Empirical tests and policy analysis of environmental degradation at different stages of economic development. World Employment Programme Research', *Working Paper* No. 238, Geneva: International Labour Office.

Robinson, S. (1976) 'A note on the U-hypothesis relating income inequality and economic development', *American Economic Review*, 66 (3): 437–40.

Schmidheiny, S. and Zorraquin, F. (1996) *Financing Change. The Financial Community, Eco-efficiency, and Sustainable Development*, Cambridge, MA: MIT Press.

Sen, A. (1999) *Development as Freedom*, New York: Alfred A. Knopf.

Shafik, N. (1994) 'Economic development and environmental quality: an econometric analysis', in *Oxford Economic Papers*, 46: 757–73.

Stiglitz, J. (2002) *Globalization and its Discontents*, London: Allen Lane.

Tisdell, C. (2001) 'Globalisation and sustainability: environmental Kuznets curve and the WTO', *Ecological Economics*, 39: 185–96.

Tobin, J. (1999) 'Interview with James Tobin: reining in the markets', 1 February, Information Access Company/Unesco, Paris.

Turner, A. (2001) *Just Capital: The Liberal Economy*, London: Macmillan.

Varian, H.R. (2002) *Microeconomics*, Venice: Cafoscarina.

Vercelli, A. (1991) *Methodological Foundations of Macroeconomics: Keynes and Lucas*, Cambridge: Cambridge University Press.

Vercelli, A. (1992) 'Probabilistic causality and economic analysis: a survey', in A. Vercelli and N. Dimitri (eds), *Macroeconomics: A Survey of Research Strategies*, Oxford: Oxford University Press.

Vercelli, A. (1998a) 'Hard uncertainty and environmental policy', in G. Chichilnisky, G. Heal and A. Vercelli (eds), *Sustainability: Dynamics and Uncertainty*, Dordrecht: Kluwer.

Vercelli, A. (1998b) 'Operational measures of sustainable development and the freedom of future generations', in G. Chichilnisky, G. Heal and A. Vercelli (eds), *Sustainability: Dynamics and Uncertainty*, Dordrecht: Kluwer.

Vercelli, A. (2000) 'Structural financial instability and cyclical fluctuations', *Structural Change and Economic Dynamics*, 11: 139–56.

Vercelli, A. (2001a) 'Epistemic causality and hard uncertainty: a Keynesian approach', in M.C. Galavotti, P. Suppes and D. Costantini (eds), *Stochastic Causality*, Stanford, CA: Stanford University Press.

Vercelli, A. (2001b) 'New globalisation and sustainability', *Discussion Paper* No 329, Siena: Department of Political Economy, University of Siena.

Vercelli, A. (2002) 'Globalizzazione e sostenibilità dello sviluppo', Inaugural Lecture to the 762nd Academic Year of the University of Siena, republished in *Economia Politica*, 20(2) (2003): 225–50.

Vercelli, A. (2004) 'Updated liberalism vs. neo-liberalism: policy paradigms and the structural evolution of western industrial economies after W.W.II', forthcoming in R. Arena, N. Salvadori (eds), *Money, Credit and the Role of the State: Essays in honour of Augusto Graziani*, Aldershot: Ashgate.

Wade, R. (2001) 'Winners and losers', *The Economist*, 28 April 2001.

Wallach, L. and Sforza, M. (1999) *Whose Trade Organisation? Corporate Globalization and the Erosion of Democracy*, New York: Public Citizen Foundation.

WCED (The World Commission on Environment and Development) (1987) *Our Common Future* (The Brundtland Report), Oxford and New York: Oxford University Press.

2 Income inequality and the environmental Kuznets curve

Simone Borghesi[1]

Non-technical summary

In the early 1990s several studies found an inverted-U relationship between environmental degradation and per capita income (the so-called environmental Kuznets curve). Since then, the literature on this subject has grown exponentially trying to overcome the limitations of the previous contributions. Some recent studies have started to question the emphasis on income growth to explain environmental degradation and argued that other explanatory variables should be included in the models beyond gross domestic product (GDP). Among the studies that introduce new regressors, only few works focus attention on inequality as an additional explanatory variable and examine its relationship with environmental degradation. For this purpose, present empirical studies generally use pooled ordinary least squares (OLS) models as preferred specification, getting mixed or conflicting results. Pooling observations, however, disregards the heterogeneity of the countries included in the panel. The aim of this chapter is to show that the results obtained in the literature may heavily depend on the chosen specification and verify how these results change if we adopt a fixed-effect (FE) model that, in our opinion, is more appropriate than the pooled OLS model in the present context.

Taking carbon dioxide (CO_2) emissions as environmental indicator, two main results emerge from the analysis. First, the FE and pooled OLS models systematically achieve different or even opposite results. The performed test rejected the hypothesis underlying the pooled OLS model in the estimated specifications, therefore pooled OLS estimations turn out to be biased in the present context. Second, inequality is always non-significantly related to CO_2 emissions in our preferred specification (the FE model). The same results hold if we use a log-linear specification (with variables in logs rather than in levels) and are also robust to alternative inequality measures. Finally, we verify whether inequality has an opposite coefficient in rich and poor countries, which may determine the overall non-significance of the inequality coefficient in the panel. For this purpose, we perform a further analysis using a non-linear model and find that the inequality coefficient is still not statistically different from zero in the FE specification.

Introduction

The relationship between environmental degradation and per capita income has attracted much attention in the literature during the last decade. In the early 1990s, some studies found that several indices of air and water pollution first increase and then decrease as per capita income grows (Panayotou 1993, Shafik 1994, Selden and Song 1994, and Grossman and Krueger 1995). This 'bell-shaped' relationship was called environmental Kuznets curve after Simon Kuznets (Kuznets 1955) who was the first to observe a similar relationship between inequality and per capita income (the so-called Kuznets curve). The literature on the environmental Kuznets curve (henceforth EKC) has grown exponentially in the last few years.[2] Recent studies have tried to overcome the limitations of early contributions by using new data sets, new functional forms and more refined econometric techniques. Moreover, some authors (e.g. Unruh and Moomaw 1998, Kaufmann *et al.* 1998, and Suri and Chapman 1998) have started to question the emphasis on income growth to explain environmental degradation and argued that other explanatory variables should be included in the models. Among these studies, a few works (Torras and Boyce 1998, Scruggs 1998, Magnani 2000, Marsiliani and Renström 2000, Ravallion *et al.* 2000, and Heerink *et al.* 2001) have examined how inequality can affect the environment–income relationship getting mixed or conflicting results. This chapter intends to contribute to this literature, bringing new evidence to stimulate discussion on the role of income distribution in the environmental problems. Taking CO_2 as indicator of environmental degradation, this work investigates the relationship between inequality and CO_2 emissions.

The following section 'Related literature' provides an overview of the literature on the environmental impact of inequality. 'Description of the data' illustrates the data, while 'Analysis of the CO_2-inequality relationship' examines the results of the empirical analysis. 'Conclusions' summarizes the main findings and indicates future lines of research.

Related literature

Boyce (1994) was the first author to investigate how inequality affects environmental degradation from the theoretical viewpoint. He set forth the hypothesis that greater inequality may increase environmental degradation in two ways: (i) via impacts on the rate of time preference, and (ii) via the cost–benefit analysis of environmentally degrading activities. As to the first point, Boyce (1994) argues that greater inequality increases the rate of environmental time preference for both poor and rich. On the one hand, when inequality increases, the poor tend to overexploit natural capital, since they perceive it as an immediate source of income that can help them secure their day-to-day survival.[3] On the other hand, economic inequality is often associated with political instability and risk of revolts. This leads rich people to prefer a policy of exploiting the environment and investing the returns abroad (where political uncertainty is lower) rather than investing in the defence of local natural resources. Thus, according to Boyce an increase in inequality induces both rich and poor to degrade more the environment they live in. As to the second point, Boyce (1994) states that in an unequal society rich people can heavily influence decisions on environmentally damaging projects. Such decisions are based on the competition between those who benefit from the environmentally destructive action ('the winners') and those who bear the costs of it ('the losers'). Boyce (1994) argues that rich people are generally the winners, while poor people tend to be the losers of the investments that have an ecological impact.[4] This political economy argument suggests, therefore, that economic inequality may enhance the possibility of environmentally damaging investments since it 'reinforces the power of the rich to impose environmental costs on the poor' (Ravallion *et al.* 2000: 6).[5]

To test the argument set forth in Boyce (1994), Torras and Boyce (1998) examine the environmental impact of per capita income and of three explanatory variables that can proxy for power inequality within a country – economic inequality (Gini index), adult literacy rates and an aggregate of political rights and civil liberties. The authors examine a set of water and air pollution variables other than carbon dioxide in a panel of countries for the period 1977–91 using a simple pooled ordinary least squares model and obtain mixed results on the environmental impact of income inequality – the Gini coefficient is positive for some environmental indicators and negative for others.

Marsiliani and Renström (2000) have recently examined how inequality affects political decisions on environmental protection. Using an overlapping-generations model, they show that the higher the level of inequality in terms of median–mean distance, the lower the pollution tax set by a majority elected representative. Inequality, therefore, may be negatively correlated with environmental protection as it leads to less stringent environmental policies. To test the model, the authors regress carbon intensity on income and inequality in two panels of seven and ten industrialized countries and find that higher inequality increases emissions intensity in a pooled ordinary least squares model (their preferred specification).

Magnani (2000) has investigated the impact of inequality on research and development (R & D) expenditures for the environment that are taken 'as proxy for the intensity of public engagement in environmental problems' (Magnani 2000: 438). For this purpose, the author tests a non-linear model where R & D environmental expenditures are a function of per capita income, income inequality and their product. The author presents estimation results obtained by pooled OLS, random effect (RE) and FE models. The latter specification, however, is mainly neglected as the Hausman test does not reject the null hypothesis of no difference between RE and FE estimators. Using a panel of 19 OECD countries in the period 1980–91, Magnani (2000) finds that higher inequality reduces environmental care, as predicted by the theoretical model set forth in the paper. The impact of inequality on environmental care, however, is statistically significant at five per cent level in the pooled OLS model only.

To test the environmental impact of inequality, Scruggs (1998) performs two cross-country empirical analyses using pooled models. First, he examines the impact of per capita income, the Gini index, and a measure of democracy on the concentration of four pollutants other than CO_2 in a panel of 22 up to 29 countries.

Then, he takes a composite index of environmental quality as dependent variable and repeats the analysis for 17 OECD countries.[6] In the first analysis, Scruggs gets conflicting results – greater inequality increases environmental degradation for one environmental indicator (dissolved oxygen), whereas the opposite holds for other indicators (particulates). In the second analysis, either inequality decreases environmental degradation or its impact on the environment is nearly zero, which seems to confirm the author's viewpoint that inequality is not necessarily related to environmental degradation. The outcome of the second analysis, however, may be affected by the way the composite index of environmental quality is constructed since, as the author also points out, it disregards many pollutants as well as recycling policies and nature's assimilative capacity. In our analysis we prefer, therefore, to focus attention on a unique pollutant, CO_2, which contributes to global warming more than any other pollutant.

The papers mentioned so far adopt a public choice approach to examine the impact that income inequality may have on environmental degradation. Other contributions, however, point out that a simple statistical argument, based on the shape of the environment–income relationship, may give important hints on the environmental effect of inequality. Heerink *et al.* (2001), for instance, adduce an aggregation argument for including income inequality in the empirical analyses on the environment–income relationship. As the authors show, when such relationship is not linear, aggregating over households with unequal incomes will generate biased estimates if inequality is omitted from the explanatory variables. If a concave (convex) relationship holds between per capita income and environmental degradation at the micro level (i.e. for all households), then income inequality is negatively (positively) related to environmental degradation. Using cross-national observations on several indicators of environmental degradation for a single year (1985), Heerink *et al.* (2001) challenge Boyce's conclusion that inequality increases environmental degradation, finding on the contrary that higher inequality may reduce environmental degradation.

Ravallion *et al.* (2000) also look at the shape of the environment–income relationship to infer the effects of income distribution on environmental degradation and claim that the relative impact of rich and poor people on the environment is *a priori* ambiguous. The authors argue that each individual has an implicit demand function for carbon emissions since consumption of almost every good implies some emissions either directly (via consumption) or indirectly (via its production). They call marginal propensity to emit (MPE) the derivative of this demand function with respect to income. If poor people have a higher MPE than rich ones, a redistribution policy that reduces inequality will increase carbon emissions. Vice versa, if poor people have a lower MPE than better-off classes, reducing inequality will also decrease the emissions level. It is difficult to say *a priori* which of these two effects tends to prevail. On the one hand, poor people generally devote their additional income to food and clothing rather than goods with large emission rates, such as motor vehicles, hence their MPE should be lower than that of the rich. On the other hand, they tend to use energy less efficiently than the rich, which entails a higher MPE. In general, therefore, the impact of inequality on emissions is ambiguous and depends on whether the MPE rises or falls as income grows, that is, on whether the CO_2-income function is convex or concave. To test the environmental impact of inequality, the authors estimate a log quadratic model where CO_2 emissions depend on average per capita income, population and a time trend, and all parameters are assumed to be a function of inequality. Using a panel of 42 countries in the period 1975–92, they find quite different results with an FE and a simple pooled OLS model and claim that the latter seems more reliable.[7] In this case, they find that higher inequality reduces carbon emissions, but increases their response to income growth.

As pointed out above, all studies examined in this paragraph use a pooled OLS model as preferred specification to investigate the link between inequality and the environment. The aim of the present work is to show that the results obtained in the literature may heavily depend on the chosen specification and verify how these results change if we adopt an FE model that, in our opinion, provides a better description of reality in the present context.

Description of the data

In the absence of a single measure of environmental quality, many indicators have been used in the literature as proxy for environmental degradation. The present analysis focuses attention on carbon dioxide CO_2 per capita emissions (metric tons per capita) as environmental indicator for two reasons: first, because carbon dioxide contributes to global warming more than any other greenhouse gas; second, because longer time-series of data are available for carbon dioxide emissions than for any other pollution indicator. The data source used for this variable is the US Oak Ridge National Laboratory (ORNL) at the Carbon Dioxide Information Analysis Center (CDIAC). ORNL provides estimates of national carbon emissions from fossil fuel consumption and cement manufacture. Data on fossil fuel consumption are based on the World Energy Data Set maintained by the United Nations Statistical Division. This data set concerns solid, liquid and gaseous fuels (primarily coals, petroleum products and natural gas, respectively). Data on cement manufacturing come from the Cement Manufacturing Data Set provided by the US Geological Survey. ORNL annually calculates emissions of CO_2 by multiplying fuel consumption by the average carbon content of each fuel type, and cement production by the average carbon dioxide released during production (Marland and Rotty 1984).

The ORNL data set has some limitations since it does not consider some important emission sources (i.e. deforestation and land-use changes), so that estimates of CO_2 emissions may depart from actual emissions.[8] However, it is widely recognized as one of the best available sources for CO_2 emissions and generally used in the literature since emissions are calculated using a uniform estimation method from a single, harmonized data set available for all countries.[9]

Data on inequality come from Deininger and Squire (1996). The authors have computed Gini coefficients and quintile shares for a large panel of countries, reporting whether inequality refers to individuals or households and whether it is computed for income or expenditures. One important feature of the work by Deininger and Squire is that the authors indicated the quality of the assembled data and the underlying criteria. Although not immune to possible critiques,[10] their data set is widely recognized as one of the most complete and updated databases of inequality currently available.

Data on the other explanatory variables (per capita gross domestic product, population density and industrial share of gross domestic product) come from the World Development Indicators (World Bank 1998). Per capita GDP is expressed in constant 1987 international dollars using Purchasing Power Parity (PPP). As Ravallion *et al.* (2000: 15) point out, '*GDP* according to PPP has the advantage of expressing income in comparable units in terms of living standards across countries (as compared to *GDP* by market exchange rates)'.[11] Population density is given by the number of people per square kilometre, whereas the industrial share of GDP is given by the industry value added as percent of total GDP.

The results that will be presented below are based on a panel of 35 countries in the period 1988–95. This sample can be considered quite representative of the large income range existing across countries since it is composed of 11 low-income, 12 middle-income and 12 high-income countries.[12] Table 2.1 shows the summary statistics for this sample. Figure 2.1 shows the scatter diagram of the sample observations on per capita CO_2 and per capita GDP. We selected only countries having high-quality data on inequality as indicated by Deininger and Squire. More precisely, we restricted to the countries that have multiple high-quality observations on the Gini index in the period 1988–95, which reduces the number of available observations to 97. This criterion differs from the one adopted by Ravallion *et al.* (2000: 15) who compute 'the average Gini index for each country, averaged over all the data available for that country from the high-quality sub-set of data'. This means that the authors have a single value of inequality for each country, whereas here we have multiple observations for each nation in the sample. Although inequality differs more across countries than within countries over time, this feature is common to all other explanatory variables used in the model[13] and we believe that treating inequality as constant may neglect part of the information. Some countries, in fact, show important changes in the level of inequality during the period that we examined.[14]

Analysis of the CO_2-inequality relationship

Model specification

Most papers in the EKC literature assume that environmental degradation is a polynomial function of per capita income. The studies generally differ in three respects: (i) the choice between linear and log-linear models, (ii) the degree attributed to per capita income in the polynomial equation, and (iii) the specification used by the authors (e.g. pooled OLS, FE, RE). As far as the first issue is concerned, both linear and log-linear models have advantages and disadvantages for the analysis of the EKC relationship.[15] Although both models were examined in this work, we

Table 2.1 Summary statistics (35 countries in the period 1988–1995)[1]

Variable	Mean	Std. dev.	Min.	Max.	Var. ratio
Per capita CO_2 emissions (tons)	5.24	5.27	0.05	27.13	17.47
Per capita GDP	6.74	6.06	0.62	21.07	8.16
Population density	2.61	7.59	0.01	48.95	4.71
Industry value added (% GDP)	32.86	9.43	10.18	60.96	40.73
Gini	36.24	8.47	20.69	54.98	26.34
Interquintile difference $(1 - Q_4 - Q_1)$	35.28	8.57	18.11	56.10	27.99

Notes

1 The original series of per capita GDP was divided by 1000 and that of population density by 100 so that these variables have the same magnitude of the others and we can avoid scale problems. The Gini index is in percent, as reported in the original Deininger and Squire (1996) data set. Q_1 and Q_4 are the cumulative income shares of the first and fourth quintile, respectively. The measure of interquintile difference is multiplied by 100 to harmonize it with the magnitude of the other variables. The last column measures the variability ratio that was computed as the standard deviation of each variable within countries divided by that across countries (expressed in percent terms).

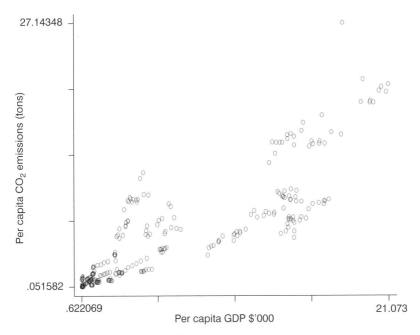

Figure 2.1 Scatter diagram of sample observations

preferred to focus attention on the linear one since its coefficients can generally provide an immediate idea of the shape of the environment–income relationship.[16] As we will point out below, however, results obtained with the linear model are robust also to the log-linear specification.

As to the choice of the functional form, most studies estimate environmental degradation as quadratic function of per capita GDP. However, several papers (e.g. Grossman and Krueger 1995, Shafik 1994, Grossman 1995, and Torras and Boyce 1998) have found that for some ecological indicators the environment–income relationship may be better described by a cubic function – environmental degradation first increases, then decreases and finally rises again. To make the present study comparable with the others, we estimated three regression models: (1) linear, (2) quadratic, and (3) cubic in per capita GDP. Each functional form was estimated by least squares with and without country- and time-specific effects.[17] Following the terminology generally adopted in the literature, we call pooled OLS model the specification that does not take country- and time-specific effects into account. The pooled OLS model is equivalent to a Least Squares Dummy Variable (LSDV) model where all country- and time-effects are jointly equal to zero. To examine whether such effects exist, we performed an F-test on the country- and time-specific effects in an LSDV model. The F-test rejected the null hypothesis that specific effects are jointly zero at one per cent significance level in all estimated models presented below (see Table 2.2).[18]

Given the existence of specific effects, we then examined whether they should be treated as fixed or random. In our opinion, despite the waste of 'between countries' information, the FE model is preferable to the RE model in the present context. The RE model, in fact, assumes that individual specific effects are not correlated with the explanatory variables. This is equivalent to assuming that country effects such as resource endowments, efficiency of the monitoring systems, number of power plants and environmental policies adopted in the country are orthogonal to the country's per capita income, which seems rather unrealistic. Our *a priori* preference for the FE model was confirmed by the Hausman test that rejected the null hypothesis of individual specific effects orthogonal to the regressors in all functional forms. When specific effects are included in the model, therefore, the estimation results below will present the FE but not the RE specification.[19]

The results of the F-test and the Hausman test jointly suggest that country-specific effects exist and are correlated with the explanatory variables, therefore pooled OLS estimates turn out to be biased and inconsistent (see, among the others, Hsiao 1986). For this reason, we prefer an FE approach to the pooled OLS model generally adopted in the studies mentioned above. In what follows, however, we will present the results obtained with both the FE and the pooled OLS model in order to compare our findings with those of the existing literature and show how results change as we pass from one specification to the other.

Beyond per capita income and inequality, we included two additional explanatory variables in the model – population density (DENS) and industry value added as share of GDP (IND).[20] Population density is generally believed to have a positive impact on polluting emissions. High population density, in fact, is often associated with high emissions due to traffic congestion. However, some authors (Scruggs 1998: 270) argue that population density could also have a negative coefficient since higher density implies higher concern for environmental problems and thus lower emissions.

The industrial value added as percent of national income captures the so-called 'composition effect' of income growth, namely how environmental degradation is

Table 2.2 Test F in estimated models[1]

Model	Linear	Quadratic	Cubic
1	$F(41.51) = 63.014$ [0.000]	$F(41.50) = 59.756$ [0.000]	$F(41.49) = 39.722$ [0.000]
2	$F(41.50) = 50.803$ [0.000]	$F(41.49) = 49.429$ [0.000]	$F(41.48) = 42.793$ [0.000]

Note

1   The F-test is: $F(g, n-k) = \dfrac{R_{\text{LSDV}}^2 - R_{\text{OLS}}^2}{1 - R_{\text{LSDV}}^2} \cdot \dfrac{n-k}{g}$. Probability values are shown in square brackets

affected by sector shifts in the composition of the economy taking place during the growth process. In general, we expect this variable to have a positive sign – as GDP grows over time, the higher the industrial share of GDP, the larger the industrial sector and the higher the emissions level.[21] This effect, however, can be counterbalanced by the reduction in emission intensity as the industrial output shifts from heavy to less polluting industries with income growth. The overall sign of the industrial share of GDP, therefore, is *a priori* ambiguous.

In the case of the cubic functional form, the pooled OLS and FE specifications of the regression model can be written as follows, respectively (Model 1):

$$
\begin{aligned}
(\text{CO}_2)_{it} = {} & \beta_0 + \beta_1 \text{GDP}_{it} + \beta_2 \text{GDP}_{it}^2 + \beta_3 \text{GDP}_{it}^3 \\
& + \beta_4 \text{DENS}_{it} + \beta_5 \text{IND}_{it} + \beta_6 \text{GINI}_{it} + \varepsilon_{it}
\end{aligned}
\tag{2.1}
$$

$$
\begin{aligned}
(\text{CO}_2)_{it} = {} & \beta_0 + \beta_1 \text{GDP}_{it} + \beta_2 \text{GDP}_{it}^2 + \beta_3 \text{GDP}_{it}^3 \\
& + \beta_4 \text{DENS}_{it} + \beta_5 \text{IND}_{it} + \beta_6 \text{GINI}_{it} + \mu_i + \lambda_t + \varepsilon_{it}
\end{aligned}
\tag{2.2}
$$

where μ_i measures the country fixed effect ($i = 1, \dots N$) and λ_t the time fixed effect ($t = 1, \dots T$).[22]

Estimation results

Table 2.3 presents the results obtained by estimating Model 1 with each functional form. The pooled OLS and FE models achieve different conclusions on the shape of the CO_2–GDP relationship. The pooled OLS model finds a cubic relationship between per capita carbon dioxide and per capita income, while the preferred specification with the FE model is a linear one (see Figure 2.2).[23] As a further check, we also performed an F-test on the joint restriction that $\beta_3 = \beta_2 = 0$ in equation (2.2) and found that the null hypothesis is not rejected at five per cent significance level. Estimation results, therefore, do not support an EKC for CO_2 emissions. This is consistent with previous studies in the literature that find that the CO_2–GDP relationship is either monotonically increasing (Shafik 1994) or it has a turning point that falls beyond the income range in the sample (Holtz-Eakin and Selden 1995; Cole *et al.* 1997).

Both pooled OLS and FE models find that the higher the industrial share of GDP, the higher the CO_2 emissions level.[24] Population density is also positively related to CO_2 emissions in both models. Its coefficient β_4, however, is not statistically significant in the FE specification, while it is statistically different from zero in the preferred (cubic) specification of the pooled OLS model.

What about the link between inequality and CO_2 emissions? In this regard, the two models achieve opposite results. The Gini coefficient, in fact, is positive but has a very low t-value in the FE model, whereas it is negative and statistically significant in the pooled OLS model. The answer to the previous question depends, therefore, on the chosen specification – *an increase in inequality is associated with lower CO_2 emissions according to the pooled OLS model, whereas it does not have a significant link to CO_2 emissions according to the FE model.* Similar results apply if we use a log-linear specification. Even when variables are expressed in logs rather than in levels, the Gini coefficient is positive but not statistically significant in the FE model, while the opposite holds in the pooled OLS model.[25] It could be argued that the high standard error of the Gini coefficient in the FE model might be determined by the existence of multicollinearity in the model. Population density, in fact, is almost constant within countries (see the last column of Table 2.1). The results of Model 1, however, were unchanged when we repeated estimations eliminating population density from equations (2.1) and (2.2), which suggests that the low t-value of β_6 in the FE model does not depend on the low variability of population density within countries.

How does the introduction of inequality affect the CO_2–GDP relationship? To answer this question, we compared estimations of Model 1 with and without the Gini index for the identical sample and found the same preferred specification in both cases – cubic in the pooled OLS specification and linear in the FE one. *Introducing inequality, therefore, does not affect the shape of the CO_2–GDP relationship.*[26]

We then examined whether the same results apply with a different inequality measure. In fact, although the Gini coefficient is the most commonly used measure of inequality, it is not sensitive to changes in the underlying income distribution – transferring a given amount from the top to the middle class has the same effect on the Gini index of a progressive transfer at the lower end of the distribution. To overcome this drawback, Deininger and Squire (1996: 567) report also the income shares of population quintiles wherever possible. We then replaced the Gini coefficient with the 'interquintile difference' that measures the difference in the income shares between the top and the bottom quintiles of the population, namely:

interquintile difference $= (1 - Q_4) - Q_1$

where $Q_i = i$-th quintile ($i = 1, 2, 3, 4$).

Replacing the Gini coefficient with the interquintile difference does not affect the results, which suggests that our findings hold also for a different inequality measure.[27] We decided, therefore, to keep on using the Gini index for two reasons. First, because Deininger and Squire provide a higher number of observations on the Gini coefficient than on the quintiles. Second, because the Gini index is a more

Table 2.3 Model 1 with variables in levels[1]

	Pooled OLS model			FE model		
	Linear	Quadratic	Cubic	Linear	Quadratic	Cubic
GDP	0.72 (16.47)	0.2 (1.11)	2.33 (6.61)	0.93 (3.78)	1.7 (3.57)	2.33 (2.95)
GDP^2		0.02 (2.8)	−0.23 (−5.87)		−0.02 (−1.87)	−0.11 (−1.3)
GDP^3			0.008 (6.7)			0.002 (1.004)
Density	0.03 (0.95)	0.05 (1.37)	0.11 (3.28)	0.51 (0.69)	0.49 (0.67)	0.62 (0.84)
Industry	0.1 (4.34)	0.13 (5.23)	0.07 (2.99)	0.07 (3.56)	0.04 (1.79)	0.04 (1.56)
Gini	−0.09 (−3.22)	−0.09 (−3.33)	−0.12 (−5.24)	0.01 (0.44)	0.01 (0.68)	0.01 (0.59)
Constant	0.58 (0.37)	0.68 (0.45)	0.81 (0.64)	−4.83 (−2.33)	−6.49 (−2.93)	−6.92 (−3.07)
Adj. R^2	0.77	0.79	0.86	0.70	0.72	0.73

Note
1   In this table as well as in the following ones t-statistics are indicated in brackets. For each model the preferred specification is indicated in bold. The R^2 of the FE model is an R^2 within.

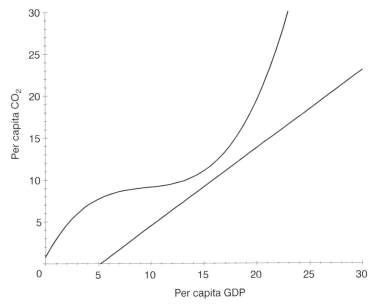

Figure 2.2   Model 1: estimated CO_2–GDP relationship with FE model (linear relationship) and pooled OLS model (cubic relationship). Flex point in the cubic pooled OLS model: GDP = 9.15, CO_2 = 8.77

complete measure of inequality than the quintiles since it is based on the whole income distribution, whereas the quintiles lose part of the information (e.g. the interquintile difference considers only the tails of the distribution).

The estimation results of Model 1 presented in this section might be affected by the presence of heterogeneity in the panel. The relationship between inequality and CO_2 emissions, for instance, might have opposite signs in rich and poor countries that tend to counterbalance in the panel, which could explain why the Gini coefficient b_6 turns out to be statistically non significant in the FE model. To investigate this problem more deeply, in the next paragraph we first examine the environment–inequality relationship for the subsamples of high- and low-income countries and then introduce a slight modification to the estimated model.

Differential effect of inequality in rich and poor countries

To verify whether inequality has a different effect on CO_2 emissions in rich and poor countries, we repeated the analysis of Model 1 for the sets of high- and low-income nations belonging to the data set that we used.[28] The results of subsample analysis suggest that according to the pooled OLS model a rise in inequality is positively related with emissions in rich countries ($\beta_6 = 0.17$) and negatively related with emissions in poor countries ($\beta_6 = -0.05$).[29] The Gini coefficient, however, is still not statistically significant in the FE model.

This analysis, however, suffers from a substantial loss of degrees of freedom since we focus attention on two subsamples of the data set. For this reason, we decided to adopt also an alternative approach to verify the differential effect of inequality in rich and poor countries by introducing a non-linearity in Model 1, as done by Barro (2000). To examine whether inequality affects growth differently in rich and poor countries, Barro (2000) allows the effect of the Gini index on economic growth to depend on the country's income level. For this purpose, he enters the Gini coefficient both linearly and as a product with (log of) per capita GDP among the regressors. Following Barro's approach, we allowed the effect of inequality on emissions to depend on the country's GDP by introducing the product of the Gini index with per capita GDP in equations (2.1) and (2.2). The cubic pooled OLS and FE models will now look respectively as follows (Model 2):

$$(CO_2)_{it} = \beta_0 + \beta_1 GDP_{it} + \beta_2 GDP_{it}^2 + \beta_3 GDP_{it}^3 + \beta_4 DENS_{it} + \beta_5 IND_{it} + \beta_6 GINI_{it} + \beta_7 GINI_{it}^* GDP_{it} + \varepsilon_{it} \qquad (2.3)$$

$$(CO_2)_{it} = \beta_0 + \beta_1 GDP_{it} + \beta_2 GDP_{it}^2 + \beta_3 GDP_{it}^3 + \beta_4 DENS_{it} + \beta_5 IND_{it} + \beta_6 GINI_{it} + \beta_7 GINI_{it}^* GDP_{it} + \mu_i + \lambda_t + \varepsilon_{it} \qquad (2.4)$$

The parameter β_6 measures the direct effect of inequality on CO_2 emissions, whereas β_7, the interaction term, measures its indirect effect through growth.

Observe that the effect of inequality on CO_2 emissions now changes at different income levels since it is:

$$\frac{\partial (CO_2)_{it}}{\partial GINI_{it}} = \beta_6 + \beta_7 \cdot GDP_{it}$$

As Table 2.4 shows, the pooled OLS and FE models achieve again opposite results. According to the pooled OLS model, $\hat{\beta}_6 < 0$ and $\hat{\beta}_7 > 7$, therefore:

$$\frac{\partial (CO_2)_{it}}{\partial GINI_{it}} \geq 0 \text{ when } GDP_{it} \geq -\frac{\beta_6}{\beta_7} \text{ and } \frac{\partial (CO_2)_{it}}{\partial GINI_{it}} < 0 \text{ when } GDP_{it} < -\frac{\hat{\beta}_6}{\hat{\beta}_7}$$

whereas the opposite holds for the FE specification.

In other words, the pooled OLS model finds that inequality increases CO_2 emissions in relatively rich countries (i.e. above a threshold level), whereas it reduces emissions in relatively poor countries (i.e. below certain income level). Table 2.4 shows the threshold income level above which the effect of inequality on CO_2 emissions is reversed. Thus, for instance, in the preferred cubic specification, the pooled OLS model suggests that greater inequality increases emissions when GDP is above 12.18 thousand dollars.

Table 2.4 Model 2 with variables in levels

	Pooled OLS model			FE model		
	Linear	*Quadratic*	*Cubic*	*Linear*	*Quadratic*	*Cubic*
GDP	−0.54	−0.82	1.57	1.05	1.71	2.42
	(1.86)	(−2.65)	(3.02)	(3.03)	(3.41)	(2.84)
GDP^2		0.02	−0.2		−0.02	−0.11
		(2.29)	(−4.78)		(−1.78)	(−1.32)
GDP^3			0.007			0.002
			(5.38)			(1.03)
Density	−0.001	0.01	0.08	0.45	0.48	0.59
	(−0.02)	(0.38)	(2.37)	(0.6)	(0.65)	(0.43)
Industry	0.11	0.13	0.07	0.07	0.04	0.04
	(4.9)	(5.51)	(3.31)	(3.49)	(1.77)	(1.56)
Gini	−0.24	−0.23	−0.18	0.02	0.01	0.02
	(−5.62)	(−5.37)	(−4.73)	(0.66)	(0.46)	(0.59)
Gini*GDP	0.03	0.03	0.01	−0.003	−0.0003	−0.002
	(4.38)	(4.02)	(1.96)	(−0.49)	(−0.05)	(−0.28)
$\frac{\partial CO_2}{\partial GINI} > 0$	GDP>6.95	GDP>7.21	GDP>12.18	GDP<7.82	always	GDP<11.55
Constant	6.18	5.76	3.17	−5.24	−6.52	−7.12
	(3.2)	(3.03)	(1.83)	(−2.33)	(−2.81)	(−2.98)
Adj.	0.81	0.82	0.86	0.70	0.72	0.73

We should be very cautious, however, in drawing any conclusion on the existence of a differential effect of inequality. Consistently with Model 1, in fact, β_6 and β_7 are statistically significant in the pooled OLS model, but FE estimations of these coefficients are not statistically different from zero in all estimated functional forms. This seems to suggest, therefore, that inequality has indeed no explanatory power for CO_2 emissions and that the low t-value observed for the Gini parameter in Model 1 is not the result of the aggregation of countries with opposite inequality effects.

The difference between the pooled OLS and FE models concerns also the significance of the other explanatory variables. In the cubic specification, the pooled OLS model finds that all explanatory variables are significantly different from zero, which also implies a cubic relationship between CO_2 and per capita income. On the contrary, FE estimations detect a linear CO_2–GDP relationship like in Model 1. Also observe that the industrial share of GDP is the only other variable beyond GDP that is statistically different from zero in the preferred linear specification of the FE model. This seems to suggest that the bulk of the variations in the carbon dioxide emissions depends on unobservable country specific effects. Similar results apply if we estimate a semilogarithmic specification by replacing the product term $GINI_{it} \times GDP_{it}$ with $GINI_{it} \times \log(GDP)_{it}$ in equations (2.3) and (2.4).

Finally, as in the previous section, we tested the robustness of our results by estimating Model 2 with all variables in logs. As Table 2.5 shows, results are basically unchanged, namely, the pooled OLS and FE model achieve opposite conclusions on the sign and statistical significance of β_6 and β_7. Once more, the FE estimations of β_6 and β_7 are not statistically different from zero in all estimated functional forms.

Conclusions

This study explored the link between environmental degradation, economic growth and income inequality within the framework of the EKC literature. To investigate this issue, we examined how inequality affects CO_2 emissions and the CO_2–GDP relationship.

Despite the large and increasing number of contributions on the EKC, only very few studies have investigated the environmental effect of inequality. These studies have generally used pooled OLS models. Pooling observations, however, disregards the heterogeneity of the countries included in the panel. For this reason, the results obtained in the literature may heavily depend on the chosen specification and may change if we adopt an FE model. This model, in our opinion, is more appropriate than the pooled OLS model in the present context, as confirmed also by the performed test that rejected the hypothesis underlying the pooled OLS model in all estimated specifications.

Our findings show that the pooled OLS and the FE models systematically achieve different or even opposite results for the relationship between inequality and CO_2 emissions. Consistently with the result obtained by Ravallion *et al.* (2000), if one

Table 2.5 Model 2 with variables in logs, effects of inequality on CO_2 emissions

	Pooled OLS model			FE model		
	Linear	*Quadratic*	*Cubic*	*Linear*	*Quadratic*	*Cubic*
ln GINI	−2.42	−2.42	−2.51	0.03	0.18	0.21
	(−6.37)	(−6.34)	(−6.73)	(0.11)	(0.59)	(0.68)
ln GINI* ln GDP	1.11	1.1	1.11	−10⁻⁵	−0.09	−0.09
	(4.31)	(4.24)	(4.43)	(0.00)	(−0.44)	(−0.45)
$\dfrac{\partial \ln CO_2}{\partial \ln GINI} > 0$	GDP>8.84	GDP>9.02	GDP>9.59	always	GDP<7.38	GDP<10.31

adopts a pooled OLS model the Gini coefficient turns out to be negative and statistically significant so that greater inequality reduces emissions. If we use an FE model, however, inequality is always non-statistically significant. This does not necessarily mean that income distribution has no effect on environmental degradation. Income inequality, in fact, can have positive and negative effects on the environment that tend to counterbalance. Thus, for instance, poor people contribute to pollution less than the rich since they have lower consumption levels, hence lower inequality reduces emissions, but they also use energy less efficiently than the rich, therefore lower inequality may also increase emissions.

Finally, we set forth the hypothesis that the overall non-significance of the Gini coefficient might depend on a differential effect of inequality for high- and low-income countries. To test whether this is the case, we performed a further analysis using a non-linear specification. The Gini coefficient, however, is still not statistically different from zero in the FE model, therefore the lack of a significant link between inequality and CO_2 emissions in our preferred specification seems independent of the aggregation of heterogeneous countries in the panel. Further investigation will be needed to examine whether inequality can have a differential effect on environmental degradation in rich and poor countries. For this purpose, future research should examine the relationship between environment and inequality in single-country studies, comparing the outcomes in developed and developing countries to analyze whether such a relationship changes at different income levels. Future empirical work should also be devoted to investigate whether CO_2 emissions are affected by inequality across countries rather than within countries. Much of the theoretical environmental literature has stressed the need of international cooperation to solve world-wide environmental problems. Large and increasing disparities across countries are likely to make international agreement on global environmental policies more difficult to achieve and thus might influence the emission path of global pollutants like CO_2.

Notes

1 I would like to thank Marzio Galeotti, Elena Gennari, Cheng Hsiao, Andrea Ichino and seminar participants at the University of Venice (CIDE conference), the European University Institute

and the EURESCO conference on 'The international dimension of environmental policy' (Kerkrade, The Netherlands, October 2000) for helpful comments and suggestions on previous versions of this paper. All remaining errors are my own. A preliminary version of the paper was published in Italian in 'Studi e Note di Economia', n. 1, 2003.

2　See, for instance, Barbier (1997), Panayotou (2000) and Borghesi (2001) for recent surveys of the literature on this topic.

3　In our opinion, however, this argument is more appropriate to describe the impact of greater poverty (rather than inequality) on the environment.

4　In an unequal society rich people can reap most of the benefits of exploiting natural resources (in terms of profits), while poor people often suffer most of the correspondent ecological costs since they rely more heavily on natural resources for their subsistence.

5　See also Boyce (2001) and Somanathan (2002) for further discussion on this issue.

6　The data set used for this second analysis is apparently made of 17 observations, that is, one per each country (Scruggs 1998: 270, table 2). The author includes two additional regressors (population density and the percentage of nuclear power in the energy supply) and rules out the measure of democracy since it has the same value in all OECD countries. He constructs the dependent variable by combining five pollution indicators – municipal waste, fertilizer use, emissions of sulphur dioxide, nitrous oxide and carbon dioxide.

7　Ravallion *et al.* (2000: 21–2) argue that the results obtained with the pooled OLS model seem more plausible than those of the FE model and that the FE estimators could be biased due to time-varying measurement errors.

8　Experts claim that 'although estimates of world emissions are probably within 10 per cent of actual emissions, individual countries estimates may depart more severely from reality' (World Resources Institute 1998: 348).

9　Galeotti and Lanza (1999a and 1999b) use an alternative data set recently developed by the International Energy Agency that does not include cement production and adopts a specific emission coefficient for each fossil fuel.

10　The data set presents international and intertemporal comparability problems because of definitional differences across countries and over time. See Deininger and Squire (1996) for a thorough discussion of these problems.

11　Other authors prefer to use GDP based on exchange rate rather than on PPP since the former 'better captures a country's control over the world product and its power in trade networks' (Roberts and Grimes 1997: 192). However, using GDP according to PPP makes our results comparable with those obtained by the other studies on the environment–inequality relationship.

12　Countries are divided by income levels according to the classification adopted by the World Bank (1998). The countries in question are: Australia, Bangladesh, Bulgaria, Canada, China, Colombia, Cote d'Ivoire, Dominican Republic, Ghana, Honduras, Hungary, India, Indonesia, Italy, Jamaica, Japan, Mauritania, Mexico, Netherlands, New Zealand, Nigeria, Pakistan, Philippines, Poland, Portugal, Romania, Singapore, Spain, Sweden, Thailand, Uganda, UK, USA, Venezuela and Zambia.

13　See the last column in Table 2.1.

14　In Bulgaria, for instance, inequality increased from 21.9 in 1988 to 34.4 in 1993. Several other countries (e.g. Hungary, Poland, Uganda, Venezuela and Zambia) experienced an increase by eight per cent or more in the same period.

15　See Galeotti and Lanza (1999a) for an extensive discussion of implications of the two models when applied to the environment–income relationship.

16　Unlike the linear specification, the log-linear model provides no closed form analytical expression for the income turning point and 'it is not possible to predict a priori the behavior of the function on the basis of the parameter signs, thus limiting their interpretability' (Galeotti and Lanza 1999a: 10).

17　Although many authors (e.g. Shafik 1994 and Ravallion *et al.* 2000) introduce a time trend as proxy for technical progress, we prefer to use time dummies since they represent a non-parametric form of the time trend, thus allowing for a less restrictive pattern than the linear trend.

18 The same result occurred when we used a much larger sample (120 countries in the same period) estimating a model without inequality.
19 The FE model has been estimated with the within estimator using deviations from individual specific means. As it is well known, the FE within estimators of β parameters coincide with the LSDV ones. The latter, however, may be computationally unfeasible when the number of time-invariant fixed effects to be estimated is too large.
20 Notice that per capita income has a very low correlation coefficient with the Gini index (–0.14) and with the industrial share of GDP (–0.01). In our opinion, therefore, the CO_2 impact of inequality and of the industrial share are not implicitly captured by the income variable.
21 Taking sulphur dioxide emissions as environmental indicator, Panayotou (1997: 472) argues that the industrial share of GDP is 'expected to enter with a positive sign since it is correlated with energy use, the main source of SO_2 emissions'.
22 Obviously, it will be $\beta_3 = 0$ in the quadratic model and $\beta_3 = \beta_2 = 0$ in the linear specification.
23 To select the preferred specification we started from the richest functional form, i.e. the highest degree polynomial, and reduced progressively the model according to the statistical significance of the parameters. Thus, the cubic model is the preferred specification if β_3 is statistically significant at five per cent level. If not, we move to the lower degree (quadratic) polynomial and look at the t-value of β_2, and so on.
24 As to the FE model, we obviously refer to the preferred (linear) specification.
25 The estimated impact of the other explanatory variables is basically unchanged as we pass from the linear to the log-linear specification of the pooled OLS model, while only slight modifications occur in the FE model. Estimation results are available from the author upon request.
26 Results are available from the author upon request.
27 Scruggs (1998) uses an alternative inequality measure to test the results obtained with the Gini index, namely the 80/20 income ratio: Q_4 / Q_1. Similarly to Scruggs, we find that no major changes occur in the results replacing the Gini index with Q_4 / Q_1.
28 The 12 high-income countries are: Australia, Canada, Italy, Japan, Netherlands, New Zealand, Portugal, Singapore, Spain, Sweden, UK and USA. The 11 low-income countries are: Bangladesh, China, Cote d'Ivoire, Ghana, Honduras, India, Mauritania, Nigeria, Pakistan, Uganda and Zambia. Income ranges between 8.4 and 21.07 thousand dollars for the former set of nations and between 0.6 and 2.3 thousand dollars for the latter.
29 In the pooled OLS model the effect of inequality on CO_2 emissions turns out to be higher in absolute terms in rich than in poor countries as opposed to the result obtained by Torras and Boyce (1998) with other environmental indicators.

References

Barbier, E. (1997) 'Introduction to the environmental Kuznets curve special issue', *Environment and Development Economics*, 2: 369–81.

Barro, R. (2000) 'Inequality and growth in a panel of countries', *Journal of Economic Growth*, 5: 5–32.

Borghesi, S. (2001) 'The environmental Kuznets curve: a critical survey of the literature', in M. Franzini and A. Nicita (eds), *Economic Institutions and Environmental Policy*, Aldershot: Ashgate. Previously published as *Fondazione ENI Enrico Mattei Nota di lavoro* No. 85.99, Milan: Italy.

Boyce, J.K. (1994) 'Inequality as a cause of environmental degradation', *Ecological Economics*, 11: 169–78.

Boyce, J.K. (2001) 'Power inequalities and the political economy of environmental protection', paper presented at the conference on Inequality, Collective Action and Environmental Sustainability, Santa Fe Institute, September 2001.

Cole, M.A., Rayner, A.J. and Bates, J.M. (1997) 'The environmental Kuznets curve: an empirical analysis', *Environment and Development Economics*, 2: 401–16.

Deininger, K. and Squire, L. (1996) 'A new data set measuring income inequality', *The World Bank Economic Review*, 10(3): 565–91.

Galeotti, M. and Lanza, A. (1999a) 'Desperately seeking (environmental) Kuznets', *Fondazione ENI Enrico Mattei Nota di lavoro* No. 2.99, Milan: Italy.

Galeotti, M., Lanza, A., (1999b) 'Richer and cleaner? A study on carbon dioxide emissions in developing countries', *Energy Policy*, 27(10): 565–73.

Grossman, G.M. (1995) 'Pollution and growth: what do we know?', in I. Goldin and L.A. Winters (eds), *The Economics of Sustainable Development*, Cambridge: Cambridge University Press.

Grossman, G.M. and Krueger, A.B. (1995) 'Economic growth and the environment', *Quarterly Journal of Economics*, 110: 353–77.

Heerink, N., Mulatu, A. and Bulte, E. (2001) 'Income inequality and the environment: aggregation bias in environmental Kuznets curves', *Ecological Economics*, 38: 359–67.

Holtz-Eakin, D. and Selden, T.M. (1995) 'Stoking the fires? CO_2 emissions and economic growth', *Journal of Public Economics*, 57: 85–101.

Hsiao, C. (1986) *Analysis of Panel Data*, Cambridge: Cambridge University Press.

Kaufmann, R.K., Davidsdottir, B., Garnham, S. and Pauly, P. (1998) 'The determinants of atmospheric SO_2 concentrations: reconsidering the environmental Kuznets curve', *Ecological Economics*, 25: 209–20.

Kuznets, S. (1955) 'Economic growth and income inequality', *American Economic Review*, 45: 1–28.

Magnani, E. (2000) 'The environmental Kuznets curve, environmental protection policy and income distribution', *Ecological Economics*, 32: 431–43.

Marland, G. and Rotty, R.M. (1984) 'Carbon dioxide emissions from fossil fuels: a procedure for estimation and results for 1950–1982', *Tellus*, 36B: 232–61.

Marsiliani, L. and Renström, T.I. (2000) 'Inequality, environmental protection and growth', *CentER Working Paper* No.2000-34, Tilburg: Tilburg University.

Panayotou, T. (1993) 'Empirical test and policy analysis of environmental degradation at different stages of economic development', in *World Employment Programme Research, Working Paper* No. 238, Geneva: International Labour Office.

Panayotou, T. (1997) 'Demystifying the environmental Kuznets curve: turning a black box into a policy tool', in *Environment and Development Economics*, 2: 465–84.

Panayotou, T. (2000) 'Economic growth and the environment', *Center for International Development, Working Paper* No. 56, Cambridge, MA: Harvard University.

Ravallion, M., Heil, M. and Jalan, J. (2000) 'Carbon emissions and income inequality', *Oxford Economic Papers*, 52: 651–69.

Roberts, J.T. and Grimes, P.E. (1997) 'Carbon intensity and economic development 1962–91: a brief exploration of the environmental Kuznets curve', *World Development*, 25(2): 191–8.

Scruggs, L.A. (1998) 'Political and economic inequality and the environment', in *Ecological Economics*, 26: 259–75.

Selden, T.M. and Song, D. (1994) 'Environmental quality and development: is there a Kuznets curve for air pollution emissions?', *Journal of Environmental Economics and Management*, 27: 147–62.

Shafik, N. (1994) 'Economic development and environmental quality: an econometric analysis', *Oxford Economic Papers*, 46: 757–73.

Somanathan, E. (2002) 'Inequality and environmental policy', paper presented at the International School of Economic Research, XV Workshop, 16–23 June 2002, Siena.

Suri, V. and Chapman, D. (1998) 'Economic growth, trade and energy: implications for the environmental Kuznets curve', *Ecological Economics*, 25: 195–208.

Torras, M. and Boyce, J.K. (1998) 'Income, inequality and pollution: a reassessment of the environmental Kuznets curve', *Ecological Economics*, 25: 147–60.

Unruh, G.C. and Moomaw, W.R. (1998) 'An alternative analysis of apparent EKC-type transitions', in *Ecological Economics*, 25: 221–9.

World Bank (1998) *World Development Indicators 1998–1999*, Washington, DC.

World Resources Institute (1998) *World Resources 1998–99*, New York: Oxford University Press.

3 Beyond accumulation and technical progress

Negative externalities as an engine of economic growth

Stefano Bartolini

Introduction[1]

The overall thesis of this chapter is that the erosion of social and environmental capital due to negative externalities may not be a limit to growth but may instead stimulate it. Hence negative externalities may be an engine of growth.

This statement is entirely at odds with the theory of endogenous growth, which emphasizes the role played in growth by positive externalities. And it is also at odds with two other bodies of literature of relevance to this study, those on sustainable development and on social capital.

The concept of sustainable development revolves around the doubts that began to arise in the second half of the last century concerning the limits to growth imposed by the finiteness of natural resources. Such doubts can be summed up by the question: do the limits of the world in which we live impose limits on the expansion of economic activity, and how stringent are those limits? The imprinting of this question on the sustainable development literature, and therefore on models of growth with environmental resources, has impeded exploration of the possibility that the depletion of natural capital may be a stimulus for growth rather than hampering it.

Nor has the literature on social capital ever considered the possibility that the erosion of the latter may be not a limit on growth but an engine for it. In fact, such literature generally considers endowment of social capital to be an important factor in determining growth, and that its erosion may damage the prospects of growth itself. This may perhaps be due to the imprinting of the concept of social capital, which has been developed to take account of the importance of socio-cultural factors for development, enabling explanation of why the market system performs so differently in countries having similar endowments and technology.

Although they will come as a surprise to the main bodies of literature referred to above, the ideas set out in this chapter have a long and interdisciplinary history. Here I shall mention only Polanyi and Hirsch, as the authors who have made the most outstanding contribution to shaping this view.

The chapter is organized as follows. 'Theoretical problems of current growth theory' sets out some theoretical problems concerning growth theory, while 'Empirical problems: Why do people strive so hard for money?' and 'Why are people so unhappy?' are devoted to some empirical problems. 'Negative externalities as the tertium movens of economic growth' argues that negative externalities may be the engine of growth that growth theory has overlooked and which may solve its theoretical and empirical problems. 'Explanation based on positional externalities' and 'Explanation based on externalities reducing free goods: the GASP models' analyse the two different kinds of negative externality that may operate as engines of growth: positional negative externalities, and those that reduce the availability of free goods as final or intermediate goods. 'Defensive expenditures in consumption' deals with the aspects of growth that have been neglected by current growth theory. 'Defensive expenditures in production' examines the growth mechanisms driven by negative externalities affecting productive capacities. 'Policy implications: the two explanations compared' compares the policy implications of the two different kinds of negative externality that may act as engines of growth. 'Implications for environmental economics' outlines the implications for environmental economics of the growth theory based on negative externalities that reduce free goods. 'On the possibilities of improving the human condition' deals with the possibilities of improving the human condition while 'Summary' summarizes the theses set out in the chapter.

Theoretical problems of current growth theory

Current growth theory is founded on the idea that growth is driven by increased labour productivity. Two causes are identified for this increase – physical and human capital accumulation and technical progress – which are therefore the engines of growth, its *primum* and *secundum movens*. However, this explanation of the long-term dynamics of per-capita output suffers from serious theoretical and empirical problems.

The theoretical problem is that an increase in labour productivity is not a sufficient condition to generate growth. Individuals may in fact devote a substantial part of increased productivity to increasing their leisure, thereby reducing the return on their investments in capital and new knowledge. This may slow growth down and in the long run bring it to a complete halt. Hence explaining why an economy grows indefinitely means also explaining, besides an increase in productivity, why individuals do not choose to devote a substantial part of this increase to augmenting their leisure. Yet it is exactly this feature that endogenous growth models are unable to explain – once the labour supply is made endogenous, they predict that individuals will use the long-term increase in the labour productivity to augment their leisure, not their output. In fact, perpetual growth tends to disappear in these models when the choice between work and leisure is made endogenous, and this comes about for the following reason – individuals tend to react to increased productivity by reducing their labour supply (particular hypotheses on preferences aside).[2]

The vulnerability of endogenous growth models to the endogenization of the labour supply implies that they fail to explain why an economy follows a perpetual growth path. Even less of an explanation may be provided by the majority of growth models which assume a fixed labour supply, and therefore assume what they are supposed to explain, namely that the increase in labour productivity is preponderantly devoted to increase output rather than leisure.

Likewise, the fact that the marginal productivity of capital does not decrease (as in models of endogenous growth) is not a sufficient condition for the saving rate to be sufficiently sustained over time to ensure perpetual growth. In economies that grow ever richer, in fact, individuals may choose to reduce their efforts to accumulate. Indeed, it is precisely this prediction that endogenous growth models tend to make when the labour supply is endogenized. Perpetual growth also flags because individuals reduce their saving rate – agents tend to respond to increased wealth by reducing their work effort devoted to accumulation (Bartolini and Bonatti 2003a).

In short, the result of perpetual growth seems rather vulnerable to inclusion of a work/leisure choice in models. The plausible mechanisms emphasized by endogenous growth models that ensure a non-decreasing marginal productivity of capital over the long period are insufficient to generate perpetual growth. In order to generate it, individuals must work and accumulate, i.e. must be interested in money, more than endogenous growth models predict. According to these models, in fact, individuals react to a long-term increase in labour productivity by enjoying life more than is necessary to ensure perpetual growth.

This is as regards the theoretical problems. We now turn to the empirical ones, which consist in the difficulty of explaining why the promises held out by growth of more freedom from work and greater happiness have not been fulfilled.

Empirical problems: why do people strive so hard for money?

Keynes predicted that by 2030 the average working week in Britain would amount to only 15 hours. In reality, the initial promise of industrialism that it would progressively free mankind from its Biblical condemnation to a life of drudgery seems to have been largely betrayed. In the advanced societies, work continues to take up most of people's vital energies.

The evidence shows that industrialism is associated with a huge utilization of labour. The beginning of growth processes – the transition from a rural to an industrial economy – has always been associated with a mobilization of human resources taking the form of explosive growth in the participation rate, in working time, and so on (Williamson 1995, Krugman 1995, Bartolini and Bonatti 2002, 2004a, and Antoci and Bartolini 2004). Moreover, as regards the long-term trend of industrial economies to reduce the labour input, the evidence shows that this, in the best of hypotheses, is weak and non-monotonic.[3] Nor does the post-industrial economy seem to encourage optimism as to any increase in leisure. In fact, a large body of data on working hours in the USA seem to indicate that they have increased in the last decades (Schor 1991, Robinson and Godbey 1999, and Bluestone and Rose 2000; see Figart and Golden 2000, for a critical review of the controversy on this argument).

Why 'industrialism has the tendency to produce goods rather than leisure time'? (Cross 1993: 7). What are the reasons for the signal failure of growth to maintain its promise of increasing leisure? Why is 'time pressure' a typical problem of contemporary society? Why do surveys invariably find that people suffer from a 'time squeeze'? Why have new categories of the socially deprived like the 'time poor' appeared? What is it that induces people to work so hard in economies which grow ever more productive?

The difficulty of growth theory in answering these questions is the obvious empirical correlate of the theoretical problem discussed in the preceding section. Since the inclusion of the work/leisure choice in endogenous growth models yields the counterfactual prediction that working time will be highly responsive in the long run to technological advances, such models are unable to explain these empirical patterns of growth, neither the sudden increase in the labour supply during industrial revolutions, the weak and non-monotonic decline in the input of labour over the very long run, nor the increase of working hours in the greatest post-industrial economy on the planet.

As regards the saving rate, too, endogenous growth models seem to predict its greater reactivity to increased wealth and productivity than is actually the case. In fact, also the tendency for the saving rate to decline is doubtful, and in any case weak if compared to the long-term increase in wealth and productivity.[4]

In conclusion, people in real economies seem to be much more interested in money than endogenous growth models predict. We do not know what prevents them from enjoying life more by working less and accumulating less. Current models seem to lack an engine of growth – a *tertium movens* of growth, which induces people to be so interested in money. 'Why do people strive so hard for money?'

Why are people so unhappy?

The second empirical anomaly is the betrayal by growth of its promise of greater well-being. A man of the nineteenth century would probably be astonished that Western societies emancipated from mass poverty would be populated by a mass of dissatisfied individuals. And the billions of human beings who still suffer from poverty would probably find it just as astonishing.

But this seems to be what is happening. The empirical evidence concerning rich countries overwhelmingly demonstrates that growth has betrayed its promise of well-being. A great quantity of data, both subjective – i.e. relative to the degree of satisfaction with their lives expressed by individuals[5] – and objective as regards suicides and mental illnesses, induce scholars in various disciplines to conclude that there is practically no correlation between income and happiness. Whether one considers the post-war decline in the number of Americans who report themselves as being 'happy' (Lane 2000: 3), or the contemporary epidemic of depression, anxiety and panic, or the increase in suicides among the young, growth has evidently failed to increase happiness.

Why are people so unhappy? What needs to be explained is the paradox pointed out by Lane (2000) 'the economic (...) institutions of our time are products of the utilitarian philosophy of happiness but seem to have guided us to a period of greater unhappiness' (ibid.: 13).

It is for this reason that the theme of happiness and the explanation of the malaise of rich societies have recently been the subject of intense debate which, besides generating a recently flourishing economic literature (the 'happiness economics'), has also involved sociologists (Baumann 2002, and Veenhoven 1993), psychologists (Kahneman 1999, and Argyle 1987) and political scientists (Lane 2000).

It is evident that current growth models, in which well-being depends entirely on what is transacted in the market, are wholly unable to explain the paradox of Lane. Any one-good model is unable to explain it because it assumes that individual well-being improves as more output becomes available for consumption.

Negative externalities as the tertium movens of economic growth

The explanation of this latter anomaly complicates explanation of the former one: 'Why do people strive so much for money if money cannot buy happiness?' This is what the literature on the topic refers to as a 'paradox of happiness'. Any joint explanation of the two empirical anomalies must in practice satisfy the requirement of explaining this paradox.

In its present state the theory of growth seems entirely unable to handle issues of such importance. A growth mechanism exclusively based on accumulation and technical progress – the *primum* and *secundum movens* of growth – fails to explain why growth has not fulfilled its promises of greater leisure and greater happiness. I argue that this inability may be because growth theory overlooks a *tertium movens* able to explain the above paradox – negative externalities.

The three trends discussed – in work, saving and happiness – have never been connected, and discussion on them has remained confined to the respective disciplinary areas, receiving no attention in the debate on growth. In the next two sections I argue that these three trends may be the consequence of the same cause – the negative externalities generated by the growth process. These negative externalities may be of two kinds – positional ones, and those that reduce the availability of free goods as final or intermediate goods.

Explanation based on positional externalities

An economy is positional in nature when individuals are interested in their relative positions rather than their absolute ones. Let us suppose that individuals are interested in relative not absolute income (or wealth). In an economy of this kind, an increase in one person's income generates a positional negative externality in the sense that it reduces the well-being of someone else.[6]

The capacity of the hypothesis that relative income matters to explain the empirical anomalies of growth theory should be intuitive. Individuals are induced to work hard and to accumulate much by positional competition. The fact that the position of people with constant incomes worsens if others increase their incomes is a powerful incentive for the former to be interested in money. But a general increase in income which leaves the relative positions unchanged cannot improve general well-being. In an economy of this kind the well-being of everyone cannot improve by definition. Hence the hypothesis of negative positional externalities is consistent with explanation of the happiness paradox. Positional negative externalities may be the *tertium movens* which explains the empirical anomalies of growth theory.[7]

Explanation based on externalities reducing free goods: the GASP models

The other explanation of these anomalies – the one based on negative externalities which reduce social and environmental capital – has been presented in a number of recent articles (Antoci and Bartolini 1997 and 2004, and Bartolini and Bonatti, 2002, 2003a, 2003b, 2004 and 2004a). According to this approach, the theoretical and empirical difficulties of growth theory are due to the fact that it fails to consider that well-being and productive capacity depend largely on goods that are not purchased in the market but are furnished by the social and natural environment. The growth process generates extensive negative externalities which reduce the capacity of the environment to furnish such goods. These negative externalities may be the *tertium movens* of growth given the capacity of the market to supply costly substitutes for the diminishing free goods. If agents can purchase costly substitutes for free resources they will react to the decline in their well-being or in their productive capacity by increasing their use of goods purchased in the market. Negative externalities force individuals increasingly to rely on private goods in order to prevent a decline in their well-being or productive capacity. In this way they contribute to an increase in output. This feeds back into the negative externalities, giving rise to a further diminution in free goods to which agents react by increasing output, and so on. A self-reinforcing mechanism thus operates whereby growth generates negative externalities and negative externalities generate growth. Hence growth takes the form of a process of substitution whereby free final (or intermediate) goods are progressively replaced with costly goods in the consumption (or production) patterns of individuals.[8]

According to these Growth As Substitution Process (GASP) models, the two anomalies of growth theory are two sides of the same coin. People strive so much for money because they have to defend themselves against negative externalities, they work so much and save so much in order to substitute – in the present and in the future – free goods with costly ones. But an increase in their income does not improve their happiness because it involves a process of substitution. These negative externalities are the factor motivating people to strive so much for money that growth theory has failed to identify. But they are also the factor that explains why people's efforts are not rewarded with increased well-being.

On this view, the dynamics of the labour supply and accumulation depends on the magnitude of social and environmental cleavages. Industrial revolutions are the paradigmatic example of this mechanism – they are the most striking processes of labour supply and accumulation increase because they are the most striking processes of social and environmental devastation recorded by economic history.

The trend of the saving rate depends on social and environmental cleavages because in this framework social wealth also includes social and environmental capital besides private capital, but agents can accumulate only the latter. Hence agents react to the progressive degradation of commons by keeping their saving rate high. At any point along a growth path, agents are poorer than appears if we consider their private wealth alone. The decline in common resources produces a negative wealth effect which boosts accumulation despite the increasing private wealth.

In this framework economic prosperity does not increase happiness. Individuals are unable to enjoy the opportunities for greater well-being offered by increased labour productivity because they are forced into over-work and over-accumulation by negative externalities. Growth thus appears to be a coordination failure.

Defensive expenditures in consumption

The idea behind GASP models is that one way to motivate people to accumulate money is to create a society in which increasingly less can be obtained for free; a society in which opportunities to acquire well-being in ways which do not pass through the market become increasingly scarce, and in which well-being can therefore only be purchased.

According to this approach, the theory of growth based on accumulation and technical progress is unable to explain the paradox of happiness because it tells only part of the story of growth – the story, that is, in which goods are luxury goods for one generation, standard goods for the next, and absolute necessities for the one after that. The history of economic growth is obviously full of examples of this process. But the other side of this story is that of free goods which become scarce and costly ones for the next generation and luxury goods for the one after that. Urbanization is widely associated with phenomena of this kind. A world in which silence, clean air, swimming in clean seas or rivers, or pleasant strolls become the privilege of uncontaminated places, and tropical paradises is a world which tends to spend considerable resources to evade the unliveable environments that it has constructed. The periodic mass migrations known as summer holidays that one observes in the rich countries, or the fact that tourism from the rich countries has become an important resource for many poor ones, may not be indicative of higher living standards but rather a response to a deterioration in the quality of life.

Of especial importance in explaining growth's betrayal of its promises of well-being is interpretation of social capital as 'relational goods', a term which denotes the contribution to well-being made by human relations (see Ulhaner 1989). That the quality of relations is of crucial importance for happiness is an assertion supported by a quantity of studies in the social sciences, as well as by evolutionary principles (Lane 2000). From this point of view, the rich societies are experiencing a gigantic *relational failure*. Loneliness is regarded as a great social and personal problem, and so too is the poor quality of relations (Lane 2000: 85). The progressive spread of market relations, exclusively based on personal advantage, seems to be associated with relational desertification (Hirsch 1976, Polanyi 1968, Hirschman 1982 and Bartolini and Palma 2002). For that matter, since its beginnings in the Industrial Revolution, the market society has been accompanied by a critique of its destructive impact on social relationships and cohesion (see the romantic and socialist critiques of the Industrial Revolution).

Urbanization, too, plays a role in determining the availability of relational goods. The urban evolution of the industrialized countries establishes the city as the center of aggregation, but only as far as production and consumption are concerned. Cities are environments constructed for the purposes of work and exchange and not as places where people can meet. The urban environment is a paradigmatic example of the poverty of relational occasions and of low-cost meeting places, and in parallel, of the abundance of costly opportunities for leisure activity. The urban distress of social groups with the freest time, most relational needs and least money – namely young people and the elderly – testify to this situation. It may be for these reasons that the city is the engine of growth (according to the World Bank) and also the crux of the mass dissatisfaction of the rich societies.

However, independently of the variety and complexity of the causes of the relational failure of the market societies, the point is that a world of relational poor individuals may seek out numerous forms of compensation in material goods – even less obvious ones like those exemplified by the enormous growth of home entertainment or drugs, the evasion *par excellence* from an unsatisfactory reality. The enormous accumulation of produced goods and the worship of everything that is private which characterizes market societies may be reactions to the erosion of everything that is common to people.

In conclusion, the time pressure and the relational and environmental failure of market societies may be at the core of explanation of both the capacity of those societies to generate growth and of the latter's betrayal of its promise of happiness.

Defensive expenditures in production

The previous section discussed the processes by which the free goods entering the utility functions are substituted. But it is likely that environmental capital, and especially social capital, is also of great importance in determining the system's productive capacities.[9] Does the consideration that social capital also enters production functions, and that negative externalities may therefore affect productive capacities, alter the assertion that negative externalities can be an engine of growth, and the explanation of the paradox offered thus far based on the substitution of free goods by costly ones?

The GASP model presented in Bartolini and Bonatti (2004) shows that also in the case in which social (and/or environmental) capital enters the production function, negative externalities may give rise to a substitution process whose result is an increase in output. The reason is that individuals may undertake expenditures to defend themselves against negative externalities also when these affect their productive capacities. Many transaction costs, in fact, are intrinsically a defence against opportunism. The erosion of social capital may lead to a spread of opportunism and therefore to an increase in many transaction costs. The decline in trust, in the perception of shared social norms, in values like honesty or business ethics greatly complicates transactions (see for instance Fukuyama 1995). Agents may defend themselves by shifting to transactional modes employing private goods rather than public ones. For example, one may substitute for trust in someone else with security cameras controlling him. The increased output consequent on the possibility to purchase defence against negative externalities produces a further decrease in social capital which feeds back the mechanism. Hence, if individuals react to the erosion of social capital by expanding the production of private goods, the unintended result will be a further erosion of social capital, and this may trigger a process of self-fuelling growth.

Hence, even when social (and environmental) capital enters the production function, negative externalities may generate a growth process. In this case, the increase in output may comprise intermediate goods whose use is made necessary by the growth process. One can easily imagine examples of this kind – expenditures on business and legal advisors, on the enforcement of property rights, of industrial secrets, on protection against crime, the costs of monitoring, of writing and enforcing contracts, information costs like expenditure on personnel recruitment or the search for commercial partners, the acquisition of personal knowledge to defend oneself against opportunism (living in a world of sharks may be very costly, and not only psychologically). Expenditure of this kind may not be a sign of the 'modernization' of transactions but instead a response to the decline in social capital.

This mechanism confirms that it is possible to explain the happiness paradox in terms of a substitution process. The need to defend productive capacities against the erosion of social capital may boost the labour supply and the level of activity. But the growth of output overestimates the increase in final goods and therefore in well-being, given that the output also comprises intermediate goods. The difference from the GASP models in which social and environmental capital enters utility functions is that in that case growth overestimates the well-being because it does not take account of the destruction of final goods.

Policy implications: the two explanations compared

In this section I compare the policy implications of the two explanations provided here for the paradox of happiness – the one based on positional negative externalities and the other relying on the externalities that affect free goods, as in GASP models.

First note that the latter explanation does not refer to anything positional – an increase in others' incomes induces individuals to work hard and accumulate much because it worsens their absolute and not relative position. The inability of growth to increase happiness is due to the fact that the erosion of free resources worsens the absolute positions of agents, not their relative ones. The interest of individuals in money, and their inability to improve their happiness, are due to negative externalities that have nothing positional.

Why should positional negative externalities be kept distinct from externalities that erode social and natural capital? The answer is because they have very different policy implications.

In their turn, the policy implications of the hypothesis of positional externalities differ greatly depending on how the positional psychology of agents – that is, their interest in positional goods – is founded. There are two motivations that may explain the interest of individuals in the relative position – envy and emulation. A biological or a cultural explanation can be given for each of them.

According to the biological explanation, the degree of satisfaction that individuals feel with their lives depends on the extent to which they are able to satisfy their needs. These needs depend on what individuals consider being possible. Hence happiness is modelled on what is deemed to be reasonably obtainable. The evolutionary psychologist Steven Pinker (1997) writes: 'How do we know what can reasonably be attained? A good source of information is what other people have attained. If they can have it, perhaps so can you' (ibid.: 390). Happiness is therefore intrinsically relative. In this set-up the positional psychology of individuals is therefore biologically founded in the cognitive processes that plot the horizon of the possible in the human species.

Of course, the policy implications of this set-up are entirely discouraging. In the envy-ridden or emulative world of the human species, growth inevitably engenders a senseless and exhausting rat race. Given that individuals' interest in positional goods is biologically founded, and therefore intrinsically bound up in human nature, it is impossible to increase the happiness of everyone.

The policy implications of the assumption that relative position matters are different if the positional psychology of individuals is culturally founded. According to numerous authors, a society based on competition tends to generate a system of values which are by their nature relative, such as success, power, etc. The values generated by a market society produce an endogenous change in preferences that makes a generalized increase in happiness impossible.

The policy implications of a cultural explanation for the interest of individuals in positional goods are less pessimistic. There is a way to increase general happiness, but it is reached along the arduous road and long-drawn-out time-scale of cultural policy (for example educational policy).

Instead, in GASP models, the inability of growth to improve happiness derives from an institutional problem, and not a biological or cultural one. The price system does not receive signals about the importance of fundamental needs which do not pass through the market. Individuals are unable to control resources crucial for their happiness. The fact that money does not buy happiness stems neither from biology nor from culture; money is unable to buy happiness amid a pattern of growth with excessively high social and environmental costs.

Implications for environmental economics

It is curious that the stagnation/decline of happiness over the very long period in the industrial economies has never been cited as evidence for the argument that current patterns of growth are not sustainable. However the literature on sustainable development would seem to be a candidate to explain a disappointing trend in well-being, interpreted as an unsustainable well-being.

Let us examine the answers furnished by this literature to the following question: on what depends the fact that a generation does or does not consume crucial resources whose depletion in some sense restricts the possibilities of future generations to satisfy their needs? The conventional environmentalist wisdom tells us that the sustainability of a given pattern of growth depends: (i) on the level of the discount rate present in the economy, (ii) on the degree of substitutability between natural capital and output.

Both these answers are profoundly questioned by the results of the GASP models. This is the argument of the next two sections.

Discount rate and sustainability

The environmentalist literature treats the problem of sustainability as a problem of (intertemporal) ethics – that is, of intergenerational equity. The problems of sustainability are attributed to the excessively high discount rate of present generations. Individuals, it is argued, give insufficient importance to the future of subsequent generations to be ensured an equal level of possibilities, whatever this means (possibilities in terms of income, well-being, consumption, or whatever 'sustainability' may mean). The propensity of present generations to exploit resources crucial for the future exceeds their right to do so, defined on the basis of some plausible criterion of intergenerational equity. According to this approach there is an 'ethical' discount rate which is lower than that of individuals. Note that the possibility of posing the problem of sustainability in ethical terms rests entirely on the assumption that the dynamic of economic systems reflects the discount rate of the individuals.

This explanation runs into a major difficulty – the incompatibility between high discount rates and the presence of substantial saving rates. Why do agents save so much if they have high discount rates? Why do they accumulate so much if their interest in the future is so low as to consign subsequent generations to a threatening and difficult future (see Vercelli 1992)?

Some GASP models may provide an explanation for the problem of sustainability which resolves the above-mentioned difficulty. They may do so because explanation of the problem of sustainability is based on the idea that the behaviour of economic systems does not reflect the discount rates of individuals (see Bartolini and Bonatti 2003a and 2003b).

These models predict that the long-term welfare of individuals tends to decline the higher their rate of time preference is – the greater the concern of living individuals for their descendants, the more they worsen the prospects of the latter.[10]

This apparent paradox can be understood if we analyse the structure of the intertemporal allocation decision problem that individuals must resolve. In these models there are two assets of importance for present and future well-being – output accumulated and the environmental and social resource. Only the former can be accumulated privately, given that the latter is a common. Hence individuals can defend their future well-being against decline in the common resource by accumulating the only asset that they are able to accumulate – the private good. In this context the dynamic of the economic system does not reflect the temporal preference of agents. The more that individuals are concerned for the well-being of their descendants, the more they will save, given that they anticipate the depletion of free resources.

But this greater accumulation of privately owned assets does not compensate for lesser social and environmental quality that it unintentionally causes, and it thus produces a decline in long-term well-being.

Hence, in GASP models the decline in long-term well-being is due to a coordination failure, not to the intertemporal greed of each generation. These models depict a world of people interested in their own well-being and that of their descendants, people who clearly perceive that well-being also depends on things that cannot be bought, primarily the quality of the environment and of human relationships. In short, they perceive the importance of living in a better world, where the expression 'better world' denotes an improvement in social and environmental quality. Because they are interested in the well-being of their direct descendents they want to bequeath a better world to them. But they do not know how to do so; that is, they feel it to be impossible. Being unable to leave them a better world, they try to leave them money. As individuals seek to acquire the money that enables them and their descendants to escape an unliveable world, each of them makes her/his small contribution to worsening the world – that is, to produce a decline in long-term well-being.

Accordingly, the more individuals are concerned about their descendants, the more willing they will be to make sacrifices to leave them a better world. Being unable to do so, they will make more efforts to leave them money. Consequently, their small personal contribution to worsening the world will be greater, and the future will be that of a worse world. This explains why the greater the efforts made by agents to improve the future of their descendants, the more the unintentional result of their intertemporal defensive actions will be a worsening of the well-being of their descendants.

According to this approach, the problem of sustainability does not arise from intergenerational conflict but from a failure among individuals belonging to the same generation to coordinate their efforts. The negative impact on long-term well-being of this coordination failure is the more severe, the more the problem of intertemporal allocation is important for individuals – that is, the stronger their preference for the future.

This argument should not be confused with a claim for a higher discount rate. I am simply claiming that respect for the discount rate of individuals may suffice for sustainability; long-term decline in well-being may arise from the inability of the economic system to reflect the time preference of agents. Individuals may have a rate of time preference that is lower than the one exhibited by the economic system, and a signal of this preference may be precisely the fact that they have substantial saving rates.

The traditional environmentalist claim for a lower discount rate is misleading if the dynamics of the economic system do not reflect the time preference of individuals. In the view put forward here the problem of sustainability is a problem not of ethics but of efficiency. In other words, it is an institutional problem. A coordination failure generates inefficiencies in the intertemporal allocation of resources. By claiming that sustainability is not an ethical question, I do not wish to argue that present generations have the right to compromise the future; rather, that they might not have the desire to do so. The problem of the sustainability of an economic system may therefore be solved by changing its institutions.

This explanation of the problems of the sustainability of well-being contains a policy message very different from the traditional environmentalist account based on the intertemporal selfishness of human beings. The paternalistic appeal of Calvinist stamp to the virtues of abstinence implicit in the traditional explanation is misleading because the problem lies not in human nature – that is, in its alleged intertemporal greed – but in the economic system. There is no intrinsic conflict in human nature between generational interest and species interest. It is the economic and social organization that should be changed.[11]

Substitutability and sustainability

One of the key results of growth models with environmental resources is that the sustainability of a given pattern of economic growth depends on a technological problem – the degree of substitutability between 'man-made' goods and natural resources; the higher this is, the greater the welfare for future generations.[12] The overall finding of this literature is therefore that the conditions which an economy must respect in order to be sustainable are the more stringent, the more pessimistic are assumptions about the degree of substitutability between produced goods and environmental goods.

In contrast, GASP models show that the possibility of substituting man-made goods for environmental assets can trigger a self-reinforcing process of growth in output that leads to a worsening of individual well-being. In fact, the growth process is described as a process of substitution of environmental and social goods with produced goods in which growth 'goes too far'.

The main implication is that the sustainability of well-being may not be a technological problem but instead an institutional one. A coordination failure may induce agents to over-exploit the possibility of substituting social and environmental resources, thereby fuelling the deterioration of those resources and generating undesired growth. In these models, substitutability guarantees the sustainability of growth, but not of well-being. The implication is that high substitutability provides no guarantee that well-being can be sustainable in the absence of policy.

On the possibilities of improving the human condition

The gradual decline in Western culture of trust in progress has probably been influenced by economic growth's betrayal of its promises. To what extent is there justification for the idea that it is possible to improve the human condition?

From the policy point of view, the GASP models imply a call for collective action that may assume different forms – for example, it may support the view that rich economies are over-worked and the demand for legislation to reduce working time. It may also support the view that a pure market economy is characterized by an excessive depletion of environmental assets, and then support demand for extensive environmental policy.[13] Given the emphasis on the importance of relations for human happiness, this approach further suggests that social policies intended to improve relations should be introduced. In short, the GASP models suggest that collective action is important for control of the inefficiencies generated by the economies described.[14]

The policy implications of the various strands of argument put forward in this chapter all lead in the same direction. According to the GASP models, current experience and the future risk of diminished well-being are neither a biological problem nor a cultural, ethical or technological one; they are an institutional problem.

The questions to be asked when assessing the possibilities of improvement in the human condition do not concern the extent to which the competitive or emulative spirit of individuals is due to biological or cultural conditioning; nor do they concern the ethical limits to the right to exploit resources of each generation or the origin of the intertemporal greed of human beings, nor the limitations of technology in devising substitutes for environmental resources. Rather, they concern the extent to which human societies are able to generate the institutional change necessary to improve the relational and environmental conditions of individuals.

It is probable that many of the problems to which GASP models allude could be greatly alleviated by focusing social policies on the humanization of relations among people, and between people and the environment. To what extent is this likely to happen?

It is anything but obvious that optimism is justified when answering the question. In general, there is no guarantee that the mechanisms that shape collective consciousness and choices do not impose particular interests to the detriment of those of broad social strata. Neo-institutionalist historiography is replete with examples of societies whose decline has been due to collective decisions serving the interests of the few at the expense of the interests of the many (North and Thomas 1973, and North 1981). The 'logic of collective action' (Olson 1971) tends systematically to distort collective choices with respect to interests of great importance. The laws that regulate the pressure capacity of interest groups tend systematically to bias collective action with respect to objectives of enormous public interest.

Hence, the crucial questions regarding the likelihood of an improvement in the human condition largely concern the success of the market democracies in representing the interests of broad strata of the population – interests coincident with the creation of institutions for the maintenance and expansion of social and environmental resources.

Summary

Current models of endogenous growth face two major empirical anomalies. The first is that once the labour/leisure choice is included, they lead to the counterfactual prediction that the labour supply will be highly responsive to technological advances in the long run. Individuals will tend to allocate the increase in labour productivity due to accumulation and technical progress preponderantly to increasing their leisure. However, this does not seem to be supported by the empirical evidence. In the industrial economies the overwhelming majority of increased productivity has been allocated to increase output, and the weak tendency for leisure to increase seems to be declining or indeed has gone into reverse in the USA in recent decades. The second empirical anomaly is that endogenous growth models predict that the well-being of agents will increase as more output becomes available. Also this prediction is counterfactual. A large body of empirical evidence shows that the rich countries are experiencing a veritable betrayal of the promises of greater happiness held out by growth.

Why, then, do people work so much? Why do they strive so much for money? Growth literature provides no answer to this question, or to the other very important one of why people are so unhappy. Moreover, providing a joint answer to the two questions seems particularly puzzling. Why do people strive so much for money if money cannot buy happiness? How can one explain the above 'paradox of happiness'? Why has growth reneged on its promise to increase leisure and happiness? The silence of economic theory on these questions is deafening. I argue that the empirical difficulties of growth theory are due to the fact that it ignores the role of negative externalities as an engine of growth. In fact, growth theory identifies a *primum* and *secundum movens* of growth – accumulation and technical progress – but it omits the *tertium movens* of negative externalities. These externalities can be of two kinds. The first are positional negative externalities, i.e. those due to the fact that individuals may be interested in relative not absolute position. In an economy of this kind, an increase in one person's income generates a positional negative externality in the sense that it reduces the well-being of someone else. Individuals are induced to work hard by positional competition. However, in a positional economy a general increase in income which leaves the relative positions unchanged cannot improve general well-being. Hence positional negative externalities may be the *tertium movens* which explains the empirical anomalies of growth theory.

The second kind of negative externalities are those which reduce free goods. Some recent models, both evolutionary or with optimizing agents, show the role of these externalities as an engine of growth. This approach emphasizes that the growth process generates extensive negative externalities which reduce the capacity of the social and natural environment to furnish free goods. In these models individuals have increasingly to rely on private goods in order to prevent a reduction in their well-being or in their productive capacity due to decline in social and natural capital. This generates an increase in output which feeds back into the negative externalities, giving rise to a self-reinforcing mechanism whereby growth generates negative externalities and negative externalities generate growth. According to these models, the two anomalies of growth theory are two sides of the same coin. People strive so much for money because they have to defend themselves against negative externalities. In other words they work so much in order to substitute free goods with costly ones. But an increase in their income does not improve their happiness because it involves a process of substitution whereby free final (or intermediate) goods are progressively substituted with costly goods in the consumption (or production) patterns of individuals. For this reason these models are labelled GASP models.

The policy implications of both views are compared. The policy implications of the presence of positional negative externalities depend on the way in which the interest of agents in relative position is founded. A biological or cultural explanation may be provided. In the former case the policy implications are entirely discouraging. In the envious and/or emulative world of the human species, the happiness of all can never be increased. In the case where the interest of agents in relative position is given a cultural foundation the policy implications are less depressing, but an increase in general happiness has to be reached along the arduous road and long-drawn-out time-scale of cultural policy.

Instead, in GASP models the inability of growth to improve happiness derives from an institutional problem, and not a biological or cultural one. The price system does not receive signals about the importance of fundamental needs which are not satisfied by market goods. Individuals are unable to control resources crucial for their happiness. The fact that money does not buy happiness stems neither from biology nor from culture in these models; money is unable to buy happiness amid a pattern of growth with excessively high social and environmental costs.

I finally draw implications for environmental economics. The conventional environmentalist wisdom poses the problem of sustainability in ethical and technological terms. In fact the sustainability of a given pattern of growth depends: (i) on the level of the discount rate present in the economy, (ii) on the degree of substitutability between natural capital and output. Both these answers are questioned by the results of the GASP models.

According to the first answer, the excessively high discount rate of present generations may be responsible for the problems of sustainability. The question of the discount rate is an ethical issue; that is, it concerns intergenerational equity, because the voraciousness of present generations in their consumption of resources is prejudicial to the rights of future generations in terms of their ability to satisfy their needs. Of course, the possibility of posing the problem of sustainability in ethical terms rests entirely on the assumption that the dynamic of economic systems reflects the discount rate of the individuals.

In contrast, according to some GASP models the problem of sustainability does not arise from intergenerational conflict but from a failure among individuals belonging to the same generation to coordinate their efforts for accumulation. These models depict a world of people interested in their own well-being and that of their descendants; people who clearly perceive that well-being also depends on things that cannot be bought, primarily the quality of the environment and of human relationships. In short, they perceive the importance of living in a 'better world'; because they are interested in the well-being of their descendants they want to bequeath a better world to them. But they do not know how to do so (because the proper institutions are missing); that is, they feel that it is impossible. Being unable to leave their descendants a better world, they try to leave them money. As individuals seek to acquire the money that enables them and their descendants to escape an unliveable world, each of them makes her/his small contribution to worsening the world; that is, to producing a decline in long-term well-being.

Hence in GASP models the dynamics of economic systems do not reflect the discount rate of individuals – the decline in long-term well-being is due to a coordination failure, not to the intertemporal greed of each generation. The problem of the sustainability of an economic system may therefore be solved by changing its institutions. There is no intrinsic conflict in human nature between generational interest and species interest. It is the economic and social organization that should be changed

As regards the second of these two points, the technological possibilities of substituting environmental and social resources, the GASP models, in contrast with the conventional wisdom on the argument, show that if man-made goods can substitute for environmental assets, a self-reinforcing process of growth in output may be triggered which leads to a worsening of individual well-being. The main implication of this is that the sustainability of well-being may not be a technological problem but rather an institutional one. A coordination failure may induce agents to over-exploit the possibility of substituting social and environmental resources, thereby fuelling the deterioration of those resources and generating undesired growth.

Notes

1 I am especially indebted to U. Pagano, A. Leijonhufvud, L. Punzo and R. Lopez for their useful comments. The usual caveats apply.

2 Bartolini and Bonatti 2003b show that if a Ramsey-Rebelo AK model is augmented by treating the units of time devoted to work, h ('capital operating time'), as a choice variable, the resulting AKh model does not generate endogenous growth in the absence of negative externalities. Duranton 2001 shows in an endogenous growth model with overlapping generations that when the labour supply is made endogenous, production remains bounded if leisure and consumption are (gross) substitutes.

3 See Bartolini and Bonatti 2003a. While working hours seemingly exhibit a century-long tendency to decline, with the debatable exception of the USA since the 1960s, per-capita labour input displays a much weaker tendency to diminish, with major and prolonged reversals of tendency. The reason for this is that per-capita labour input (annual average working hours x total employment/total population) is influenced by the historical trend for the participation rate to increase.

4 Also a matter of controversy – like working hours in the USA during recent decades – is whether the trend in the saving rate is increasing or decreasing. Whilst in the case of working hours the dispute mainly concerns what the most reliable data are, the debate on saving rate centres on what should be considered the 'right' variables to measure. For example, if we include capital gains in saving, the 1995–8 saving rate in the USA was the highest since the 1960s (Gale and Sablehouse 1999). After the recent crisis of the stock market, the personal saving rate has begun to rise again in the USA.

5 'Classical' papers on the topic are for instance Easterlin 1974 and 1995 and Oswald 1997.

6 The main precursors of the idea that relative position matters are Veblen 1899/1934 and Hirsh 1976. According to Hirsh, well-being in the rich economies depends increasingly on positional goods. The clearest definition of pure positional good has been provided by Pagano 1999, according to whom consumption by an individual of a positive amount of a positional good involves the consumption of an equal negative amount by someone else. Examples of pure positional goods are power, status, prestige. This definition implies that increased consumption of a positional good by someone produces a negative externality on someone else.

7 The role of relative wealth effects as an engine of growth is shown in Corneo and Jeanne 2001. Among the growth models including the concern of individuals for their relative position see for instance (Fershtman *et al.* 1996, and Corneo and Jeanne 1999), which focus on the impact of the initial distribution of wealth on the growth rate.

8 Antoci and Bartolini 1997 and 2004 show, under various conditions concerning pay-offs and negative externalities, how the latter act as a *tertium movens* of growth. In an evolutionary game without accumulation and technical progress, they demonstrate that negative externalities can generate growth of per capita output because of their simple impact on the labour supply. In Bartolini and Bonatti 2004a these results are obtained in a world with optimizing agents. Consequently, the proposition that negative externalities can generate growth does not depend on assumptions about the bounded, or otherwise, rationality of agents. These three papers show the mechanism of substitution between free and costly consumption in the pure state; that is, they demonstrate the logical possibility of obtaining an increase in per capita output in models without accumulation and technical progress. These three models therefore imply that the presence of accumulation and/or technical progress is not a necessary condition for growth. Bartolini and Bonatti 2002 analyze in the version with optimizing agents of this framework the conditions that generate multiple equilibria and the role played by the cultural attitudes prevalent in a society in selecting of the growth path. Bartolini and Bonatti 2003a and 2003b incorporate the mechanism of substitution between free and costly consumption into the main paradigms of growth theory: exogenous and endogenous growth. Bartolini and Bonatti 2003a introduce this mechanism into an exogenous growth model a la Solow-Ramsey, finding that negative externalities boost the labour supply and accumulation and consequently the steady-state level of activity. Bartolini and Bonatti 2003b show that if the labour supply is endogenized in a Ramsey-Rebelo AK model of endogenous growth, the resulting model does not generate perpetual growth in the absence of negative externalities. Accumulation and technical progress are not a sufficient condition for endogenous growth to come about, unless negative externalities are introduced into the model. These negative externalities engender a process of substitution between free and costly consumption which gives rise to unbounded growth. The feature shared by all six of these models is that the substitution mechanism takes place in consumption. Social and environmental capital enter utility functions alone, and growth is fuelled by its substitution with produced final goods. Bartolini and Bonatti (2004) show that substitution mechanism may also operate in production. Using an exogenous growth model in which social and environmental capital enters only the production functions and the labour-leisure choice is included, they show that, under certain conditions, the erosion of social and environmental capital may enhance growth, i.e., increase the steady-state level of activity. Hence growth can be a process whereby not only final goods but also intermediate free goods are substituted with costly ones. The possibility of growth as a substitution process is generalized from the case in which negative externalities affect consumption to the case in which they affect production. On this point see also Smulders 2000.

9 Natural capital tends to have a significant productive role only in economies which rely largely on traditional agriculture. Industrial economies instead mainly use the environment as a repository for waste, so that it is unlikely that resources depletion will restrict production. Instead, social capital plays a productive role of great importance in the rich economies.

10 In Bartolini and Bonatti 2003a and 2003b, infinitely lived dynasties are assumed. Under this assumption the discount rate expresses the interest of individuals in both their own futures and those of their descendants.

11 For a presentation of the 'right-based approach' to sustainability see Bromley 1998, who argues that this approach implies a claim for an institutional change ('an environmental regency') 'that will protect the interest of future persons'. Hence, asserting that the interest of future generations must be protected against the voraciousness of present ones, as implied by the right-based approach, or arguing that an economic organization should be created which is able to reflect the interest of the present generations for future ones, as implied by GASP models, may lead to policy options that are similar yet founded on profoundly different motivations.

12 In this literature, the degree of substitutability between 'man-made' capital and natural capital is considered crucial for sustainability. If they are perfect substitutes, the condition for sustainability is that the aggregate stock of capital ('man-made' plus natural) should not decline ('weak' sustainability) (see, for instance, Hartwick 1986). If they are not perfect substitutes, sustainable development requires that there be no net damage to environmental assets ('strong' sustainability) (see, for instance, Pearce *et al.* 1990).

13 This claim for collective action is perfectly compatible with the existence of an 'environmental Kuznet curve', i.e. the inverted U-shaped relation between per-capita income and environmental degradation. In fact, we agree with those who maintain that explanation for this relation lies in the progressive extension of the environmental policies normally observed in rich countries (Grossman and Krueger (1995), Arrow *et al.* (1995), Ayres (1995), and De Bruyn *et al.* (1998)). Since a reduction in the depletion of the environment is due to policy responses, to proclaim that growth is a substitute for environmental policy is a dangerous misunderstanding.

14 Obviously, also the definition of property rights which enables the formation of a market for resources is a collective action. In fact, it requires institutions that define the new rights and institutions that enforce them. The property rights solution is the one that requires the least amount of collective action, compared to any other institution, for example a public regulatory authority. However, as often noted, environmental policy may require extensive public intervention due to high transaction costs which render the market solution costly and inefficient. Moreover, the GASP models are consistent with an interpretation that emphasizes the role of the enlargement of market relationships in causing a deterioration of relational goods. From this point of view, it is difficult to view the formation of markets as a general solution for the loss of well-being treated by these models.

References

Antoci, A. and Bartolini, S. (1997) 'Externalities and growth in an evolutionary game', *Discussion Papers*, No. 10, Trento: Università di Trento.

Antoci, A. and Bartolini, S. (2004) 'Negative externalities, and labor input in an evolutionary game', *Environment and Development Economics*, 9: 1–22.

Argyle, M. (1987) *The Psychology of Happiness*, London: Methuen.

Arrow, K. and Bolin, B., Costanza, R., Dasgupta, P., Folke C., Holling, S. Jansson, B.-O., Levin, S., Mäler, K.-G., Perrings, C. and Pimentel, D. (1995) 'Economic growth, carrying capacity and the environment', *Science* 268: 520–1.

Ayres, R.U. (1995) 'Economic growth: politically necessary but not environmentally friendly', *Ecological Economics* 15: 97–9.

Bartolini, S. and Bonatti, L. (2002) 'Environmental and social degradation as the engine of economic growth', *Ecological Economics*, 41: 1–16.

Bartolini, S. and Bonatti, L. (2003a) 'Undesirable growth in a model with capital accumulation and environmental assets', *Environment and Development Economics*, 8: 11–30.

Bartolini, S. and Bonatti, L. (2003b) 'Endogenous growth and negative externalities', *Journal of Economics*, 79: 123–44.

Bartolini, S. and Bonatti, L. (2004) 'Social capital and its role in production: does the depletion of social capital depress economic growth?, *Quaderni del Dipartimento di Economia Politica* No. 42, Siena: Università degli Studi di Siena.

Bartolini, S. and Bonatti, L. (2004a) 'The mobilization of human resources as an effect of the depletion of environmental and social assets', Mimeo, Florence-Bergamo.

Bartolini, S. and Palma, R. (2002) 'Economia e felicità: una proposta di accordo', in L. Bruni e V. Pelligra (eds.), *Economia come impegno civile*, Roma: Città Nuova.

Baumann, Z. (2002) *La solitudine del cittadino globale*, Milano: Feltrinelli.

Bluestone, B. and Rose, S. (2000) 'The enigma of working time trends', in Golden, L. and Figart, D.M., *Working Time: International Trends, Theory and Policy Perspectives*, London and New York: Routledge.

Bromley, D.W. (1998) 'Searching for sustainability: the poverty of spontaneous order', *Environment and Development Economics*, 24: 231, 240.

Corneo, G. and Jeanne, O. (2001) 'On relative wealth effects and long-run growth', *Research in Economics*, 55: 349–58.

Corneo, G. and Jeanne, O. (1999) 'Pecuniary emulation, inequality and growth', *European Economic Review*, 43: 1665–78.

Cross, G. (1993) *Time and Money: The Making of Consumer Culture*, London and New York: Routledge.

De Bruyn, S.M., Van den Bergh, J.C.J.M. and Opschoor J.B. (1998) 'Economic growth and emissions: reconsidering the empirical basis of environmental Kuznets curves', *Ecological Economics*, 25: 161–75.

Duranton, G. (2001) 'Endogenous labor supply, growth and overlapping generations', *Journal of Economic Behaviour and Organization*, 44: 295–314.

Easterlin, R. (1974) 'Does economic growth improve the human lot? Some empirical evidence', in P.A. David and M.W. Reder (eds.), *Nations and Households in Economic Growth: Essays in Honour of Moses Abramowitz*, New York and London: Academic Press.

Easterlin, R. (1995) 'Will raising the income of all increase the happiness of all?', *Journal of Economic Behaviour and Organization*, 27: 35–48.

Fershtman, Murphy, Weiss (1996) 'Social status education and growth', *Journal of Political Economy*, 104: 108–32.

Figart, D.M. and Golden, L. (2000) 'Introduction and overview: understanding working time around the world', in L. Golden L. and D.M. Figart (eds), *Working Time: International Trends, Theory and Policy Perspectives*, London and New York: Routledge.

Fukuyama, F. (1995) *Trust: The Social Virtues and the Creation of Prosperity*, New York: Free Press.

Gale, W.G. and Sablehouse, J. (1999) 'Perspectives on the household saving rate', *Brookings Papers on Economic Activity*, 1: 181–224.

Grossman, G.M. and Krueger, A.B. (1995) 'Economic growth and the environment', *Quarterly Journal of Economics*, 110: 353–77.

Hartwick, J. M. (1986) 'Intergenerational equity and the investing of rents from exhaustible resources', *American Economic Review*, 67: 972–4.

Hirsh, F. (1976) *Social Limits to Growth*, Cambridge, MA: Harvard University Press.

Hirschman, A.O., (1982) 'Rival interpretations of the market society', *Journal of Economic Literature*, 20.

Kahneman, D., (1999) 'Objective happiness', in Kahneman, D., Diener, E. and Schwarz, N. (eds.) *Well-Being: The Foundations of Hedonic Psychology*, New York: Russel Sage Foundation.

Krugman, F. (1995) *Pop Internationalism*, Cambridge, MA: MIT Press.

Lane, R. (2000) *The Loss of Happiness in Market Democracies*, New Haven, CT and London: Yale University Press.

North, D.C. (1981) *Structure and Change in Economic History*, New York and London: Norton & Company.

North, D.C. and Thomas, R.P. (1973) *The Rising of the Western World: A New Economic History*, Cambridge: Cambridge University Press.

Olson, M., (1971) *The Logic of Collective Action: Public Goods and the Theory of Groups*, Cambridge, MA: Harvard University Press.

Oswald, A.J. (1997) 'Happiness and economic perfomance', *Economic Journal* 107: 1815–31.

Pagano, U. (1999) 'Is power an economic good? Notes on social scarcity and the economics of positional goods', in Bowles, S., Franzini, M., Pagano, U. (eds), *The Politics and the Economics of Power*, London and New York: Routledge.

Pearce, D.W., Markandya, A. and Barbier, E. (1990) *Sustainable Development: Economy and Environment in the Third World*, London: Earthscan Publications.

Pinker, S., (1997) *How The Mind Works*, New York: W. W. Norton.

Polanyi, K. (1968) *The Great Transformation*, Boston, MA: Beacon.

Robinson, K.A. and Godbey, J. (1999) *Time for Life: The Surprising Ways Americans Use their Time*, University Park, PA: Penn State Press, State College.

Schor, J. (1991) *The Overworked American: The Unexpected Decline of Leisure in America*, New York: Basic Books.

Smulders, S. (2000) 'Economic growth and environmental quality', in H. Folmer and H.L. Gabel (eds.), *Principles of Environmental and Resource Economics*, Cheltenham: Edward Elgar.

Ulhaner, C.J. (1989) 'Relational goods and participation: incorporating sociability into a theory of rational action', *Public Choice*, 62: 253–85.

Veblen, T. (1899/1934) *The Theory of the Leisure Class*, New York: Modern Library.

Veenhoven, R. (1993) *Happiness in Nations: Subjective Appreciation of Life in 56 Nations 1946–1992*, Rotterdam: Erasmus University Press.

Vercelli, A. (1992) 'Sostenibilità del debito pubblico e sostenibilità dello sviluppo', in Ente 'Luigi Einaudi' (ed.), *Il disavanzo pubblico in Italia: natura strutturale e politiche di rientr*,Bologna: Il Mulino.

Williamson, J.G. (1995) 'Migration and city growth during industrial revolutions', in H. Giersch (ed.), *Urban Agglomeration and Economic Growth*, Berlin: Springer Verlag.

Part II

Unequal effects of environment changes

4 Navigating in a second-best world

Ecological distribution, historical liability and social choice

Sylvie Faucheux and Martin O'Connor

Technology risks and unequal ecological distribution

Science and technological advances, seen widely as among the motors of competitiveness and as the cornerstone of the 'knowledge society', can be expected to continue with striking speed in the coming decades (IPTS 1999, and 2000). This innovation coupled with the scale of goods and services production, transportation and consumption activities will undoubtedly bring benefits and attractive novelty to many sectors. But, no doubt, it will also contribute significant new sources of bother, inconvenience and risks (negative health and environmental effects, societal tensions and stresses). It is easy to make a list of 'risks' already anticipated from current technological innovation trends:

- Increasing quantities of by-products and combustion emissions related to the use of hydrocarbons (oil and gas products, as well as coal), e.g., for high speed air and surface mobility;
- A rise in the use of scarce elements, including rare earths and other substances, of varying toxicities, linked to the specialized requirements of information technology and communications systems;
- Continuing increase in chemical residuals (including fertilizer by-products, pesticides and medicinal drugs for animals) linked to intensive agriculture and livestock raising practices;
- The possible production of new types of complex wastes, whose environmental and health impact is difficult to evaluate, resulting from metallic composites, from materials (re)processing at various stages of the nuclear fission cycle, and so on;
- Increased disruption of terrestrial ecosystems and occupation of rural territories due to the continuing expansion of existing and new types of transport infrastructures;
- New ecological and health risks linked to the use of products from genetic engineering, on the one hand the creation of new animal and plant forms, on the other hand the arrival in major quantities on the market of foodstuffs and other products that depend, directly and indirectly, on the use of these GMO components.

In this chapter, we consider these phenomena as issues of 'ecological distribution' and look at the question of their regulation or governance as an aspect of the economics problem of 'social choice'.

Ecological distribution refers to the social, spatial, and inter-temporal patterns of access to the benefits obtainable from natural resources and from the environment as a life-support system, and also exposure to the dangers and harms from adverse environmental conditions. The determinants of ecological distribution are in some respects natural (for example climate, topography, land quality, minerals and rainfall patterns), but are in other respects social, political, and technological. Ecological distribution issues must therefore be characterized, simultaneously, in terms of 'objective' physical realities and 'subjective' dimensions of societal choice.

On the 'science' side, the task is to define the frontiers of what is feasible for an economy and, more especially, the trade-offs (opportunity costs) imposed by the constraints on what is feasible. Here we encounter the phenomena of systems complexity and uncertainty, of irreversibility and of having to live with the consequences of what we have already done. On the 'social' side, the task is to decide a good or acceptable (or least bad) course of action for members of the society, within the bounds of what is feasible. Here we encounter the diverse considerations of justice and justification: who decides what is desirable, for whom, by what criterion, according to whom?

Sustainability policies address, among other things, the challenge of inter-temporal (or inter-generational) equity. This is not just the natural resource depletion concern that present-day high rates of resource consumption may leave less for future prospects of consumption. It is also the problem of deep uncertainties about outcomes, of the (sometimes certain, sometimes uncertain) arrival of 'bads' – as well as goods – as components in the spectrum of the possible outcomes, and of charting a collective course in the sometimes degraded conditions of life that are the legacy of decisions in the past.

Modern systems science tells us that, wherever technology is employed to obtain a desired outcome – e.g., a production process, a consumption activity, the construction or modification of infrastructures – there will be 'side effects' of various sorts. If these are benign or beneficial (such as the diffusion of knowledge from research and innovations), this is not too problematical for society (although it may be an important concern in the regulation of intellectual property rights and other aspects of knowledge management). But, sometimes, there are negative (but unintended) effects that, over time, become more significant than the short-term benefits that were the original purposes. We will discuss the example later on of radioactive wastes, whose management has a far longer time horizon than the period of power generation itself.[1] We find ourselves in situations where *the emergent systems effects* – related to what, in negative terms, Ivan Illich already in the 1960s and 1970s termed the 'counter-productivities' of professional services and high performance systems – are at least as significant as the directly intended effects.

What makes for an adequate and appropriate way of framing social choice and governance processes for this new generation of ecological distribution problems? 'Some considerations about ecological distribution' develops the key concept of ecological distribution through a variety of examples. 'Economics and ethics of sustainability' links the ecological distribution concern to the inter-temporal equity principle that is commonly espoused as a guideline for policies of a 'sustainable development. 'The dialectics of intended and unintended effects' reviews our knowledge of our incomplete knowledge about possible long-term consequences of production and technology choices, and presents some considerations in favour of a more reflexive perspective on the eventual contributions of science and technology innovations as factors/vectors of progress in society. 'Sustainability politics (1): precaution and deliberation' draws the preceding threads together and suggests the pertinence of a deliberative political process for the problem of 'navigating together in a second best world'. 'Sustainability politics (2): living with the past' introduces historical liability as the distinctive context in which public policy choices must now take place. Our current technologies may bring long lasting consequences – benefits and burdens – to which those on the receiving end have never given consent. Contemporary analysts of social choice must not only address *ex ante* the increasingly visible, and controversial asymmetries in the exposure – or likely future exposure – of different constituencies (including future generations) to risks and to 'bads'. They must also address *ex post* the requirements of living with the costly and sometimes painful legacies of the past. 'Navigating in the second-best world of radioactive wastes' and 'Resolving an (unintended) coexistence problem' illustrate these considerations through the topical question of strategies for long-term radioactive waste management. Coexisting with the wastes will require the emergence of new institutions and societal conventions for maintaining vigilance long after nuclear power stations are shut down. 'Social choice and stakeholder deliberation' concludes, with a short discussion of the roles of stakeholder deliberation for discovering and evaluating new ways of charting a common future and, more particularly, of living with our past.

Some considerations about ecological distribution

We use the term ecological distribution to refer to all roles of the non-commodity environment as sources of human well-being and, more especially, to the patterns of access – the social, spatial and temporal asymmetries – in the non-marketed use by humans of environmental resources and services, such as wild and agricultural biodiversity, and in the burdens suffered, such as pollution. For example, an unequal distribution of land, and pressure of agricultural exports on limited land resources, may cause land degradation by subsistence peasants working on mountain slopes, accentuating inequalities of economic and ecological distribution. The inequalities in per capita exosomatic energy consumption would be an instance of social ecological distribution. The territorial asymmetries between SO_2 emissions and the burdens of acid rain, which reduce the quality or availability of environmental services, are a case of spatial ecological distribution. The intergenerational inequalities between the enjoyment of nuclear energy (or emissions of CO_2), and the burdens of radioactive waste (or global warming) are asymmetries of temporal ecological distribution.

Since the 1980s, a variety of analyses have emerged around this theme of ecological distribution. While the term itself is of relatively recent origin – being coined by Martinez-Alier during the 1980s, as far as we know – these analyses typically extend and adapt traditional themes of political economy and welfare economics to contemporary preoccupations with the environment – and thus rejoins environmental themes with older themes of justice, land and labour that are constitutive of traditional political economy.[2]

Thus, fossil-fuel resources are being used up within a few generations in processes that endanger the earth with pollution and global warming; large quantities of radioactive materials are being destabilized into toxic fission products; tropical forests shrink perceptibly each year; soil erosion and desertification proceed at an increasing pace; aquifer water is mined; incineration of solid waste transfers harmful substances into the air; pesticides cause problems of drinking-water pollution; and so on.

The social and environmental burdens of this innovation process are unevenly distributed. Under pressures of commercial survival, firms may be expected to seek lower input costs (including labour costs) and to seek to off-load environmental and social performance burdens onto other social partners – e.g., onto the state and taxpayers, onto workers (in terms of bad working conditions, commuting costs, etc.) onto future generations and non-human nature (as analysed, notably, by ecomarxist and ecofeminist activists and scholars). Eco-feminists such as Salleh (1997), Mies (1986) and Waring (1989) have examined in depth the parallels between the occultation of women's work behind market and public policy conventions, and the non-inclusion of environmental costs of resource depletion and pollution damages.

Equity issues are often very local issues, but they also take on international proportions. One facet of the universal ideology of development, after the Second World War, was that all nations should progressively attain material affluence – the 'under-developed' nations should therefore 'catch up'. Unfortunately, by the 1970s it had already become apparent that the vaunted economic growth, fuelled by the transfusions of capital and knowhow from industrialized countries to the poor, was not having the employment-creation results that had been hoped of it. In addition, as the Club of Rome in 1972 sought to insist, a continuation of rapid growth fuelled by ever-increasing energy and natural resources use, threatened to bring some appalling environmental side-effects.

In the current context of observations about globalization and military/economic hegemonies, much increased attention has been given to instances of 'international externalities', cases of alleged cost-shifting by economic players separated by very large distances. Many of these involve multinational firms, such as mining companies – increasingly coming under attack in the courts and in the boardrooms for the adverse social and ecological impact of their operations. These and other sorts of experiences are giving rise to a growing body of literature on '*unequal ecological exchange*' between the North and South countries (Gedicks 1993, Faber 1993, and Sachs (ed.) 1993).

Take the example of genetic diversity in crop plants and long-term world food security (Boyce 1996, and Hobbelink 1991). This diversity has been, until now, sustained mainly in the field by poor farmers in developing countries who receive no payment for providing this external benefit to humankind. The pressures of free trade undermine the viability of these in situ centres of agricultural genetic diversity, and threaten rural livelihoods as well as the continued provision of the genetic diversity as a world benefit. The conflicts of interest are brought out by the case of Mexican maize whose viability is threatened under the North American Free Trade Agreement. The market price of Mexican maize is higher than US maize, partly due to better soils and growing conditions in some US regions, but also partly due to US farm subsidies and the externalization of pesticide and groundwater degradation problems by the US farm sector. In a short period of time (a few years or decades), the heritage of 5000 years of Mexican agricultural husbandry could be irretrievably lost.

A highly developed country with a significant component of service industries, banks, insurances and so on, may appear to have a low per capita environmental impact because it imports its needed (depletable) primary materials and energy and has succeeded in exporting polluting production industries. A part of the pollution and ecological damage associated with the industrial world's economic dynamism is shifted 'offshore'. Thus, more generally, a nation may be the cause of environmental damage outside its own territorial borders, or it may bear damage due to actions outside its borders. The distinction between damage 'borne' on a nation's territory and the damage 'caused by' the nation's economic activity can be extremely important in setting policy targets. In terms of national welfare, the damages borne by the nation can seem a rational reference point. However, this can lead to policies deliberately aiming to off-load or export environmental pressures onto other countries (e.g., relocation of 'dirty' industries, and dumping of toxic wastes offshore). In terms of participation in an international community, the damages caused – namely, a nation's contribution to total environmental pressures – will be an unavoidable reference point. This can be seen in such examples as negotiations over the distribution of burden for reductions in CFCs, greenhouse gas emissions, acid rain, etc.

Starting from the theoretical distinction between environmental costs caused and costs borne by a nation, a variety of indicators of environmental load displacement through trade have been developed in the body of literature (Muradian and O'Connor 2001). In addition to environmental statistics for nationally registered environmental pressures (such as energy resource exploitation, forest cutting, fish catch, pollutant emissions and land use changes), the corresponding effects have to be calculated which are linked with imports and exports of raw materials and goods. For example, analyses have been conducted for a range of countries to quantify the ecological footprints left by production and consumption in rich countries, in terms of land area, water and photosynthesis requirements, compared with the availability of these resources in the producing and consuming countries (Wackernagel and Rees 1995, and Wackernagel *et al.* 1999). Some analyses add a temporal dimension. Now that the limits to the 'sink' capacity of the planet for carbon dioxide emissions have become the object of international debate, it has been argued that the industrialized countries have appropriated the environmental services in an historically inequitable way, in this sense taking from their less developed neighbours as well as imposing a cost on future generations (Azar and Holmberg 1995, and Agarwal and Narain 1991).

If, making allowance for system boundary definition and measurement difficulties, an unequal burden of environmental costs can be identified, and this can be linked back to prevailing market and other institutional arrangements for goods and services production, consumption, transportation and international trade, then one can speak of patterns of ecologically unequal exchange. If we go further and postulate liability for imposition of uncompensated costs, we may speak of an ecological debt, as for example the factory owner who, after he makes a good profit, is held liable to make some sort of recompense for the fact that effluent from the factory poisons the fish upon which a population downstream depends for its livelihood. Of course, notwithstanding such principles as 'polluter pays' (adopted officially by OECD countries for 30 years), the debt is often just theoretical, a compensation is not necessarily paid. This is partly a power problem: a question of *might not right*.

Economics and ethics of sustainability

Economic and ecological distribution issues are intrinsic to contemporary 'sustainability' concerns. Let us develop a simple framework of analysis in terms of 'supply' and 'demand'. On the supply side, the task is to define the *frontiers of what is feasible* for the economy and, more especially, the trade-offs (opportunity costs) imposed by the limits to what is feasible. On the demand side, the task is to assess *what will be judged desirable* by members of the society. Suppose a simple economy that can produce two types of goods, those favoured by 'us' and those favoured by 'them' (O'Connor 2002). Limited resources mean a trade-off between the two types of goods. What, then, is the right balance between 'us' and 'them'? In an economy dominated by 'us', the preferred mix of goods would plausibly be different from the mix for an economy where status is given to the preferences of 'them'.

Traditional concerns with productive efficiency, resource discovery and technological progress have put the emphasis on, first, getting onto the frontier of feasibility and, going beyond that, pushing out the frontier of possibilities over time. But, the emergence of concerns for: (1) the 'ecological limits' to expansion of economic production, and (2) the adverse side-effects and 'environmental costs' associated with economic expansion, has somewhat changed the profile of the social choice question.

In the textbook neo-classical economics treatments, economic goods and services are produced through bringing together three classes of inputs, the factors of production, which are human capital (labour), produced economic capital and natural capital. Analyses are conducted of feasibility and policy requirements for achieving sustained growth in output of produced goods and services. The path taken by an economy will depend on, among other things, the partitioning of produced capital between re-investment (savings) and final consumption. Analysis thus centres on the 'opportunity costs' of using natural and produced economic capital in different ways – notably, the trade-offs between present and future production/consumption. In dynamic modelling approaches, technological and resource considerations determine whether or not the economy is capable of following a sustainable development time-path. One can think of the models as simulating 'societal choices', as signified by population growth, individuals' preferences and institutional arrangements governing endowment or income distribution, subject to the defined technical and resource constraints. Population change is usually treated as exogenous, so the emphasis is placed on production feasibility (the inter-temporal production possibility frontier) and on the social determinants of investment and consumption over time.

Since the 1970s, a great variety of models have been constructed in which: (1) there exists the technological capability for unlimited growth in the value of economic capital over time by substituting away from a renewable or non-renewable natural capital, but (2) achievement – or not – of consumption sustainability is a social choice. The focus here is on the distribution not just of wealth but also of anti-wealth – that is, the production of dangers, damages and of 'risks' (prospects of future penury, difficulties and damages) that may fall on others elsewhere or in future generations (e.g., Muir 1996). Achieving sustainability would depend, one way or another, on environmental and economic resource management choices made on behalf of future generations, investments whose payoff is diffusely distributed into the future. And, because quantification of such impacts is highly speculative, images of the inter-temporal feasibility frontier showing the trade-off between 'us' in the present and 'them' the future generations, fluctuate like video-game projections before our eyes.

The dialectics of intended and unintended effects

Determining what might be feasible in ecological economic futures is partly a matter of science and technological know-how. But, the 'space of feasible outcomes' is characterized *ex ante* by an inherent indeterminacy and *ex post* by irreversibility.

The phenomenon of 'adverse environmental impacts' associated with the expansion of industrial economics and mass consumption has been widely remarked since at least the 1960s. In the past, it was commonplace to admit the existence of risks from failures, if something goes wrong (a machine breaks down, a bridge collapses, and so on). It was also commonplace to admit risks associated with uncertainty, associated with incomplete information and also incomplete understanding (which is not the same as 'information' but includes the explanatory frameworks, etc.). More and more, however, this uncertainty is not about an independently existing natural world 'out there', but about complex systems whose change is partly induced by our own deliberate actions. We throw stones in the pond, but the full effects are unknown; the ripples travel out and down with repercussions further than we can look. What might be a tremendous result locally, in the short term and on a small scale, can be a disaster in its longer-term indirect consequences or if applied on a larger scale. Ecosystem perturbations and toxic chemicals, which nature or society can cope with or ignore when occurring at small scales, can accumulate to serious threats when the scale of production or of perturbation is enhanced (global climate change, tropical forest destruction and so on).

What the scientific record itself has by now made clear, is that this emergence of unplanned side-effects – often destructive and more or less irreversible in their consequences – is not just due to negligence or abuse, but is *inherent* in the potentialities of science and technology themselves. We summarize this knowledge of the dynamics of knowledge as follows:[3]

1   The permanent process of pushing back the frontiers of knowledge and science-based interventions also confronts us, in new ways, with the limits both to our knowledge and to our intervention capacity.

2   Our knowledge advances permit sophisticated interventions in ecosystem functioning and in the components of life itself; yet our scientific understanding of the physical environment and of the impacts of human activity on life process and ecosystems remains very incomplete and in many cases lags far behind our interventions.

3   Science-based innovation has, in the past, contributed to industrialization processes that have proven highly disruptive to ecosystems at local and global levels. Some of the new commercially attractive technologies may also be incompatible with ecological stability and environmental quality goals.

4   On a socio-economic plane, there are evident fears that some forms of commercially driven innovation and technology transfer can work to heighten socio-economic stratification, and perhaps even worsen poverty for disadvantaged populations rather than reduce it.

5   Some new forms of knowledge give a significant potential for 'mass terrorism', not limited to a small variety of circumstances. Going beyond the now classical risks such as blackmail by taking hostage a few hundred people in a hijacked plane or in a building, and the problem of 'proliferation' of fissionable materials, there are a huge variety of options for the 'bringing down the house' (or threatening to), through allying a few well-focused perturbations (notably chemical, biological and informational) to techniques of electronic communication and rapid mobility.

We have gone far beyond the macroscopic intervention in materials (such as building a dam – although this sort of construction is still important), and are now capable of intervening in organization at the scales of atoms (nuclear fission and fusion), of molecules, and of cellular structures (notably in genetic heritage, e.g., gene spicing and cloning technologies). The new forms of organization (or disorganization) are dynamic (ecosystem change, hydrological cycles, atmospheric circulation), or have a long active life (toxic wastes, including radioactivity), or are potentially self-renewing (modified life forms). Our affirmed technological prowess can thus constitute a self-renewing source of problems. More science and new technology applications can sometimes solve, or at least mitigate, the emerging problems. But, as we have already highlighted, the unintended 'side-effects' can come to be more significant than the original purposes. This is well publicized for risks in the electronuclear industry and in biotechnology applications based on genetic engineering. It is also true for the complicated yet fragile systems of food production, health care and communication upon which modern societies depend, and hence for a wide range of technologically mediated interventions in politics and human relations.

Paradoxically, a strong trust or belief in the capacity of science and technology to produce desired results, can lead – and in fact often has led – to reliance on ever more vulnerable systems, and to a dramatic underestimation of what have been called 'virtual' or 'hypothetical risks', that is, the typical risks of modernity that are characterized by complex causation networks, time lags and severity of impacts which is prohibitive to any kind of laboratory testing (a nuclear melt down, the deliberate release of an invasive plant, etc.). These 'virtual' risks are unproven until they materialize, but at that point they cannot be managed (or only at very great costs). Moreover, the perceived uneven, unfair, and un-negotiated imposition of disadvantages, damages and burdens (including future clean-up costs or enduring health problems, etc.) is, for many people, unaccepted and unforgiven – and hence much more significant than any notion of a 'net benefit' to society.

Sustainability politics (1): precaution and deliberation

Social choice is about the principled distribution of bads and risks, as well as of wealth, entitlements and economic goods. The considerations of the preceding sections explain why, in technology, environmental and wider sustainability policy, an ever-increasing weight is being given to ambiguous potency of technological interventions. New governance conventions for science and technology deployments are required to address the 'post-normal' situation[4] characterized by:

- Irreducible uncertainties (unpredictability of complex systems, real yet non-quantifiable risks to health, environmental damage, loss of economic opportunity);
- Plurality of social values and hence divergent concerns and justification criteria;
- High decision stakes (including commercial and military interests, risks of social disruption, possible severe irreversible impacts on health of populations and/or life-support systems) and long risk/impact time-horizons;
- Systems complexities that, on the 'down sides', may manifest themselves in unintended effects and counter-productivities that, as historical liabilities, jeopardize community livelihoods, health and future economic prospects for long periods of time.

What should be our attitude about the possibly of adverse consequences imposed on others (elsewhere or in the future) by present-day production and consumption decisions? The question may be not even asked if the 'demands' of those persons upon whom penury, degraded environmental conditions, health damage or other costs are imposed, have no rights, or are simply not able to be heard.[5] Sustainability is about commitment to justice and coexistence in various forms of extended community. The Brundtland Report formulation of sustainable development seeks to reconcile present day needs with the requirements of future generations (WCED 1987). Other definitions put to the fore the maintenance of biosphere life-support systems, species diversity, economic justice between North and South nations, political self-determination and tolerance of diversity in cultural and political conventions. The articulation of sustainability as a problem of social choice – sustaining of what, why, for whom? – thus highlights a tension between two forms of discourse and action:

- On the one hand, self-centred attitudes associated typically with discourses of control or of domination, which seek to pursue or to impose one's own set of purposes with the exclusion or discounting of any contradictory claims of what is good or valuable, to be respected or merits to be done;
- On the other hand, generous attitudes that propose to search out possibilities of coexistence based on tolerance of and respect for a plurality of antagonistic or seemingly contradictory considerations.[6]

The two forms are in dialectical relation, in the sense that every organism or cultural form affirms its specificity in relation to the rest of the world, while at the same time inhabiting (and depending on) that world in its richness and diversity.[7] Nonetheless, discourses of self-interest have a tendency sometimes to simplify towards formulae (more or less disguised) of 'Might is Right', and intolerant aggression is also a hallmark of certain cults and self-identifying elites. A domination ethic tends to consider the outside world, including other people, as means to an end and/or as obstacles to achieving one's purposes. A coexistence ethic, by comparison, would seek out forms of courtesy and dialogue. Discourses in favour of coexistence can be as simple as a pleading of 'equal rights' for everything and everybody. But, more reflectively, it is clear that a precept of coexistence is an open question. There is tolerance of tensions, an admission of antagonisms is inevitable, but the desire to find a form of life where each leaves a space for the others (notwithstanding the antagonisms and differences). In this regard, as Latouche (1989: 139) suggests, the conviction in the merits of a philosophy of coexistence can arise almost paradoxically:

> … as there is no hope of founding anything durable on the short-change of a pseudo-universality imposed by violence and perpetuated by the negation of the other party, the venture is warranted that there is indeed a common space of fraternal coexistence yet to discover and construct.

Taking into account the 'monopoly' presence of the present generation of powerful economic interests, it will be up to the present generation's policymakers and articulate members of the public to affirm by proxy the 'entitlements' (if any) of future generations, of endangered species and ecosystems, of vulnerable peoples and so on. Provision for the 'needs of future generations' (and for all other forms of diversity) can be assured only through generous choices of resource use (investment and protection decisions) whose intent is to enhance the opportunities and environmental security of the 'others' (including those to come). Such a commitment may be given practical effect in a variety of ways, through communal and political choices, for example:

- Specific ecological and amenity 'protection' decisions;
- Time, labour, and economic resources expended in environmental repair and enhancement;
- Infrastructure and durable public assets investment;
- Provision for extensive and ongoing community involvement in decision-making processes, sometimes known as costs of democracy;
- Educational investments aimed at fostering ethics of care and environmental interest;
- Investments in research and technological development intended to furnish understanding, information, and practical know-how that may enhance simultaneously the economic opportunities and environmental security of generations to come.

This is a rather traditional list, and versions of it are easily found in the eco-development, green economy and North–South justice literatures of the 1970s. We can add to this list, as a more recent arrival, the Principle of Precaution as a guideline in regulatory policy. In the Rio Declaration (at the 1992 Earth Summit), for instance, it is stated: 'Where there are threats of serious or irreversible damage, lack of full scientific certainty shall not be used as a reason for postponing cost-effective measures to prevent environmental degradation' (Rio Declaration on Environment and Development (June 1992), Principle 15).

This precautionary principle can be justified by a variety of arguments in terms of duty or responsibility, respect or esteem for others (notably future generations) as members of an extended community. The idea is that actions carrying a possible (but as yet undemonstrated) risk of serious and long-lasting damage to future human interests should not be permitted. As such, the principle is clearly founded on ethical considerations that take on their distinctive force in the new context where science and technology progress are no longer regarded as ordinarily beneficial and where powerful forces of change are being engaged under conditions of inability to exercise mastery over eventual outcomes.

In a stylized way, we can present our societies' attitudes towards technological progress as polarized dialectically around a question of the burden of proof.

Those evoking the traditional discourses of progress and perfectibility (and others invoking mere adventurism) will argue that 'the future can look after itself' and that all interesting technological risks may be run.

Those evoking a 'precautionary' attitude will argue about the risk of so-called 'Type II Error', emphasizing that absence of proof of danger is not the same as proof of the absence of danger. And, where deep uncertainty and possibly grave dangers reside, the risk should not be run.

Neither of these positions, in their pure forms, is satisfactory. Often, it is not possible to furnish definitive proof of danger, nor definitive proof of non-danger.

How far should precaution be pushed? (some risks must be run; otherwise there are the dangers and contradictions of paralysis). The role of the precautionary principle here is to furnish a 'counter-weight' against the apparently heedless rush of contemporary innovation and commerce into ecological, geophysical, metabolic and chemical novelty that, to many people, appears as an excessive enthusiasm for making trouble. So, we have an interesting situation where neither 'rule' can, strictly speaking, be applied; yet each precept acts as a caution on (or, indeed, a refutation of) the other, creating a sort of dilemma or impossibility.

This 'impossibility' is an example of a decisive property of 'social choice' situations generally. As is well known, the attempted axiomatization of the abstract social choice problem for economic policy analysis, as formulated by Kenneth Arrow in 1950, led to an apparent impasse – the so-called Impossibility results (see Arrow 1963). Briefly, and roughly speaking:

- If the attempt is made to advise on what is 'best' for the society, on the basis of a 'general' rule (or set of criteria), then the choice comes down to one between Dictatorship or Inconsistency;
- If both Dictatorship and Inconsistency are to be avoided by weakening the rule system, then either the advice may be indecisive and/or the possibility is opened of dishonourable outcomes.

The 'impossibility' result does not mean that a reasoned base for policy is impossible. Rather, it implies that, if reasoned basis for action is to be established, then forms of deliberative procedure must be sought that permit those involved – the stakeholders – to maintain a permanent 'dialogue' or 'argumentation' between the several non-reconciled principles or positions.

An analyst in such circumstances needs to be like a 'midwife of problems' (Rittel 1982: 35–48), helping to raise into visibility, 'questions and issues towards which you can assume different positions, and with the evidence gathered and arguments built for and against these different positions'. There will generally coexist a plurality of evaluation or justification principles that – while being all reasonable and pertinent in some way(s) – cannot all be applied simultaneously (or, at best, may lead to divergent recommendations).[8]

This view of a collective 'working out' of impossible social choice problems is what underpins much of the current focus on multi-stakeholder deliberation as a political cornerstone for the pursuit of sustainability. The argument of this (rather large) contemporary literature is that decision quality may be enhanced through integrating scientific, technical and economic expertises within a *permanent communication process*.[9]

Sustainability politics (2): living with the past

Precaution may be considered as one reasonable and pertinent principle for orientating social choices in favour of sustainability. Nonetheless, this principle is, par excellence, to be applied *ex ante*. It does not say much about how a society

should orient itself and cope with historical liabilities – the burdensome consequences of past decisions and events (including serious misfortunes such as the
Chernobyl nuclear reactor meltdown, once they have come to pass).

The case of radioactive waste management is already widely recognized in
this regard (O'Connor and van den Hove 2001) and will be our chosen example
in the sections to follow. Other examples are problems of saline intrusion to
groundwater, land instability, and underground water and soil pollution arising
from abandoned coal, salt and metal mining operations (Faucheux and Hue 2000,
and 2001). Species extinction on a large scale is already a *fait accompli*. Scientists
currently speculate on the possible impacts of greenhouse-gas enhanced climate
changes. The emergence of new infectious agents provoking health disorders or
significant ecological disruptions, are among the categories of 'virtual risks' of
unintended and perhaps irreversible disruptive consequences of wilful genetic
experimentation.

In public policy as in practical life, it is becoming more and more necessary to
come to judgements about how 'we' are to live with, or cope with, or get along
with, those effects that have already (perhaps imprudently) been produced.
Frequently lip service is paid to principles of 'fair compensation' for burdens
imposed on an innocent third party. But, when insurance funds are limited and
taxpayers are already overwhelmed, an ample compensation is rarely paid. In the
case of major misfortunes, the people most directly concerned are rarely able to
put the losses and burdensome conditions completely behind them. They will not
make life 'as before'. They will live with the memories, the scars, and the pain of
things lost, the hesitations and uncertainties of building a new life. The concept of
historical liability therefore introduces several distinctive features into the problem
of social choice. First, there are the *requirements of memory* associated with the requirements of monitoring and eventual intervention for different sorts of contaminated
sites and unstable situations whose 'risks' extend decades (or, in some cases, many
centuries) into the future. Second, there is the problem of *community and partnership
building in the face of adversity*. This is partly an economic resources problem. But it is
also a cultural and (inter) subjective problem of purposes and meanings.

Public policy in situations of historical liability must contribute to repairing,
revitalizing and rebuilding communities. What are the human factors that permit
people, in the face of economic loss, environmental adversity, health damage or
other misfortune, to pick up the pieces and become again purposeful and enthused
in their efforts in society?[10]

Trust, hope and confidence are three very human factors. We can characterize
trust as the willingness of a person, group or community, to make itself vulnerable
in the expectation (or hope) of a benefit coming from association with others that
would not otherwise be forthcoming. The conditions of trust in government, as in
commercial enterprise, as in science and technology advances more generally, all
relate, on the one hand to hopes for benefits and, on the other hand to confidence
in the capacity and will of society's leaders and innovators, and other potential
partners, to assure the sharing of those benefits. Concepts of fairness, good, justice
and right are the speciality of philosophers and other social scientists. Ordinary

people in all walks of life also have their sentiments of what is good, fair and right. Successful policy, like successful diplomacy, will arise from effective dialogue leading to confidence in the prospects of a worthwhile common future.

Multi-stakeholder deliberation in this context does not aim merely at an efficient exchange of information. It does not aim only to obtain a structured and transparent evaluation of options by different sectors of the affected communities. There is an underlying model of human nature that proposes inter-subjective communication as a profound process of culture and community building. The contact of persons with each other, the work, the learning that takes place, all of this brings the evolution of perceptions, beliefs, relationships and attitudes. So it is not just a 'discussion' of how the society might chart a course for the future, it is actually *a contribution to (re)building this future together*.

Navigating in the second-best world of radioactive wastes

Let us now consider in a stylized way the characterization of deliberation processes that might bring together the two sides of the topical social choice problem of how to manage high level long-life radioactive wastes. These two sides are, respectively, *systems science* and *social signification* (namely, the meaning and weight attributed to events, actions and conceivable consequences).

The systems science side addresses the *ways and means* of controlling the exposure of present and future generations to radiation, relative to what is considered safe or otherwise satisfactory. Systems science, drawing on various aspects of physics and chemistry, biology, epidemiology and related subjects, will also advise on what should be considered a safe level of exposure (and why). This is the material question of the dose.

Can we deduce from statistics and scenario speculations about the present and possible future levels of exposure, what 'should' be done? The short answer is, no. The radioactive wastes in question constitute a socially constructed risk situation. As in the case of most socially mediated risks, the significance – and hence the acceptability or not – to an individual, to members of a community, to a society of exposure (or a danger of exposure) to a dose depends very much on how, by whom and why the dose has been produced. Correspondingly, in order to assess to what extent or on what basis the members of a society will judge acceptable (or not) a given strategy for management of high level long lived radioactive wastes, we will have to consider the distinctive meanings and *relationships* (in social, economic, cultural and symbolic terms) that the alternative strategies might establish between the people – individuals, classes, interest groups, succeeding generations, whole nations – implicated in the situations of production, storage and monitoring of the wastes.

To explore this question – the *social dimension* of radioactive waste management – we draw on an instructive example that was highlighted at the OECD Nuclear Energy Agency's 'Forum on Stakeholder Confidence' Workshop held in Ottawa, Canada, in October 2002.[11] This is the experience of the communities of Port

Hope, on the shores of Lake Ontario, whose townships have been contaminated with (mostly low level) long-lived radioactive wastes due to past factory activities of radium and uranium refining.

The striking feature of this 'case study', made clear by key stakeholders themselves and reinforced by CD-Rom multi-media presentations, is that the Port Hope (and neighbouring) communities have set about to *build a social – and societal – relationship with the wastes*. Emerging from more than 20 years of inconclusive discussions, suggestions and deliberations is a clear affirmation by the Port Hope community that it accepts 'ownership' of the contamination problem. It is a *historical liability* that the community *affirms as a part of its identity*. The community has actually refused certain proposed solutions for long-term waste management that depend on expertise and knowledge that they feel is not sufficiently accessible to them – that is, that would place the problem 'out of their hands'.[12] They prefer a *solution that they can see and understand*.

The preferred solution concept is to accommodate the radioactive wastes as modern-day burial mounds. The radioactive wastes, piled together and suitably 'capped', will become landscape features integrated into the everyday life of the community. The managed wastes thus become features in a kind of theme park this becomes (it is hoped) a tourist attraction rather than a reason to shy away.

It is recognized by all concerned, that this solution has been facilitated by the fact that the radioactive wastes in question are due to factory activities (radium and uranium refining) that engaged many of the past generations of the town's inhabitants and, thus, that contributed fundamentally to the building of the local economy and community. An objection might be made that, even if the 'theme park' concept might work for Port Hope, it is not necessarily an appropriate solution concept for the bigger problem of long-run management of large quantities of high-level radioactive wastes. The point is that, once it is admitted that relationships will (one way or another) come to be built and maintained, one sees the crucial importance of the question – political and sociological at the same time – whether and to what extent the 'forms of relationships' and the conventions and mechanisms by which they are established and maintained, are, or can be made, should be – or inevitably will be (even without knowing it in advance) – matters of societal choice and of social construction of meanings. We are creating durable relics for later generations of archaeologists. Our civilization is constructing the 'sites' that will be observed and assessed by later civilizations, and ascribed their distinctive meanings as the durable traces of our current way of life.[13]

The 'appropriation' of the waste/contamination problem by the 'local' stake-holders and their identification of a solution concept *that they can live with* are key ingredients for the economic, social and political viability of a solution. Equally necessary is the engagement of the relevant national authorities, establishing *a political/economic partnership*, as now is visible in the terms of the Port Hope Area Initiative bringing together the complementary local and national resources and forms of authority. So, taking Port Hope as an example, we see that there are three key components for a viable solution to a radioactive waste management problem. These are:

- The Science Dimension/Capacity to Measure and to Manage the Dose: the development and maintenance of scientific knowledge and technical competency to measure and to control the present and eventual exposure of living beings to radioactivity;
- The Social Dimension – Building Social/Societal Relationships with the Wastes: the envisaging and invention, in social and symbolic terms, of how the relevant community (or communities) will relate to and interact with the sites and the wastes;
- The Building of Political/Economic Partnerships: permitting to mobilize the relevant knowledge and resources for the implementation of an agreed societal solution to the disposal and watching over of the wastes.

We will not discuss the first component, the technical/scientific aspect of responsibility for 'managing the dose', which has been present since at least the 1950s in the objectives and statutory obligations for radiation security in the handling of raw and refined fuels, the operation of nuclear power stations and the storage and disposal of radioactive wastes.

Concern for the third component, partnership building, has emerged all over the world since the 1980s as a pragmatic response by public authorities (and, sometimes, by nuclear industry actors themselves) confronted by the ineffectiveness of the standard technical expertise model for viable waste management decisions. In many of those countries directly concerned by an obligation of radioactive waste management associated with nuclear energy production, there is an incontestable '*deficit*' *of stakeholder confidence* concerning the decisions proposed by the established expert and government bodies for the 'long-term disposal' of radioactive wastes. For example, in the UK, France, Germany and Canada, public outcry and dispute has forced the abandonment of envisaged programmes and/or a major reconstruction of the institutional and policy framework.[14] Confronted by public disquiet about the risks, and the very long time-frames involved in monitoring wastes, the authorities have turned to various forms of 'stakeholder consultation'.

At the heart of the social dimension of any agreed solution for waste management is the question of the nature of the relationships to be established and maintained by society with the sites and the radioactive wastes. Rather strikingly, there is little evidence of discussion of this component in authoritative documents on disposal and management options. This is not because this component of policy formulation is absent. Rather, it is because a specific answer – the type of 'relationship' envisaged – has already strongly been presumed and is *taken for granted*. We refer here to the concepts of *containment* and of provisional and permanent '*disposal*' of wastes through the competent action of an authority, respecting the precept, '*Out of public sight, therefore out of the public's mind*'. The comfort and safety of the public are assured by technological means implemented by a delegated authority, through the controlled collection and then expulsion of the noxious elements outside the society.[15]

In effect, since the 1950s the prevailing solution concept for radioactive waste disposal was the operation of a suitably designed and situated 'Modern-model rubbish dump'. As such, the solution was framed in essentially technical terms, and its implementation was not seen to involve the public directly. The *social dimension* of the solution was 'buried' inside the technocratic model of reputable *scientific/technical* expertise responding to the performance requirements of public administration.

This solution concept, based on a presumed partnership of administrative and scientific expertise and the precept '*out of public sight, therefore out of the public's mind*', was a reasonable one when formulated in the 1950s. But it is clear that the concerned public *today* do not have much confidence in this model. This lack of confidence arises from many factors – partly from the accumulation of experience with nuclear energy, radiation and spent nuclear fuel (including, notably, the difficulties of long-term and secure containment); partly from growing general awareness of the problems of waste management in modern societies; and partly in the wider context, discussed in earlier sections, of our societies' increasing awareness of the myriad, often uncontrollable and often long-lasting, side-effects of technological (physical, chemical, genetic and ecological) inventions.[16]

Resolving an (unintended) coexistence problem

Some radioactive wastes are highly dangerous and very long lived. Since the waste management problem is a long-term issue, confidence is partly a matter of hope and trust.[17] In this regard, concerning radioactive wastes we can observe that many people *are not willing to trust the waste to stay put* (for thousands and thousands of years); and, many people *are not willing to trust the experts* when they say that, suitably contained, the wastes will stay put.

In short, the interested public are not willing, at the present time, to go along with the model '*out of public sight, therefore out of the public's mind*'. The enduring presence of the hazardous wastes is bothersome, but it is not easily forgotten. So, a solution that the public will feel able to *trust* must engage a permanent process of vigilance – living with and '*watching over the wastes*'.[18]

Around the world, in the process of trying to achieve safety, satisfy regulatory requirements, and put at rest the public mistrust, many thousands of millions of dollars have been spent on scientific investigations, technical experiments and a variety of deep and surface storage feasibility studies. Simulation models and quantitative risk assessments are projected hundreds and thousands of years into the future. The chemical, thermal and physical properties of minute fissures in geological formations are studied with assiduity, in the hope of proving (or disproving) a containment prospect. And, the more the scientific and technical frontiers are pushed back, the more complex (and complicated) the systems science questions become.

An object that engages such extensive, costly and meticulous scientific attention, that has become the focus of deep societal controversy for more than 50 years, and that is expected to remain the object of permanent surveillance for hundreds or even thousands of years, cannot be considered still to be just a 'waste'! Radioactive wastes are something else! They are a class of artefacts that most people have heard about but never seen, and that have become mythical – folkloric in the deepest sense of the term. 'Nuclear waste' is an *icon*, a *symbol* of the great adventure (and the uncertain destiny) of our technological civilization. These artefacts are a *historical liability* not just for us but also for entire future societies (and not just future generations of our forms of society) that will inherit the requirement for *watching over our wastes*, as a part of the cultural (and not just material) legacy of our times.

Suppose the construction of an eventual underground storage site, maybe Yucca Mountain as proposed in the USA. If the installation is presented like a rubbish dump, then the communities 'hosting' the installation will be able to affirm – not without justification – that they are being 'dumped upon'. If it is explained to them that placing the installation in their community is the 'best' alternative in terms of the overall balance of costs and benefits to the nation, this will only be adding insult to injury.[19]

Once we put aside as inadequate the old model 'out of sight, out of mind', we have to reconsider from the start the consequences of a solution concept, and of its implementation, for the relationships of people to each other. If people complain about being 'dumped upon', then this is not just a problem of economic opportunity or risk of physical injury (e.g., potential exposure to radioactivity in the case of transport accidents, plant malfunction or hostile attack). It is also a matter of status, pride, dignity, and prestige. Suppose that there are jobs attached to the long-term task of watching over the wastes and salaries to be paid. In what terms will the jobs of site warden be advertised? Who will be recruited? Will there be job opportunities for the locals? What will be the sorts of skills required? What skin colour? What salary scale? What will be the relation of the radioactivity wardens to the local community, and the perception of their role by the rest of the society?

We propose a short (and so far not very systematic) anthropology of 'social models' that might be proposed for 'watching over the wastes'. Here are a few that come to mind:

- Build a mausoleum/shrine/temple/tomb;
- The orphan-site (or the waif?);
- The Haunted House: abandonment of the disposal (burial) site to the ghosts;[20]
- Construction of the installation as a theme park (cf. Port Hope), and development of a tourist operation exploiting concepts of a technological museum, vicarious risk, etc.;
- A nursing home for the long-term care of unruly residents who, by chance, could get confused and get out of hand.

Variations of the shrine/temple concept have been offered by many different commentators for some years. The concept has appeal partly because it evokes the 'eternal' character of the guardianship task. One could imagine generation after generation of monks roaming the corridors in a solemn contemplation, each generation handing down, by ceremony and song, a unique competence to the one that follows, maintaining an eternal vigil accompanied perhaps by an existential anguish.[21]

Each 'model' for watching over (or neglecting) the wastes privileges different aspects of social life, different types of prestige and status, different communities, different relationships. The shrine/temple concept could have appeal because, by the establishment of the new priestly caste, it could offer a high status rehabilitation option in the case of long-term structural unemployment of highly trained nuclear engineers. The rather contrasting nursing home concept brings a quite different set of connotations – patience, compassion, meticulous care, weariness, maybe even mourning, anger and sadness with the pain of a long condemnation to watch over the aging residents of the rest home who, dreadfully, do not know how to die.

Social choice and stakeholder deliberation

With the benefit of the nuclear wastes example, now let us come back to the central theme of our discussion, the role of multi-stakeholder deliberation to formulate and resolve problems of 'social choice' about economic and ecological distribution.

Rittel (1982) in his discussion of 'wicked' problems that do not lend themselves to clear-cut and once-and-for-all solutions based on simple principles of optimal choice, developed the metaphor of navigation in turbulent conditions: 'let us embark on the risk together'. The lesson of historical liability is that, whether we chose it or not in the past, we are now 'embarked' on the risks together.[22]

There is certainly a need for science and technical competence for the design and the piloting of a boat – in the present case, concerning a very real material problem of the risks of excessive and inadvertent exposures to a radiation dose. But, how do we manage human relations during the voyage? What are the purposes that we will find, invent and share along the way? Without attention to the social and symbolic dimensions, the necessary political/economic partnerships cannot be built and the relevant knowledge (which includes human as well as technical sciences) will not be obtained or will not be mobilized.

No individual or institution (however expert or humanly wise) holds all alone a completely satisfactory blueprint for 'what should be done' for a community embarked on its voyage. The deliberation process is pragmatic and permanent, an attempt not only to mobilize existing wisdom and purposefulness but also to let these qualities emerge and be renewed along the way. Consider, for example, the possibility of carrying out a sort of multi-stakeholder multi-criteria appraisal of solution concepts for vigilance concerning radioactive wastes.[23] Three axes can be used to frame a simple methodological schema for an evaluation process:[24]

1   The exploration of options: radioactive waste policy or management perspectives are explored in terms of a small number of scenarios each of which expresses distinct technological, economic and governance features.
2   The diversity of stakeholders: the scenarios of distinct possible futures are to be evaluated explicitly from distinct stakeholder perspectives.
3   Multiple evaluation criteria: the stakeholders will make evaluations of each

scenario in terms of a range of key governance issues, using a variety of different criteria reflecting the full diversity of societal concerns.

The general idea is that a (relatively small) number of options, here described as 'scenarios', are identified as wanting to be assessed in a *comparative way* by people bringing a variety of preoccupations, expertises and points of view. In the present example, we could focus on a selection of qualitatively different social models for watching over the wastes – the rubbish dump, the temple/shrine, the haunted burial site, the nursing home, etc. Then, we can consider each of these solution concepts as – prima facie – *ethically principled actions*, meaning to identify the ways in which, as individual and collective actions, they satisfy or respond to particular criteria of good or sound practice that are suggested by members of the community. For the radioactive wastes, current examples of 'ethical bottom lines' could include:

- National autonomy/responsibility ('take care of your own wastes' at national scale);
- That 'the polluter pays' (but, how much, to whom, etc.);
- A principle of inter-generational responsibility (do not pass on problems to others that you cannot cope with yourself);
- Health security to workers and the public (reasonable steps to avoid an excessive dose);
- Enhance the prestige of the host communities for any waste site;
- Security against attack in the face of external or internal sources of aggression.

Each distinct stakeholder group will bring a different balance of preoccupations to the deliberation process. The general idea is that a *comparative evaluation* of the scenarios would take place from a variety of *different points of view* corresponding to distinct preoccupations. Each stakeholder group may express different criteria of adequacy or quality in relation to each of the 'governance issues'. Tensions, conflicts of interests, uncertainties and dissent (amongst scientists as well as decision-makers, administrators and stakeholders from different walks of commercial activity and civil society) can be explored by comparison of the judgements made about the good and not so good features of each solution concept or implementation strategy. In effect, the scenario set becomes the platform for a *multi-stakeholder deliberation* about the *social meanings* as well as the *scientific/technical* quality associated with the different decision options and policy choices.

This schema for a deliberation process is, in itself, a political model which carries value judgements. Which value judgements? It is conceivable that an 'ethical assessment', as a social science exercise, could be carried out for strategic purposes, in order to design better propaganda and more effective manipulation of public opinion and fears. We should not discount this possibility.[25] But we choose to focus here on the role of such analyses, dialogue and reflection not for more effective coercion but in a societal search for common grounds of coexistence.

The search for novel and compromise solutions, as possible ways forward together, depends not so much on technical expertise (although this can certainly be helpful, e.g., repairing a boat, working out how to contain the reactor wastes) but more especially on *mobilizing human know-how and resources* in a social process. The viability of any voyage-in-common depends somehow on goodwill, respect and trust; these are the *conditio sine qua non* for any effective and successful partnership. But *trust*, here, is rather more than just confidence that a person will pay his or her bills or do his or her job. Respect for divergent criteria does not mean the dissolving of all differences and conflicts. It means willingness to accept limits, to accept vulnerability, and to make compromises based on the hope of benefits coming from coexistence. Whether or not, in the face of very different attitudes and convictions, lack of interest, and the myriad fears (including, but not limited to concerns about radioactivity) that populate the landscapes of everyday life, our societies can develop and maintain this willingness, remains to be seen.

The idea of a respectful coexistence is a delicate and pertinent point to discuss in the current climate of geopolitical tensions about Right and Wrong. There will evidently be many situations where people, different cultures, or different species of plants and animals, simply cannot, or do not want to, find a basis for durable coexistence. Reflective deliberation as advocated here may work to highlight appreciation of tensions, but it does not necessarily find a way to put an end to them.

Notes

1 For this example and others, we could define a sort of 'coefficient of irreversibility' which compares the lifetime of the active wastes, with the productive lifetime of the nuclear energy generation process.

2 Entrées to the contemporary literature are provided by, inter alia, Kapp (1983), Beckenbach (1989/1994), Martinez-Alier (1995), Martinez-Alier and O'Connor (1996), and O'Connor (ed., 1996).

3 This synthesis is partly adapted from the overviews of science, complexity and risk governance developed by Funtowicz *et al.* (1998) and by Gallopín *et al.* (2001); we owe some parts of our formulation also to Joachim Spangenberg.

4 See Funtowicz and Ravetz (1990, 1991, and 1994), O'Connor and van den Hove (2001), and Faucheux and Hue (2001).

5 If future interests are regarded as having standing then, in the standard economist's language, we may have a situation of 'market failure' due to 'missing markets'. But, this sort of market failure is also cost-shifting success from the point of view of those parties benefiting from the 'non-internalization'. So missing markets can be a significant support to the profitability of powerful players in the existing markets and may even be designed by them. A zero-price may signal not non-scarcity or ignorance about a damage or risk imposed, but simply a relation of power in a situation of conflict.

6 A time honoured example of this sort of attitude is the Buddhist precept, 'Do not take life unnecessarily'. Everything reposes, of course, on what constitutes 'unnecessarily'.

7 This dialectical distinction between domination ethics and coexistence ethics is developed by various analysts (e.g., Latouche 1984, 1989, Salleh 1997, and O'Connor 1999) and is really as old as the hills (although perhaps somewhat out of fashion in the modern world of crass utilitarianism and instrumental rationality). It engages epistemological and existential as well as overt ethical dimensions. There are some links, too, with themes of communicative rationality and the 'ideal speech situation' developed by Habermas (1979). However, an exposition of the (many) philosophical variations will not be developed here.

8 Although we do not always find this point discussed in standard economics policy textbooks, it is not really such a new problem for economists. John Stuart Mill had encountered it many times (see O'Connor 1995/1997); environmental philosophers currently discuss it (e.g.,

Holland 1997, and Stone 1987). Several generations of institutional economists such as Commons (1934) and Samuels (1992) have insisted on the importance of empirical and theoretical analysis of the instituted processes of 'working out' responses to various social choice and coordination dilemmas. For example Commons, in his *Institutional Economics* (1934: 712), writing in advance of Arrow's mathematical axiomatization, insisted that no general formula could be relied upon to produce 'reasonable' outcomes in application to all sets of problems of fairness and justice in resource allocation. Reasoned and reasonable compromises would have to be deliberated and worked out in a permanent social process.

9　Whether or not 'stakeholder' is an adequate term for all situations of conflict, negotiation and political argumentation is certainly open to debate, but not a question we address here. For some recent developments around themes of multi-stakeholder deliberation for sustainability, see Dryzek (1994), Holland (1997), Jacobs (1997), Sagoff (1998), Bailly (1998), De Marchi and Ravetz (1999), De Marchi *et al* (2001), Le Dars (2001), and van den Hove (2000, and 2001).

10　Rather than being simply tired and fatalistic about the never-ending delays, repairs and patch-up jobs (as with motorway systems where the grand scheme is never really operational and the prevailing experience is of road works, traffic jams, accidents, photochemical pollution, etc.) that are the reality produced by the various forms of technocracy and commercial enterprise that dominate the scenes of modern economic life.

11　The discussion that follows is adapted from parts of O'Connor (2003). For further details of the NEA's Forum on Stakeholder Confidence and the programme of workshops since 2000, see www.nea.fr/html/civil/welcome.html.

12　For example, the community rejects a solution concept, argued by some experts to be technically superior, for 'disposal' of the contaminated material in a cavern hollowed out under the lake. For various reasons they do not completely trust this solution.

13　Are the Port Hope storage/disposal sites to be considered as analogous to ancient burial mounds, or as a new form of trash mound, or something else? This is still an open question; time will tell. Archaeologists give us some anachronistic reference points. The term *'barrow'* designates a variety of forms of burial mound that are features of sites of prehistoric civilizations. Long barrows are generally Neolithic structures and the round barrows generally Bronze Age or later. The long barrow is an elongated roughly rectangular structure and may contain many burial chambers. Round barrows, more common than long barrows, typically contain only a single burial or two or three individuals. A typical example would be a roughly hemispherical mound formed by piling the earth up at the centre of a circular ditch. Building material varies according to location; if there was only a thin top soil then the mound might be formed by piling boulders into cairns. Another type of round barrow is the pond barrow formed by digging the earth out from the centre of the site and piling it up in a bank around the site. The central area would then be used for burial. The *'midden'*, by contrast, is the term used for soil incorporating decomposed food waste (including shell and animal bone), ash, charcoal and other organic debris, and tools and other living debris, built up at places where people have lived or worked. 'Shell midden', for example, is midden soil with significant quantities of shellfish shells, characteristic of coastal settlements. What will be the typical forms and composition of our nuclear barrows?

14　If there were not this deficit of stakeholder confidence, the Nuclear Energy Agency's Forum for Stakeholder Confidence would not have a reason to exist. Some elements of overview are found in the NEA's FSC documents; see www.nea.fr.

15　A waste is any sort of product or by-product of economic activity that is in surplus relative to society's needs. According to what we may call the 'Modern-model rubbish dump' model, it suffices that the society invest some effort in collection methods, organization and transport services, and it is possible, once and for all, to get rid of the wastes. As long as the members of society follow the rules (about 'putting out the rubbish for collection'), they do not have to think about what happens next.

16　The public's refusal to place one's confidence in decision-makers and experts can have many origins. In the nuclear waste case, there are certainly some doubts expressed that the proposed storage solutions will really work as described. This doubt is then allied to reluctance to accept or approve the consequences in the event of failure. There may also be the view that the solution proposed, even if it works as intended, is in some fundamental way inadequate, undesirable or inappropriate. Consider the following metaphor. Suppose that a person has an infected leg. Cutting off the leg is one solution and it may work as planned. But an injection of antibiotics may permit the person to keep living with the leg. In such a situation, it may not be desirable (from the patient's point of view) to give monopoly decision power to experts in amputation. For 50 years in the nuclear sector, the principal decisions have been taken authoritatively, and the assurance of 'quality' has been the designated – or self-designated – responsibility of a limited circle of expertise. The sector, military and civil, has therefore been characterized by what some call a 'deficit of dialogue' or even a 'deficit of democracy'. This in itself is enough to contribute to suspicions (as to, e.g., cover-ups, vested interests, inadequate weight to citizens' concerns, blind spots, group-think, failure to listen to 'weak' signals about system weaknesses and risks, etc.). Some parts of public mistrust can be overcome by procedural reforms, scrupulous science and better communication. But, as the infected leg image is intended to make clear, these may not be enough on their own.

17 Our definition of trust is the willingness to be, or become, vulnerable in order to have the possibility to benefit from some outcome that is not achievable otherwise. This highlights the importance of identifying what is the 'benefit' that is being proposed or sought. The production of radioactive wastes in large quantities is now a historical fact, and what society seeks is to formulate a satisfactory way of living with the wastes.

18 This *mistrust* of both nature (the material wastes) and human nature (the possible failings of the experts) has – among other things – contributed to the push to introduce the concept of *reversibility* (including retrievability) into the formulation and evaluation of waste management options. The *mistrust* that an unobserved waste might not 'stay put' is probably more significant in the emergence of 'reversibility' than the argument put forward by experts of a possible economic or security benefit from retrieval at a future date. People are not necessarily willing to trust the experts when they suggest adaptations to the 'Modern model' of storage, that a variety of provisions for '*reversibility*' of the containment (etc.) can be incorporated into a waste management strategy. Rather – as in the example of Port Hope for low-level wastes and also in the case of public outcry over the UK deep disposal proposal – the social demand seems to be that the wastes should in some way remain 'visible' and 'accessible to the society' and that the communities or society in question should thus be able to maintain an active relationship with the site(s).

19 This may be one source of the visible stand-off between the USA federal authority and Nevada State. The US situation can be contrasted with the case of Finland, where a sort of symbolic as well as economic partnership seems to have been negotiated, with a reciprocal affirmation of the status of local and national authorities in the implementation of a disposal strategy.

20 If people mistrust nuclear, if they mistrust the wastes, if they mistrust the authorities (which authorities, in what context?), what is it that makes them afraid, that nourishes the mistrust, that makes them uncomfortable? There is a very large body of literature, both scholarly and popular, on the eternal subject of the haunted house, the haunted burial site, the roaming of souls, spirits and shadows not yet reconciled to cross the boundary between the Living or the Dead. To explore the concerns expressed in society about 'orphan sites' and about the problems of 'invisible' hazardous wastes, some careful social science enquiry would provide some important insights.

21 One could imagine the monks and acolytes watching the computer screens for a signal of alarm or a flicker of untoward movement just as, in the 1976 film *Il Deserto dei Tartari* ('The Desert of the Tartars') by Italian director Valerio Zurlini, the soldiers gazed at the horizon waiting eternally for an eventual invasion by nomad Tartars. (According to one website review, 'The characters are full of suppressed emotion and inner turmoil, the surrealistic fort a metaphor of their spiritual imprisonment and the huge expanse of desert a tangible, day by day, year by year reminder of their fears and lost aspirations …').

22 The voyage-in-common metaphor is also taken up by the recent ULYSSES project funded by the European Commission and addressing public participation in climate change policy formulation and evaluation (see Guimarães Pereira and O'Connor 1999).

23 In some contexts this is referred to as an 'ethical assessment' (cf. Fleming 2003) which, in this context, is not a personal moral judgement but rather a profiling of the spectrum of principles for judgement put forward in the deliberation situation. Usually, indeed, an 'ethics' question is seen to arise only when there is an *absence of consensus* about criteria of choice or action. When there is not consensus, it is easy to say that those with whom I disagree are being 'unethical'. But, in a philosophical or social science point of view, assessment means exploring and documenting the preoccupations and principles (the 'bottom lines') of the people making up the affected communities.

24 This is a highly generic schema. An example of its application, known as 'The Deliberation Matrix', is the multi-media interactive 'Deliberation Support Tool' (DST) implemented by researchers in the *GOUVERNe* Project ('Guidelines for the Organization, Use and Validation of information systems for Evaluating aquifer Resources and Needs') funded by the European Commission and led by the C3ED research institute (see www.c3ed.uvsq.fr).

25 Just as technologies have their distinctive risk profiles, so social science methodologies open up distinctive domains of risk.

References

Agarwal, A. and Narain, S. (1991) *Global Warming in an Unequal World: A Case of Environmental Colonialism*, New Delhi: Centre for Science and Environment.

Arrow, K. (1963) *Individual Values and Social Choice*, 2nd edn, New York: Wiley.

Azar, C. and Holmberg, J. (1995) 'Defining the Generational Environment Debt', in *Ecological Economics*, 14: 7–20.

Bailly, J.-P. (1998) 'Prospective, débat, décision publique', in *Journal Officiel de la République Française: Avis et Rapports du Conseil Economique et Social, Extrait du Rapport*, 16: 13–129.

Beckenbach, F. (1989/1994) 'Social Costs of Modern Capitalism', in *Capitalism, Nature, Socialism*, No. 3: 91–105, revised and reprinted in M. O'Connor (ed., 1994) *Is Capitalism Sustainable? Political Economy and the Politics of Ecology*, New York: Guilford.

Boyce, J. (1996) 'Ecological Distribution, Agricultural Trade Liberalization, and In-Situ Genetic Diversity', in *Journal of Income Distribution*, 6(2): 265–86.

Commons, J.R. (1934) *Institutional Economics: Its Place in Political Economy*, reprinted (1961) Madison, WI: University of Wisconsin Press.

De Marchi, B. and Ravetz, J. (1999) 'Risk Management and Governance: A Post-Normal Science Approach', in *Futures*, 31(7): 743–57.

De Marchi, B., Funtowicz, S. and Guimarães, Pereira Â. (2001) 'From the Right to be Informed to the Right to Participate: Responding to the Evolution of European Legislation with ICT', *International Journal of Environment and Pollution*, 15(1): 1–21.

Dryzek, J. (1994) 'Ecology and Discursive Democracy: Beyond Liberal Capitalism and the Administrative state', in M. O'Connor (ed.) *Is Capitalism Sustainable? Political Economy and the Politics of Ecology*, New York: The Guilford .

Faber, D. (1993) *Environment under Fire: Imperialism and the Ecological Crisis in Central America*, New York: Monthly Review Press.

Faucheux, S. and Hue, C. (2000) 'Politique Environnementale et Politique Technologique: Vers une Prospective Participative', *Nature, Science Sociétés*, 8(3): 31–44.

Faucheux, S. and Hue, C. (2001) 'From Irreversibility to Participation: Towards a Participatory Foresight for the Governance of Collective Environmental Risks', *Journal of Hazardous Materials*, 86: 223–43.

Faucheux, S. and O'Connor, M. (2000) 'Technosphère versus écosphère. Quel arbitrage? Choix technologiques et menaces environnementales: signaux faibles, controverses et décision', *Futuribles*, No. 251.

Fleming, P.A. (2003) 'Stakeholder Confidence: Observations from the Viewpoint of Ethics', in *Public Confidence in the Management of Radioactive Waste: the Canadian Context* (NEA Forum on Stakeholder Confidence, Workshop Proceedings, Ottawa, Canada, 14–18 October 2002), Paris: OECD: 169–76.

Funtowicz, S. and Ravetz, J. (1990) *Uncertainty and Quality in Science for Policy*, Dordrecht: Kluwer Academic Press.

Funtowicz, S. and Ravetz, J. (1991) 'A New Scientific Methodology for Global Environmental Issues', in R. Costanza (ed.), *Ecological Economics: The Science and Management of Sustainability*, New York: Columbia University Press.

Funtowicz, S. and Ravetz, J. (1994) 'La science post-normale et les systèmes complexes émergents', *Revue Internationale de Systémique*, 8(4–5): 353–77.

Funtowicz, S., Ravetz, J. and O'Connor, M. (1998) 'Challenges in the Use of Science for Sustainable Development', *International Journal of Sustainable Development*, 1(1): 99–107.

Gallopín, G., Funtowicz, S., O'Connor, M. and Ravetz, J. (2001) 'Science for the 21st Century: From Social Contract to the Scientific Core', *International Journal of Social Science*, 168: 209–29.

Gedicks, A. (1993) *The New Resource Wars: Native and Environmental Struggles against Multinational Corporations*, Boston, MA: South End Press.

Guimarães Pereira, A. and O'Connor, M., (1999) 'Information and Communication Technology and the Popular Appropriation of Sustainability Problems', *International Journal of Sustainable Development*, 2(3): 411–24.

Habermas, J. (1979) *Communication and the Evolution of Society* (English translation), London: Heinemann.

Hobbelink, H. (1991) *Biotechnology and the Future of World Agriculture*, London: Zed Books.

Holland, A. (1997) 'The Foundations of Environmental Decision-making', *International Journal of Environment and Pollution*, 7: 483–96.

Institute for Prospective Technological Studies (IPTS) (1999) 'Technology Map', *Futures Report Series* 11, Joint Research Centre, Seville: European Commission.

Institute for Prospective Technological Studies (IPTS) (2000) 'A Survey of National/Regional Prospective Technological Studies in Germany and Spain and the Exploitation of their Results in the Policy-Making Processes', EUR 19574 EN, Seville: European Commission.

Jacobs, M. (1997) 'Environmental Valuation, Deliberative Democracy and Public Decision-making Institutions' in J. Foster (ed.), *Valuing Nature? Economics, Ethics and Environment*, London: Routledge.

Kapp, K.W. (1983) *Social Costs, Economic Development, and Environmental Disruption*, Lanham, MD: University Press of America.

Latouche, S. (1984) *Le Procès de la Science Sociale*, Paris : Anthropos.

Latouche, S. (1989) *L'Occidentalisation du Monde: Essai sur la Signification, la Portée et les Limites de l'Uniformisation Planétaire*, Paris : La Découverte; English translation, *The Westernisation of the World*, London: Polity Press.

Le Dars, A. (2001) 'Mettre en place une gouvernance participative pour la gestion des déchets nucléaires à vie longue et à haute activité: quels moyens pour quels fins?', in G. Froger (ed.), *Gouvernance 1: Gouvernance et Développement Durable*, Basle, Geneva and Munich: Helbing & Lichtenhahn.

Martinez-Alier, J. and O'Connor, M. (1996) 'Distributional Issues in Ecological Economics', in R. Costanza, O. Segura and J. Martinez-Alier (eds) *Getting Down to Earth: Practical Applications of Ecological Economics*, Washington, DC: Island Press: 153–84.

Martinez-Alier, J. (1995) 'Political Ecology, Distributional Conflicts and Economic Incommensurability,' *New Left Review*, 211: 70–88.

Mies, M. (1986) *Patriarchy and Accumulation on a World Scale*, London: Zed Books.

Muir, E. (1996) 'Intra-Generational Wealth Distributional Effects on Global Warming Cost Benefit Analysis', *Journal of Income Distribution*, 6(2): 193–214.

Muradian, R. and O'Connor, M. (2001) 'Inter-country Environmental Load Displacement and Adjusted National Sustainability Indicators: Concepts and their Policy Applications', *International Journal of Sustainable Development*, 4(3): 321–47.

O'Connor, M. (ed.) (1996) Symposium on the Economic Analysis of Ecological Distribution, *Journal of Income Distribution* 6(2): 145–326.

O'Connor, M. (1995/1997) 'La Réciprocité Introuvable: L'utilitarisme de John Stuart Mill et la Recherche d'une Ethique pour la Soutenabilité', in *Economie Appliquée*, XLVIII No. 2: 271–304; English version 'J.S. Mills's Utilitarianism and the Social Ethics of Sustainable Development', in *European Journal of History of Economic Thought*, 4(3):478–506, 1997.

O'Connor, M. (1999) 'Dialogues and Debate in a Post-normal Practice of Science: a Reflexion', *Futures* 31: 671–87.

O'Connor, M. (2002) 'Social Costs and Sustainability', in D.H. Bromley and J. Paavola (eds), *Economics, Ethics and Environmental Policy: Contested Choices*, Oxford: Blackwell Publishing, .

O'Connor, M. (2003) 'Building Relationships with the Waste', in *Public Confidence in the Management of Radioactive Waste: the Canadian Context* (NEA Forum on Stakeholder Confidence, Workshop Proceedings, Ottawa, Canada, 14–18 October 2002), Paris: OECD: 177–90.

O'Connor, M. and van den Hove, S. (2001) 'Prospects for Concertation on Nuclear Risks and Technological Options: Innovations in Governance Practices for Sustainable Development in the European Union', *Journal of Hazardous Materials*, 86: 77–99.

Rittel, H. (1982) 'Systems Analysis of the "First and Second Generations",' in P. Laconte, J. Gibson and A. Rapoport (eds., 1982) *Human and Energy Factors in Urban Planning*, NATO Advanced Study Institutes Series, The Hague: Martinus Nijhoff: 153–84.

Sachs, W. (1993) *Global Ecology*, Zed Books: London.

Sagoff, M. (1998) 'Aggregation and Deliberation in Valuing Environmental Goods: a Look beyond Contingent Pricing', *Ecological Economics*, 24(2–3): 213–30.

Salleh, A. (1997) *Feminism as Politics: Nature, Marx and the Postmodern*, London: Zed Books.

Samuels, W.J. (1992) *Essays on the Economic Role of Government: Vol.I Fundamentals; Vol.II Applications*, London: Macmillan.

Stone, C. (1987) *Earth and Other Ethics: The Case for Moral Pluralism*, New York: Harper & Row.

van den Hove, S. (2000) 'Participatory Approaches to Environmental Policy-making: The European Commission Climate Policy Process as a Case Study', *Ecological Economics*, 33: 457–72.

van den Hove, S. (2001) 'Approches participatives pour la gouvernance en matière de développement durable: une analyse en termes d'effets', pp. 53–89 in G. Froger (ed.), *Gouvernance et Développement Durable*, Basle, Geneva and Munich: Helbing & Lichtenhahn.

Wackernagel, M. and Rees, W.E. (1995) *Our Ecological Footprint: Reducing Human Impact on the Earth*, Gabriola Island, BC and Philadelphia, PA: New Society Publishers.

Wackernagel, M., Onisto, L., Bello, P., Callejas, A., Lopez, I., Mendez, J., Suarez A. and Suarez G. (1999) 'National Natural Capital Accounting with the Ecological Footprint Concept', *Ecological Economics*, 29: 375–90.

Waring, M. (1989) *Counting for Nothing*, Sydney: Unwin.

WCED (World Commission on Environment and Development) (1987) *Our Common Future*, (The Brundtland Report), Oxford and New York: Oxford University Press.

5 Poverty alleviation environment and sustainable development

Implication for the management of natural capital

Anil Markandya[1]

Introduction

The purpose of this chapter is to see how the ideas of sustainable development fit into the vision for development articulated by Stiglitz in his Prebish lecture at UNCTAD in 1998 (Stiglitz 1998). This is quite a challenge; Stiglitz barely mentions the term sustainable development in his entire lecture. Further he only twice refers (briefly) to the environment or natural capital, which are the specific issues to be covered in this chapter. It is hard to imagine that these concepts were high on his mind when he prepared the lecture.

In this chapter, I will begin by looking at the literature on sustainable development, focus on the role of natural capital, and see what implications it has for poverty alleviation. 'Sustainable development and natural capital' will look at the ideas for economic development outlined by Stiglitz and see what one can draw out in terms of implications for sustainable development and natural capital management. 'Conclusions and recommendations' addresses the specific questions the organizers want answered, which relate to the Stiglitz paper and the guiding principles of sustainable development.

Sustainable development and natural capital

The term sustainable development has its origins in the IUCN 1980 World Conservation Strategy report, but it was with the World Commission on Environment and Development, entitled, 'Our Common Future' (1987) that the term gained broad currency.[2] The Commission defined sustainable development as 'development that meets the needs for the present without compromising the ability of future generations to meet their own needs'. This definition, while useful in drawing attention to the concern with the long-term implications of present day development, asks as many questions as it answers. What constitutes 'needs', and how will these change over time? What reductions in the options available to future generations are acceptable and what are not? The operational aspects of sustainable development were not answered by the Brundtland Commission, although the Report itself gave strong hints that the environmental degradation resulting from today's economic policies was a major source of concern from a sustainability viewpoint.

The first attempts to make the concept more precise were theoretical rather than practical. They focused on the economic and the environmental dimensions of the debate. From the economic perspective, some of the earlier contributions (Pearce *et al.* 1990) suggested sustainable development should imply that no generation in the future would be worse off than the present generation. In other words society should not allow welfare to fall over time. Experience tells us that this does not always happen; countries experience growth and decline and their citizens' welfare does indeed fall from time to time. In the last 170 years or so, some OECD countries have achieved a rate of economic growth of one to two per cent *per capita per annum* measured in terms of GDP (Maddison 1995). While this does not guarantee that welfare never fell from one year to another, or from one generation to another, it makes it more likely that future generations would, 'on average', be better off then the present one.[3] But these records have only been constructed, painstakingly, for a few advanced countries and we cannot judge others over such a long stretch. The best we can do is look at the last 33 years or so. Here the World Bank is an invaluable source. Out of 148 countries in its database, GDP figures are available for 1965–97 for 111 of them (World Bank 2000a). Of these, 28 countries had negative *per capita growth* over the period. Half were in Africa (Central African Republic, Chad, Congo, Cote D'Ivoire, Ghana, Madagascar, Mauritania, Mozambique, Niger, Senegal, Sierra Leone, Sudan, Togo and Zambia), one in Asia (Mongolia), three in the Middle East (Iran, Jordan, Kuwait and United Arab Emirates), four in Eastern Europe (Bulgaria, Georgia and Romania) and six in Central and South America and the Caribbean (El Salvador, Haiti, Jamaica, Nicaragua, Peru and Venezuela). Furthermore, of the 37 countries for which we do not have data, it is likely that many of them have had a decline in GDP – a number are newly created states of the Former Soviet Union, which have had precipitate declines in national income).

Of course, *per capita* GDP is a very rough measure. Among its many failings, it does not tell us how particular groups in society fared over that time, especially the vulnerable and poor. In this regard one can say that if society as a whole is getting worse off then the poor will hardly ever better their position; being at the bottom of the pile their lot will almost certainly decline. The converse, too, which is less obvious, seems to hold to some extent. While not all groups will have improved their welfare in the 83 countries that have had positive economic growth in the last 33 years, most have, especially if the rate of growth has been high enough. The World Development Report for 2000 shows convincingly that several aggregate indicators of poverty decline as economic growth increases. The closer the growth rate is to zero, the more likely is it that poverty will not decline for all groups in society.

So far we have discussed sustainable development in relation to economic growth and said nothing about natural resources or natural capital.[4] The 'founding parents' of sustainable development were equally concerned about both aspects –

sustainability and development. The worry with the former was that society may be enjoying high and increasing welfare at the expense of running down its capital, particularly its natural capital.

To address this, economists have turned to looking at changes in the stock of wealth, where wealth is defined to include natural, human, physical and social capital (World Bank 1997). If society's wealth *per capita* is declining then it is leaving future generations less with which to sustain present levels of consumption. Unfortunately it is notoriously difficult to measure all these forms of capital for any one country and even more difficult to do so in a way that permits comparison across countries. Nevertheless some brave attempts have been made (World Bank 1997, Hamilton and Clemens 1999, and Hamilton 2000). The last and most recent of these has looked at changes in wealth *per capita* by looking at changes in genuine savings, for the period 1990–7. The analysis shows a considerable increase in the number of countries with negative changes. With the exception of China, the majority of countries (47 of them) lying below median world income have declining wealth *per capita*. Of course, this is a short period, and it is dangerous to extrapolate from it to the future. Non-zero population growth rates can easily yield alarming and nonsensical results if projected far enough into the future. There are also concerns that the measures of capital do not take enough account of the productivity of different types of capital. For example, the measures constructed by Hamilton include Australia as a country having negative wealth increase and the USA as on a 'knife edge' – under some parameters it too has an increase in wealth less than its increase in population. Given the stellar performance of the US economy during the period under consideration, this result may be difficult to accept but it reflects the relatively low savings as well as the unusual increase in population. It does not account, however, for the technology changes that have increased productivity so sharply in the 1990s.

Questions have also been raised as to the validity of constructing a single measure of wealth by adding up human, physical, natural and social forms of capital. Problems of converting some forms of capital into monetary units are well known. Some economists have raised concerns about the message that is being given if, for instance, natural capital is being depleted but physical capital accumulated so that total wealth is increasing (Daly 1990). If the losses of natural capital are particularly critical to the functioning of the ecosystem, and thereby to the economic systems that depend on them, their loss may be incalculable.

In summary, the literature on real wealth and sustainable development provides us with some early warnings about what may go wrong if we do not look at the trends in all types of capital, including human and natural capital. But the data are for short periods and do not capture all aspects of economic development, notably the huge benefits from technological change. Hence they cannot point to unsustainability in a definitive way. Many of the factors that result in negative increases in *per capita* wealth can be reversed over the medium term, especially if the integrity of ecosystems is maintained and enough investment is taking place in human capital. In the very long term, of course, no one can ever say with any certainty what will happen.

Poverty and sustainability

What does the literature on sustainable development have to say about poverty? Directly it says little, but in the Brundtland definition, there is an implicit recognition of the issues of equity within and across generations. Intra-generational equity arises because we want to 'meet the needs of the present'. Any reasonable definition of such needs must include the elimination of 'pronounced deprivation in well-being', which is the World Bank's definition of poverty in its 2000 Development Report. Intergenerational equity refers to the needs of future generations and again no one would disagree with the view that this requires the elimination of poverty. One can ask why we should focus on poverty, rather than equity in a wider sense. No one has really provided a serious analysis of this but there are two possible reasons. One is that there is a clear point at which we can define pronounced deprivation as measured, say, in access to resources. The use of 'a dollar a day' serves this purpose and is based on some definition of what is needed to meet basic necessities. Although this has some superficial appeal, the 'cut-off' remains arbitrary and one could argue, with some persuasion, that welfare increases gradually and continuously as consumption rises above the poverty line and falls gradually and continuously as consumption falls below it. The other, more likely reason is that politically it is much more appealing to talk about alleviating poverty rather than reducing inequality in a more general sense, even if the latter is a better guide to social welfare.

Whatever the reason, there is almost universal agreement that a focus on poverty is justified, even if, at times, the measures used are not particularly those of poverty but more general indicators of inequality or deprivation. Given this focus, we are interested in the linkages between poverty and natural capital. In this section I explore these linkages, drawing in particular on work by Ekbom and Bojo (1999), Duraippah (1996) and Markandya (2000). In doing so it is helpful to set out a number of propositions that are commonly made about these linkages and to evaluate them.

An increase in poverty results in an increase in degradation

It is popular among policy-makers in the development field to claim that poverty leads to environmental degradation. There are a few studies that have documented a temporal association between increased poverty and increased environmental damage. De Janvry and Garcia (1988) have looked at a wide variety of experiences in Latin America. They state:

> Even if the masses of rural poor are not the major agents of environmental degradation, important environmental problems in many regions of Latin America are associated with their activities …

Other authors note a similar association (Southgate 1988, and Mink 1993). A key issue of interest is, of course, the causality. Is it increasing poverty, caused by any one of a number of factors, that results in the degradation, or is it degradation, following natural disasters or policy-induced changes, that results in increased poverty? But even before one can address that there is a more basic question of fact. What correlation is there between changes in poverty and changes in the ambient environment? The literature does not pose the question in quite that way. In fact I could not find a single development-related study that had documented an increase in poverty and correlated it with a change in the ambient environment.[5] Given the central role such a hypothesis should have in this area, this is a surprising omission. Hence it cannot be said with any certainty that increases in poverty are correlated with increases in degradation, let alone that they are the cause of the degradation.

An environment inhabited by the poor will be more degraded than one inhabited by the rich

This thesis implies that, in a cross-section of communities, the level of the ambient environment will be superior in a richer community than in a poorer community. Or, to be more precise, a poverty-affected community will have a more degraded environment than one that is not so affected. Some cross-section studies addressing this issue exist. Jaganathan (1989) looked at rates of deforestation and the level of poverty in West Java and land use and poverty in Nigeria. He found little evidence that poverty was a driving force in the deforestation or in the damaging changes in land use. This study, however, looked (vaguely) at the levels of poverty against changes in the environment (rates of deforestation). More recently, Deninger and Miniten (1999) have studied the relationship between forest cover and poverty in the Chiapas and Oaxaca regions of Mexico. They find, using probit regressions, that the higher the level of poverty in any region, the lower the probability of a plot of land being under forest cover. The results are well determined but do not of course, establish causality. Nor do they establish that an increase in poverty will result in increased loss of forest cover.

At the farm level, two interesting papers that have addressed this question are Aheeyar (1998) and Linde-Rahr (1998). Aheeyar has looked at investment in soil conservation in Mahaweli region of Sri Lanka. Investment and annual expenditures on soil conservation were analysed for different income groups, both in cash terms as well as in terms of the imputed value of labour time. As expected, the lower income households spent less cash, but they made up for this to a large extent by higher levels of 'in-kind' expenditure on soil conservation, with the result that the aggregate level of annual expenditure on soil conservation did not show any significant relationship with the level of income. Nevertheless, the lack of cash expenditures was seen as a constraint on effective soil conservation, and an analysis of soil erosion and annual income did reveal a negative relationship between the two (again, however, without an implication of causality).

The study by Linde-Rahr looked that the farm-level determinants of reforestation in Vietnam. The factors which determine whether farmers plant trees as part of their land management activity has been looked at in a number of previous papers (Dewees 1993, and Patel *et al.* 1995). However, the direct link to incomes and poverty has not been clearly established in them. Linde-Rahr's paper is particularly interesting in that it analyses the effects of income and gender on tree planting. He finds tree planting increases with the female number of household members and decreases with female income, but decreases with the male number of household members and increases with male income. The overall implications for poverty and tree planting are not evident, but the paper is suggestive of a rather complex relationship in which gender composition will be of some importance.

The above examples are all from rural areas. For the urban environment we may think we know the answer. The slums and poor neighbourhoods are surely the most environmentally degraded parts of the towns and cities. But even here, systematic studies are not obvious in their results. The recent work by Brooks and Sethi (B&S) (1997) and other US studies (Tietenberg 1996) have looked at community exposure to pollution or polluting activities and correlated them with the levels of poverty (among other variables). B&S find that race and poverty are both important determinants of exposure. Poverty, however, had a 'quadratic effect', so that at very low levels of poverty the exposure was lower than average, but at levels above a threshold it was positive.[6] Both Tietenberg and B&S note the significance of race, so that exposure goes up as the percentage of black people in the community increased, with no threshold effects.

No such studies are available for the developing world. Were they to be undertaken, it would be interesting to know both what is the situation with respect to the urban environment as well as to the rural. Are the poorest communities the ones where the environment has been most degraded? They often have the more fragile land, but that does not mean that it is more damaged than land held by less poor people. As with much of the literature in this area, there are lots of theories but very serious empirical data.

Important social changes have resulted in concurrent increases in poverty and environmental degradation in a number of developing countries

Social and economic changes that impinge on the poverty-environment link are divided into those that are directly policy-related (such as agricultural prices, tariffs, land tenure arrangements, etc.) and those that are related to phenomena that are less directly a function of policy – population changes, changes in institutional arrangements, etc. Lopez (1992) refers to the two as 'external' factors and 'internal' factors respectively. Although the distinction is not completely clear-cut, it is useful to divide these factors in this way.

External factors

A popular line of reasoning among researchers begins by noting that a number of undesirable agriculture-related policies have been introduced in the recent past, especially in developing countries. The consequence of these has been to increase, through a variety of channels, the degradation that is caused by poor rural communities. Lopez (1992) blames the promotion of large-scale agriculture, export-oriented forestry and major public infrastructure as the main factors. Such policies result in a permanent change in the circumstances of the poor, making it more difficult for them to retain adequate land on a secure basis. Moreover, even if the policy is subsequently reversed, or the project or programme arrested, the damage to the poor cannot be undone – there is a prevalence of hysterisis in environmental destruction. The mechanism is mainly a displacement of people to make way for the new projects or for expanded, more efficient, agriculture. The displaced often migrate to new areas, which are not suited to sustainable agriculture and, even to the extent that they could be used sustainably, the limited land rights do not encourage the migrants to use them in that way. Whether the poor are made poorer by this process remains unclear. But they certainly become more environmentally damaging in what they do.

Similar reasons are given by other scholars. De Janvry and Garcia (1988), in a review of rural poverty and environmental degradation in Latin America, were among the first to analyze issues clearly. The proximate causes of environmental degradation by the poor are:

- soil erosion by small-holders as a rational strategy of survival;
- 'semi-proletarianization' of the rural population and a collapse of local institutions;
- deforestation as a result of migrants seeking land.

When asked why these developments have occurred, a number of answers are offered. Foremost among these is the claim that, in Central and South America at least, the governments pursued economic policies and strategies which are unfavourable to agriculture. The main factor was the high level of taxation ('disprotection') of the sector. This lowered the return to land, making investment in soil conservation less attractive. At the same time, subsidies to inputs such as fertilizer and pesticides, which increased the attractiveness of agriculture, rarely reached small producers. Credit subsidies, for example, which were tied to mechanization and livestock, did not help the poor. Furthermore, subsidies to mechanization reduced employment possibilities in the sector. As a result, the agricultural sector has not fulfilled the employment creation potential of the sector.

Second has been the failure of institutions to respond to the changing demographic and technological changes. Land tenure has remained concentrated and the demise of the rental market has been damaging to small farmers. Security of tenure remains a major issue for many of the poor, making investment in conservation an unattractive option. The situation has been exacerbated by what the authors call an 'anti-peasant bias' in rural institutions. Subsidized institutional credit and new technological options are not easily accessible to small-holders.

Local institutions have broken down because of the process of 'modernization and the competitive pressures it entails'. It is unclear what this means, but the examples offered show that allocating time to the maintenance of common resources in rural communities is falling. This is partly because of the poor return to conservation in the changing circumstances, and partly because new institutions are needed to ensure that the benefits of any common action can indeed be captured by the community (on this see the discussion on institutional change, below).

More recently Heath and Binswanger (1996) have gone over the same ground and come up with similar conclusions. Looking in detail at Colombia, but drawing on wider experience in rural development, they focus on the presence of too many farmers working fragile land as the cause of both increased poverty and increased degradation. When asked why this is happening now, the reasons are similar to the above – the fact that modern agriculture absorbs too little labour, the subsidies for capital inputs discriminate against small farmers and the reduced scope for tenancy farming and sharecropping. The whole structure is exacerbated by the increase in the number of farmers, as the rural population increases.

The paper referred to above draws on the experience in South America. For Central America, similar considerations are believed to be valid.[7] Lopez and Scoseria (1996) discuss the poverty-environment linkages in Belize, where population growth and migration from other Central American countries have increased pressure on the forest resources. Although such use of land is not the largest cause of deforestation, it accounts for about one third of the loss of forest. Why is the level as high as it is? Partly it is the need for land to accommodate more farmers, and partly the fact that methods of cultivation are land-intensive. Prices of crops such as corn and beans are more attractive than those of vegetables, which are more labour-intensive. If price incentives were different, land needs could be less and the damage associated with this sector correspondingly smaller. Given the limited resources of small farmers, they need strong incentives if they are to practise sustainable agriculture.[8] The lack of secure rights to the land provides exactly the opposite; it encourages mining of the land and moving to new areas when the present plots are exhausted. In this context, however, the process of land privatization has not benefited such farmers. It has a requirement that land be leased before purchase and the formula has resulted in higher prices per hectare for small plots than for large plots. Most have not been able to afford the acquisition of land through this scheme.

Internal factors

Population growth. Undoubtedly the most controversial of the internal factors is that of population growth. Many commentators point to the effects of increases in overall population in terms of pressure on land and increases in environmental degradation. (De Janvry and Garcia 1988, Cleaver and Schreiber 1994, Lopez 1992, and Lopez and Scoseria 1996 all identify an increase in the population as a contributing factor in many situations.) The literature does not, however, agree on the role of population. Opposing the views of the above authors, is the Boserup hypothesis (Boserup 1965), which states that, as land becomes more scarce relative to labour, agriculture is intensified and productivity per unit area goes up. Rather than deteriorating, the land resource base improves in the process. Studies in Africa, such as Pingali *et al.* (1987) (Africa-wide) and Tiffen *et al.* (1994) (Kenya, Machakos District) are cited as evidence that population growth can result in improved productivity.

The issue is complicated because the studies on the Boserup hypothesis do not isolate the effects of population growth from other factors that have given rise to the success stories. In the Machakos district, for example, Tiffen *et al.* show how a situation in the 1930s, of low population and a colonial policy of restricting most of the land to white settlers, was transformed into one where yields have increased tenfold, erosion has been arrested and the population has increased by a factor of six. The problem is to know how much of this was due to: (a) the opening of land for all users, (b) investment in infrastructure, (c) access to non-farm employment opportunities, (d) technological developments that were brought in from outside the region (especially for maize), and (e) price incentives for products that were relatively environmentally benign. In other words, if the population growth had been half of what it is, would the changes in land use have been more or less environmentally beneficial?

Heath and Binswanger (1996) contrast the case of Kenya with that of Ethiopia, where areas with an increase in population density beyond 'carrying capacity' are also areas of the greatest degradation. They point out that how successfully the population growth is accommodated depends on the policy framework. In other words, with the right policies, a substantial increase in population need not result in environmental degradation.

Clearly the issue of population on the environment is more complex than some analysts might suggest. In many countries, especially in Africa and Asia, rural population growth is a major contributor to environmental pressure on the land and to environmental degradation. After allowing for migration to urban areas, the population in these regions is increasing, and the Boserup effect is not evident. Not all such regions have faced an environmental deterioration, however. The examples of Machakos and others indicate that, with the right strategies, the larger population can be accommodated. But even in these areas, a lower rate of population growth might have made for a better quality of life and less environmental pressure.

The evidence on the effects of population on the environment is further complicated by the fact that, as urban opportunities improve, some areas of land are becoming 'depopulated'. Young men in particular are migrating to the cities, leaving behind weakened families and less allocation of labour to collective soil conservation activities. This has been a particular problem in the Andes and in Mexico (Collins 1987). A recent NAFTA-related study on the effects of a decline in the price of corn has suggested that even more migration from rural areas will result with increased environmental pressure (Nadal 1999). To some extent a similar phenomenon occurred in Europe in the post-war years, when land and buildings were simply abandoned as the occupants migrated to the towns and cities. But much of this patrimony is being revived through re-migration and as tourism and other uses of land are developed.

Where rural population growth is a matter of concern, what kind of policies can one introduce to reduce the population pressure? There is considerable evidence to suggest that education (particularly of women), the level of agricultural employment and level of nutrition and the extent of civil liberty all act to reduce the levels of total fertility (Sen 1994, and Dasgupta 1995). Policies, therefore, that act to improve these factors can be expected to reduce total fertility and, thereby, pressure on the natural resource base. Some of these will also help reduce poverty. In addition, general economic growth has been negatively associated with population growth and it has been argued that the former will act to reduce population pressures over time. The problem with this argument, however, is that while *average* population growth rates may decline with *per capita* GDP, sections of the community that depend on natural resources may find themselves locked into a cycle of poverty in which high fertility rates are maintained and that, in turn, exacerbate the pressure on the natural environment.

Dasgupta (1995, 1996) has argued that this cycle could work in the following way. As common resource management systems break down, so individuals are more able and willing to make decisions on family size that do not take full account of the social costs of child rearing, with the use of common resources treated as a free good. Over time, the natural resource base is increasingly depleted and the family unit requires more members to achieve the same level of welfare. Thus a cycle of increasing degradation is established. The theory has plausibility but needs to be tested with real data. Such studies still need to be carried out, both to test the validity of the theory and to see how it needs to be elaborated and developed further.[9]

The dynamics of institutional change. It was noted earlier that, at the heart of the environment–poverty relationship, is the question of what management systems operate for natural resources and how they evolve over time. This issue has been studied in depth by Lopez (1997), Narain (1998) and others. On the evolution of institutions, there are plausible theoretical and empirical studies which show that, contrary to some commonly held views, there is frequently an inverse relationship between rural communities' ability to cooperate in the management of common resources and the state of those resources. In other words an internal 'self-correcting' mechanism can exist, which implies that institutions evolve so as to respond to a deteriorating rural environment by increasing the level of cooperation over common resources. In a recent paper, Narain (1998) cites some evidence for this for common forest resources in the state of Gujarat in India. The key questions are: (a) under what conditions is this mechanism likely to operate, and (b) what can governments do to facilitate this process of cooperation?

In a wide-ranging review Lopez identifies a number of factors that are critical for the appropriate institutional response to increasing environmental pressure. He begins by noting that neither privatization nor elaborate traditional community regulations are sufficient to guarantee that the institutional changes will be sufficient to protect the natural resource base. Privatization can be a negative factor if it leads to a 'race for property rights', if it results in the creation of a landless sub-group, and if the rights to previously communal land cannot be maintained when the land is left fallow. It can be a positive factor if it is carried out in a way that avoids these factors.[10]

What other policies can one adopt to encourage the effective evolution of the institutions, and to slow down the social and environmental change that is damaging the natural resource base? Various proposals have been made. One is through ensuring and promoting homogeneity in the affected groups and, more generally, reducing the costs of cooperation at the community level. Actions here include support through extension services, training, poverty alleviation, etc. Education is also seen as an important influence, as is gender equality.[11] These will result in a 'new order' but one that is more sensitive to the environmental constraints and the imperative of cooperation in the management of natural resources. Another is information and public education in general. A third is legal and other government support for new and reformed property management systems. All these responses are of great importance in setting the right policy framework. Unfortunately the state of knowledge about the dynamics of institutional change, on which to base them, remains weak.

There are examples where the evolution has taken place successfully in the face of increasing pressure on the resource base. One study from Nigeria (Mortimore 1989) shows how small farmers adopted sustainable management strategies on new land even when the short-term costs of doing so were high. Another is the Kenya study referred to above (Tiffen *et al.* 1994). It was partly the effective transformation of institutions that was responsible for the success of that case. Other examples of 'success' in institutional evolution have come from India. Taking data from Western India, Chopra and Gulati (1996) have shown that property rights have evolved in such a way so as to reduce out-migration and improve the management of common resources. Similarly, Chopra and Kadekodi (1988) show how the transference of property rights from the state to village communities and from individual to 'pooled community management' has generated benefits in terms of the management of the resource base in selected Indian cases.

These are interesting and important papers, but more work needs to be done to understand the dynamics of institutional change for agricultural communities in developing countries. There is no doubt that, with the onset of major social and political changes in the post-war period, many of the systems of traditional management have broken down. If this is to be reversed, a better understanding of the dynamics and the role of environmental policy is essential.

A deterioration of the ambient environment hurts the poor more than the rich (and conversely)

The general presumption among policy-makers is that a declining natural environment hurts the poorest sections of society. By and large this is found to be so. The vulnerable are often the users of marginal resources and also the most dependent on the common resources of the community in which they live (Dasgupta 1996). Hence it is these groups that are most impacted when the deforestation, soil erosion and other negative impacts on the environment occur, often as a result of natural disasters. This common view is largely correct, but *detailed quantitative empirical evidence* on how the poor are affected relative to the non-poor, and which groups are especially vulnerable is not easy to find. There are some exceptions. Firewood scarcity has been shown to impose a greater cost on the poor than on the better off (e.g. the time spent collecting firewood has a high value relative to other components of the household's income) (Kumar and Hotchkiss 1988). Research by Kadekodi (1995) has shown that, when water shortages occur as a result of misuse of natural events, it is the poor who are the most affected. However, one cannot conclude that environmental degradation always hurts the poor more than the better off. For urban pollution problems, for example, such as outdoor air quality, the poor are more likely to live closer to highly polluted areas, but the value they place on cleaner air is less than that of the rich. Hence a general deterioration in air quality may hurt more poor people, but each has a lower value of the benefit, implying that the change in their position vis-à-vis the better off is ambiguous. This is examined further in the next section.

Policies that change the environment can hurt the poor more than the rich (or vice versa)

When measures are taken to improve a degraded environment, how are the poor affected? It depends, of course, on what the measures are. Environmental regulations that increase the costs of producing certain goods can result in increased unemployment and higher prices for the goods. How they impact on the poor will depend on what the goods are, what share they have in the budget of the poor, and who suffers the unemployment.

One of the more sophisticated attempts to see how changes in the quality of the environment have actually affected the poor versus the rich is the paper by Brooks and Sethi (1997). Using the same data referred to in 'Sustainable development and natural capital', they also look at how the changes in toxic release inventory between the date of the release of the first data set and the second (1990 and 1992 respectively) were distributed across US zip codes. Using a logit equation in which a value of one implied an increase in the level and a zero implied a decrease or no change, they found that jurisdiction poverty was negatively related to increases in toxic releases. The same applied to the presence of collective action and the level of voter turnout. On the other hand, a one per cent increase in the percentage of blacks increased the probability of a worsened release situation by 0.002. The negative sign on poverty is 'explained' in terms of lower levels of activity in poor areas. It does suggest, however, that the poor are not always worse off as the environment changes over time. Unfortunately no such data are available for developing countries.

There are a few recent studies on the distributional impacts of environmental regulations in developing countries. Eskeland and Devarajan (1996) looked at the distribution of environmental costs for the transport sector in Indonesia and Mexico. They conclude from the data that, as expenditure on private and public transport increases as a percentage of income across quintiles, measures to reduce emissions from transport (particularly private transport) will have a progressive impact.

This has been followed by a more detailed analysis of two regions of Indonesia (Jakarta and the 'Rest of Java') by Eskeland and Kong (1998). The authors develop a measure of the 'distributional characteristics' of a policy. This is an income-weighted measure of the increase in costs for different income groups resulting from measures that increase pollution control costs, or a similar measure of the increase in benefits resulting from the improved environment that results from the same measures. Environmental regulations in the areas of energy production and use, and transport are analysed in some detail. On the distributional effects of control costs the paper shows that transport policies are more 'distribution friendly' than energy policies, mainly because transport environmental controls affect the rich relatively more than do energy environmental controls. Within transport, controls on private transport have a relatively smaller impact on the lower income groups than do controls on public transport. Within energy, gas and electricity controls have the smallest impacts on the poor, and firewood, kerosene and coal have the biggest. All these differences become much smaller, however, when the indirect effects of the control measures are taken into account – i.e. when the impacts of the measures on the production costs of other commodities are allowed for.

On the benefits side the analysis is complicated by the fact that one does not know with any accuracy how the willingness to pay for the improvements changes with income. Eskeland and Kong take a range of values for the 'income elasticity of willingness to pay for environmental improvements' they estimate are the distributional effects of the benefits.[12] These are roughly the same for the energy and transport regulations. With an income elasticity of demand for the benefits of one (a commonly assumed value), the resulting net distributional effects (taking both costs and benefits) are approximately neutral for energy and positive for transport. The lower the income elasticity of demand for the benefits, the greater are the distributional impacts of the benefits, and the greater the net benefits from both strategies.

Another study for Indonesia that has looked at the income impacts of environmental policies in a computable general equilibrium framework is that of Resosudarmo and Thorbecke (1996). They analyze the 'Blue Sky Program' (BSP) that includes a number of measures to improve air quality – such as reductions in leaded gasoline, recovery of vapour emissions, higher emissions standards for vehicles, etc. Using a Social Accounting Matrix, to which pollution and health impacts sectors have been added, they show that the distributional outcome depends on what is assumed about reductions in output in the controlled sectors. With no change in output, there are negligible losses of incomes. With a fall in output, however, in the transportation sector, some low-income households could be worse off to the extent of three to four per cent. The model has a number of limitations, but the results are useful in picking out certain occupational groups and tracing through the effects of different polices on them. Such a sophisticated analysis is needed if we are to say something about the output effects of these policies elsewhere.

These results are not inconsistent with those from industrialized OECD countries, although there are some differences. The OECD experience is well-covered in recent publications (OECD 1994, and Tietenberg 1996). Studies on air pollution distinguish between mobile and stationary sources. Control costs for mobile source pollution through vehicles tend to be regressively distributed (Harrison 1975, 1977) in the USA. The difference between the USA and Indonesia and Mexico can be explained by the fact that rural car ownership is much lower in the latter two countries.[13] For stationary sources the distribution of costs is more complex to model because the incidence structure is more involved, but in essence the US studies show costs to be regressive (Gianessi *et al.* 1979). The research issue here is the adoption of more sophisticated models to study the incidence effects of such measures, especially when they are adopted across a wide range of industries and result in a number of relative price changes. For water pollution Gianessi *et al.* (1979) also found costs to be regressively distributed, in spite of the fact that part of the costs were borne by general subsidies, which come from the local/regional tax system and which are therefore (probably) mildly progressive.

On the benefits side crude estimates suggest that mobile air pollution benefits are progressive for those living in urban areas. The same does not apply, however, in suburban areas or in rural communities. Tietenberg 1996 cites some work by Asch and Seneca, who examined socio-economic data from stationary sources in three US cities and concluded that the benefits were greatest (in terms of reductions in air pollution) in the poorest areas of those cities. In the case of water regulation, however, benefits more clearly favour the better off more than the poor, although the number of studies is very few. Harrington (1981) found the benefits of the Water Pollution Control Act 1972 in the USA to be concentrated among middle income groups relative to the poor.

Market-based instruments such as taxes and permits have also been assessed for their distributional effects. Many of the studies look at instruments that have not actually been implemented; they are based on simulation results rather than historic empirical data and need to be viewed in that light. Smith, 1995, has looked at the distributional effects of 'Green Taxes' in Britain and Germany and analysed the impacts of a carbon tax across income groups. As expected the tax would be mildly regressive, more so in Britain than Germany. Taxes on petrol on the other hand are mildly progressive.

Comparisons between the distributional effects of taxes and of command and control instruments are not generally available for developing countries. Some work by the OECD (OECD 1994), has looked at trading programs for emissions and compared them (implicitly) to those of direct controls. Tradable permit schemes are generally more efficient in achieving environmental goals than command and control schemes and hence entail a smaller increase in prices. Since such price increases were found to be regressive in their impact, the smaller they are the less the regressive impact. Furthermore, most actual schemes do not involve selling the initial allocation of permits to existing polluters but providing them free of charge. This in turn can reduce the burden on industry, compared to a tax, which is not rebated. Thus the simulation analysis carried out on US schemes have shown a net benefit to low income households in using marketable permits compared to conventional command and control instruments. It should be noted, however, that the focus of studies of marketable permit schemes is not the distributive impacts on households, but rather the regional and industrial distributive effects.

A significant problem in environmental regulation in developing countries arises from difficulties in controlling small scale enterprises (SSEs), because of their limited financial and human resources, and low level of technology. Regulators frequently shy away from such regulations, from fear of the effects these may have on employment and incomes of poor households. Studies of the distributional effects of the regulation of SSEs, however, are very few. One recent attempt is Lanjouw (1997), who has analyzed this sector in Ecuador. Overall, employment in the pollution-intensive SSEs is not concentrated among the poor, but among the urban, literate population. Hence to the extent that environmental regulations in the sector impact on employment, they do not impact on the poorest. Furthermore, estimates of the impacts of large-scale losses of employment in this sector on poverty are not large. Overall he concludes that arguments against regulating the SSEs on the grounds of increased poverty are exaggerated.

Finally there are distributive effects in developing countries arising from the regulations in developed countries. These occur through changes in the direction and composition of trade. Although there are some studies that look at the effects of environmental regulations on trade, there is little work on how these changes in trade patterns impact on the distribution of income in the developing countries. The study by Verbruggen *et al.* 1995, shows, for example, how environmental export regulations in the EU have impacted on the exports of cut flowers from Kenya, and hence had a detrimental effect on the incomes of poor Kenyan farmers. A set of case studies on trade and the environment (Jha *et al.* 1999) also conclude that stricter environmental regulations in developed countries are having a bigger impact on the small and middle sized enterprises in developing countries, with a *prima facie* case that perhaps the less well-off are more impacted than the rich. But this has not been systematically studied from the income distribution point of view.

Economic development should help reduce poverty and improve the environment

There is a strand of literature (Grossman and Krueger 1991, World Bank 1992, and Barbier 1997), which suggests that the relationship between GDP and the quality of the environment is 'U-shaped', i.e. the quality of the environment deteriorates initially as GDP *per capita* increases, and then improves after a certain critical value of *per capita* GDP has been reached. This critical value varies with the pollutant, and indeed for some pollutants such as VOCs there is no 'turning point'. In fact the evidence for such a relationship is mixed with some studies even showing an inverted 'U' curve (Stern *et al.* 1996).

This model (also referred to as the 'Environmental Kuznets Curve') can be looked at in conjunction with the original Kuznets curve, which postulated a deterioration in income distribution in the early stages of economic growth, followed by an improvement later (Kuznets 1995). Taking the two together one would conclude that a declining environmental quality and increasing income inequality go hand in hand as part of the 'development process'. In the end things should work out fine, with improvements in both these indicators of human welfare.

Unfortunately, such a sanguine view is inappropriate and misleading from a policy viewpoint. First, some of the environmental degradation being observed, and sometimes being caused by extreme poverty, is irreversible and will never be recovered. Second, what is a long-term time series relationship is being inferred from cross-section inter-country data. There is no reason why a particular country should follow the path characterized by a cross-section of countries. Indeed the aim should be to follow a policy based on a comparison of domestic costs and benefits of different options, taking account of their impacts on all aspects of welfare, including poverty/inequality, environmental quality, GDP and other indicators such as those used by the UNDP in its Human Development Reports. Although the Kuznets curve is a useful empirical regularity, its existence is of little relevance in determining such a set of policies.

Poverty and sustainable development: some conclusions

Thus far the discussion has been on poverty and its linkages with sustainable development, especially through the maintenance of natural capital. We have noted first that indicators of sustainable development have to take account of all types of assets, including natural, human and social capital as well as physical capital. It is the sum total of these different forms that has to be non-decreasing if development is to be judged as sustainable. Second, we observe that societies that maintain, or increase, the level of output as measured by GDP are also societies that reduce the levels of poverty. From these two observations it is not unreasonable to conclude that development will be consistent with the long-term elimination of poverty if it is carried out in a way that ensures an adequate intergenerational transfer of all forms of capital, including natural capital. The latter is particularly important in areas where it is uneasily substituted for by other forms, such as human or physical capital.

More specifically, we have noted that there are linkages between what happens to the stock of natural capital and poverty. These are not simple, and some of the more commonly held views are not proven. In particular, the poor are not necessarily more damaging to their environment than the better off. Nor is there any support for the view that an increase in poverty always causes an increase in environmental degradation.

There is, however, support for the proposition that when changes in institutions take place, which break down common management systems for natural resources, these can result in increased poverty and increased degradation of the environment. Much depends on how society copes with the changes and how capable it is in adapting its institutions to such changes. There are 'success stories' as well as cases of failure. We need to understand this process of adaptation more thoroughly, and in this I believe there are some common grounds with the strategy for development that Stiglitz proposes.

There is also a lot of casual evidence to indicate that when there is a loss of natural capital, perhaps as a result of natural disasters, the poor suffer disproportionately more than the rich. Hence policies that prevent such losses, particularly in relation to firewood, water and soil, will benefit the poor, as long as the costs of such policies do not fall heavily on them. In general we cannot say that preservation of natural capital, or an improvement of the environment is a 'pro-poor' policy. It does depend on how the costs are distributed. Some work has been carried out to identify the kinds of measures that are pro-poor and those that are not, but more can and should be done in this regard.

Poverty, sustainability and Stiglitz's strategy for development

Let us now turn to the vision for development that Stiglitz articulated in his Prebisch lecture. From a wide ranging review of development strategies over the last 50 years, he derives a number of recommendations. Perhaps the most important idea is that we need to pay more attention to culture and institutional development, with a focus on the individual, the family and the community, in addition, of course, to the public and private sectors of the economy. As technological and economic changes unfold, they have impacts on the different stakeholders. It is imperative that these groups have a say in the way in which society responds to these changes; ownership and participation, inclusion and consensus, and social capital are the key words. This is a departure from the more conventional economic views of development, which have focused on the roles of the public and private sector and efficiency in the allocation of resources, and have had little to say on these topics.

Of course it would be wrong to assume that Stiglitz ignores these more conventional issues in development. He makes a number of key recommendations here too, in some cases, departing from the pure neoclassical orthodoxy. Briefly these are:

- The creation of a strong, competitive, stable and efficient private sector through a sound legal and regulatory environment.
- A stable macroeconomic framework that 'reduces the country's vulnerability to the inevitable shocks that are associated with global engagement'. In this regard he notes the possibly destructive impacts of short term international capital flows.
- Public provision of health, infrastructure and education services, and/or the creation of an enabling environment so that the private sector can provide some of these services.
- Openness to trade and a liberalization of international trade in goods and services with, at the same time, increased opening of developed country markets to developing country exports and a more generous approach to sharing intellectual property rights on the part of the developed countries.

Finally, he includes a brief statement to the effect that global environmental goods, such as greenhouse gases, which are in danger of being over-produced or over-used, need to be addressed collectively.

While Stiglitz does not have much to say about sustainable development and poverty, his vision does have some implications for sustainability. Principally, he sees these measures as leading to a social transformation that will be 'sustainable, strengthening the environment' and 'durable, withstanding the vicissitudes sometimes accompanying democratic processes'. On poverty he is more specific. He believes that his measures will reduce poverty and, hopefully, eliminate it at least in terms of the absolute standard.

I would not question the general thrust of that claim, but the paper does not say how these goals will be achieved. Let me offer some suggestions as to: (a) how his recommendations lead to these goals, and (b) what complementary measures need be introduced that will make the claim more likely to be realized.

The direct implications of Stiglitz's recommendations for sustainablility and poverty

Directly, the strategy he proposes is necessary if sustained growth is to be achieved. From historical experience this will contribute to the alleviation of poverty more than any other single measure. At the same time, the policies of openness, consensus and transparency should ensure that particular policies and programmes are not implemented if they have serious adverse implications for particular groups in society.

The focus on institutions is also important for the poverty/environment linkages discussed in the previous section. As we noted there, a key dimension of the response of communities to social, economic and environmental pressures is the institutional dynamic. Where this works well, the effects are positive, or at least not as damaging as they might be. Where it does not work well, the effects can be disastrous. While we do not know all the secrets of what makes for good institutional dynamics, we can say with some confidence that relations of trust, participation of all stakeholders in decision-making and a sense of ownership by all in the wider social fabric are critical.

On the environmental issues specifically, Stiglitz has only a brief paragraph, to the effect that the global community needs to address the issue of global environmental resources. No one would argue against this but it hardly offers any advice as to how this is to be done. Since there is a huge body of literature on this important subject, one can admonish the author for giving it such short shrift.

Additional measures needed if Stiglitz's vision for development is to be consistent with sustainable development

The vision for development that Stiglitz provides is just that – a vision. It does not contain detailed operational guidance on how to achieve the goals he seeks. While the full exercise of working out the operational significance of his strategy is beyond the scope of this chapter, issues relating to poverty and natural resource management are discussed further below. The principle actions that need to be taken are the following.

Tracking progress toward sustainable development.

It is imperative for policy-makers to know how consistent their actions are with the goals of sustainable development. This can only be achieved by having indicators that are regularly reported and widely disseminated. As far as natural capital is concerned, some of the wealth measures discussed in 'Sustainable development and natural capital' are useful and should be constructed, using consistent methods of valuing all assets including natural resource stock changes. Work is still in progress on this and more effort is needed if we are to have measures that can be used with the same level of confidence as, say, GDP.

But a real wealth measure is not enough. Tracking sustainable development needs physical measures for ecosystem health and warning indicators when that health is under threat. Much work has been done on such pressure indicators (Adriaansee 1993, and Markandya and Dale 2001) and we have a good idea of what information countries need. But what has not yet been done is to develop those indicators that both track the state of ecosystems and at the same time take account of the impacts of these changes on vulnerable individuals and communities. Some changes to the state of natural capital are more threatening in this respect than others. It would be useful to have an indication of the extent to which this is so.

Guidelines for evaluating policies and programmes with respect to natural capital and poverty.

Many important decisions regarding economic development are taken without paying enough attention to their implications for indicators of poverty or the state of the natural environment. Although this is changing, the capacity of developing countries to undertake such assessment is limited. Furthermore, integrated systems of assessment that look at both environment and poverty issues are very rare. It is true that development agencies have devoted considerable resources to ensuring major environmentally sensitive investment programmes are scrutinized over their environmental impacts and (increasingly) their social impacts. But it is not only such programmes that have implications for poverty and natural capital, so do policies in the areas of trade liberalization, structural adjustment and privatization; perhaps even more so. We need to develop tools of analysis that are simple and robust and that track such policies in terms of their impacts on indicators of sustainability and poverty. Furthermore such analysis should feed back into the design of the policies. We are a long way from achieving these goals.

In the design of policy the tendency has been to look for 'win-win' solutions. This is natural – policy-makers want to please all parties and avoid having to make hard choices. But we cannot hope to cover all relevant options in this way. There are simply too many situations where there are trade-offs. For example a conservation programme may improve the stock of environmental capital but at a cost in terms of increased hardship to some; or a trade liberalization or privatization measure may promote economic growth but at a cost in terms of some environmental damage and/or increased unemployment. The traditional methods of analysis of such trade-offs have been social benefit–cost and multi-criteria analysis. They should continue to be used but they need to be strengthened, especially in the way that poverty and natural resource impacts are assessed, both in terms of changes in their present and future levels. As this work evolves, we should get some broad guidance of how environmental policies can be made 'pro-poor', how what poverty reduction strategies can be made 'pro-environment' and how macroeconomic policies can be made more sensitive to both sets of concerns.

International environmental icssues

Sustainable development certainly requires us to address the global environmental challenges of climate change, protection of the stratospheric ozone layer and conservation of biodiversity. It also requires a concerted approach to transboundary environmental problems relating to air pollution, management of international waters and the like. The difficulties in these areas are clear. Countries have to cooperate but they cannot be made to do so. An agreement has to be acceptable to all parties but each party will perceive the costs and benefits differently. Thus far, in spite of the many difficulties I would take an optimistic view of cooperation in this area. Countries have managed to address some issues effectively (e.g. reducing the use of ozone depleting substances through the Montreal Protocol, regional agreements on reducing transboundary air emissions) and are making slow progress on others, such as reductions in greenhouse gases.

The poverty dimension in such deliberations has had a relatively small role but here, too, countries are beginning to evaluate options with respect to their social implications, including several that impinge on poverty. For example, work on the Clean Development Mechanism (which permits reductions in greenhouse gases in a developing country to be credited to a developed country in exchange for support in making the reductions) is developing guidelines for assessing projects, taking account of the broader social and poverty impacts (Markandya 1998). This kind of assessment can and should be extended to other international environmental problems.

Conclusions and recommendations

This chapter has discussed the linkages between poverty and environment and how they are relevant to the broader goals of economic development. From the first part, there are two broad questions: does poverty damage the environment and does environmental degradation hurt the poor? There are many versions of each that have been looked at in the chapter, but, at the cost of some loss of accuracy, the broad answer to the first question is 'no' and the answer to the second is 'yes'. Of course there are complex issues and these simple answers will not always hold but the thrust is in that direction.

The implications for policy then become clearer. Alleviating poverty will not necessarily help reduce environmental pressures, and indeed may increase them. Appropriate measures need to be taken to handle the problems that emerge when such changes take place. On the other hand, protection of the environment will often have a pro-poor benefit, the more so when it relates to green issues than to brown ones. Again this should provide an added impetus for environmental protection in a poverty based strategy.

As far as Stiglitz's vision is concerned we acknowledge that sustained growth will contribute to the alleviation of poverty more than any other single measure. At the same time, the policies of openness, consensus and transparency should ensure that particular policies and programmes are not implemented if they have serious adverse implications for particular groups in society. This focus on institutions is also important for the poverty/environment linkages.

Fleshing out his vision for sustainable development, we identify the following as important:

- Tracking progress toward sustainable development.
- Preparing and operating to guidelines for evaluating policies and programmes with respect to natural capital and poverty.
- Addressing the important international environmental issues.

Each of these areas has a poverty dimension, which we have touched upon. Much needs to be done to understand it more thoroughly and to build on that understanding.

In summary, much of what is needed is to mainstream poverty and environmental issues in day-to-day economic decision-making; to include poverty issues in environmental policy-making and vice-versa. If these measures are taken, and the reforms in economic management that Stiglitz espouses are carried out, I believe we will move substantially in the right direction.

Notes

1 I would like to thank many people who have contributed, some unknowingly, to the ideas expressed here. At the Bank, I have had helpful discussions with Jan Boyo, Gayatri Acharia and Kirk Hamilton. At Bath, Pam Mason and I have written jointly on this topic. Elsewhere, Kirsten Halsnaes and Ronaldo Seroa da Motta have worked with me on sustainable development issues. At a workshop in Ottawa on Poverty and Sustainable Development, an earlier version was presented and there was a lively debate and my discussant, Jim McNeil made some very valuable suggestions as did a number of others. Of course all errors are my own.

2 This is more popularly known as the Brundtland Report, after the Chairman of the Commission.

3 Ideally one should measure growth in consumption rather than income, but over very long periods the two should show similar trends. For a more demanding definition of sustainability in an intergenerational context see Markandya and Mason 2000.

4 I use the terms natural resources and natural capital interchangeably. Both provide a flow of environmental services from assets that are available in some form without any anthropogenic involvement. Of course, their use depends on man as does their productivity.

5 One study that looks at a cross-section of US data and correlates these two variables is Brooks and Sethi (1997). I consider those results in 'An environment inhabited by the poor will be more degraded than one inhabited by the rich' below.

6 Low exposure for very poor communities may be explained in terms of very low levels of economic activity in these areas.

7 Scholarly 'macro' level analysis of the links between policy, poverty and the environment do not appear to be available for other regions of the world.

8 Some economists have argued that the poor pay less attention to the environment because they have higher time preference (or discount) rates. The evidence for this, however, is not strong. Pender and Walker (1991) find generally high time preference rates among farmers, but not systematically higher ones for the poor. Furthermore, it should be noted that a high time preference rate does not necessarily imply a low level of investment in conservation.

9 Dasgupta (1996) cites one study by Cleaver and Schreiber (1994), which produces positive correlations between poverty, fertility and environmental degradation in sub-Saharan Africa, and another by Filmer and Pritchett (1996) for Pakistan with similar results. But much more is needed to validate this view of how these factors are related.

10 In some cases government action has been actually harmful to the effective evolution of the institutions. A case in point is the nationalization of formerly traditionally managed resources, with disastrous consequences (Bromley 1991).

11 In this context the book by Agarwal (1994) makes a strong case for the role of women's empowerment as a factor in arresting natural resource degradation.

12 The elasticities take a range of values from 0.1 to 2. A default value of one is often used and very crude income elasticity of the WTP for health benefits of 0.35 estimate has been suggested by Krupnick *et al.* 1996, based on Mitchell and Carson 1986. But this *seriously* needs to be confirmed.

13 The US regressivity can be reduced by suitable changes in policy design. Harrison suggested, for example, that lower standards be adopted in rural areas than in urban ones. This results in a significant reduction in regressivity because car ownership among poor households is much higher in rural areas than urban ones.

References

Adriaansee, A. (1993) *Environmental Policy Performance Indicators*, The Hague: Sdu Uitgeverij.

Agarwal, B. (1994) *A Field of One's own: Gender and Land Rights in South Asia*, Cambridge: Cambridge University Press.

Aheeyar, M.M. (1998) 'Small Holder Farmers, Poverty and Land Degradation: Evidence from Sri Lanka', Working Paper, HK/Agrarian Research and Training Institute, Colombo.

Barbier, E. (ed.) (1997) 'The Environmental Kuznets Curve', Special Issue, *Environment and Development*, 3.

Boserup, E. (1965) *The Conditions for Agricultural Growth*, London: Allen and Unwin.

Bromley, D. (1991) *Environment and Economy: Property Rights and Public Policy*, Oxford: Blackwell.

Brooks, N. and Sethi, R. (1997) 'The Distribution of Pollution: Community Characteristics and Exposure to Air Toxics', *Journal of Environmental Economics and Management*, 32: 233–50.

Chopra, K. and Gulati, S.C. (1996) 'Environmental Degradation and Population Movements: The Role of Property Rights', *Environmental and Resource Economics*, 9 (4): 383–408.

Chopra, K. and Kadekodi, G. (1988) 'Participatory Institutions: The Context of Common and Private Property resources', *Environmental and Resource Economics*, 1: 353–72.

Cleaver, K.M. and Schreiber, A.G. (1994) *Reversing the Spiral: The Population, Agriculture, and Environment Nexus in Sub-Saharan Africa*, Washington, DC: The World Bank.

Collins, J.L. (1987) 'Labor Scarcity and Ecological Change', in D.P. Little, M.M. Horowitz and A.E Nyerges (eds), *Lands at Risk in the Third World: Local Level Perspectives*, Boulder, CO: Westview Press.

Daly, H.E. (1990) 'Toward some Operational Principles of Sustainable Development', *Ecological Economics*, 2: 1–6.

Dasgupta, P. (1995) 'The Population Problem: Theory and Evidence', *Journal of Economic Literature*, XXXIII: 1879–902.

Dasgupta, P. (1996) *Environmental and Resource Economics in the World of the Poor*, Washington, DC: Resources for the Future.

De Janvry, A. and Garcia, R. (1988) *Rural Poverty and Environmental degradation in Latin America: Causes, Effects and Alternative Solutions*, S 88/1/L.3/Rev.2, Rome: IFAD.

Deninger, K.W. and Miniten, B. (1999) 'Poverty, policies and deforestation: the case of Mexico', *Economic Development and Cultural Change*, 47(2): 313–344.

Dewees, P.A. (1993) 'Trees, Land and Labour', *World Bank Environment Paper*, No. 4, Washington, DC: The World Bank.

Duraippah, A. (1996) 'Poverty and Environmental Degradation: A Literature Review and Analysis', *CREED Working Paper Series*, No. 8, IIED, London.

Ekbom, A. and Bojo, J. (1999) 'Poverty and Environment: Evidence of Links and Integration into Country Assistance Strategy Process', *Discussion Paper, Environment Group, Africa Region*, No. 4, Washington, DC: The World Bank.

Eskeland, G.S. and Devarajan, S. (1996) *Taxing Bads by Taxing Goods: Pollution Controls with Presumptive Charges*, Washington, DC: The World Bank.

Eskeland, G.S. and Kong, C. (1998) 'Protecting the Environment and the Poor: A Public Goods Framework and an Application to Indonesia' *Working Paper, Development Research Group*, Washington, DC: The World Bank.

Filmer, D. and Pritchett, L. (1996) *Environmental Degradation and the Demand for Children*, Research Project on Social and Environmental Consequences of Growth-Oriented Policies, Working Paper No. 2, Washington, DC: The World Bank.

Gianessi, L.P., Peskin, H.M. and Wolff, E. (1979) 'The Distributional Effects of Uniform Air Pollution', *Quarterly Journal of Economics*, 93: 281–301.

Grossman, M. and Krueger, A.B. (1991) 'Environmental Impacts of a North American Free Trade Agreement', *National Bureau of Economic Research, Working Paper* No. 3914, Cambridge, MA: NBER.

Hamilton, K. and Clemens, M. (1999) 'Genuine Saving in Developing Countries', *World Bank Economic Review*, 13 (2): 33–56.

Hamilton, K. (2000) 'Sustaining Economic Welfare: Estimating Changes in Per Capita Wealth', *Policy Research Working Paper* 2498, Washington, DC: The World Bank.

Harrington, W. (1981) 'The Distribution of Recreational Benefits from Improved Water Quality: A Micro-Simulation', *Quality of the Environment Division, Discussion Paper* D-80, Washington, DC: Resources for the Future.

Harrison, D. Jr. (1975) *Who Pays for Clean Air? The Costs and Benefit Distribution of Automobile Emissions Standards*, Cambridge, MA: Ballinger.

Harrison, D. Jr. (1977) 'Controlling Automotive Emissions: How to Save More Than $1 Billion Per Year and Help the Poor Too', *Public Policy*, 25(4): 527–33.

Heath, J. and Binswanger, H. (1996) 'Natural Resource Degradation Effects of Poverty and Population Growth Are Largely Policy-induced: The Case of Colombia', *Environment and Development Economics*, 1(1): 65–84.

Jaganathan, V.N. (1989) 'Poverty, Public Policies and the Environment', *Environment Working Paper* No. 24, Washington, DC: The World Bank.

Jha, V., Markandya, A. and Vossenaar, R. (1999) *Reconciling Trade and the Environment*, Cheltenham: Edward Elgar.

Kadekodi G.K. (1995) *Operationalising Sustainable Development, Ecology-Economy Interactions at a Regional Level*, Amsterdam: Institute for Environmental Studies.

Krupnick, A., Harrison, K., Nickell, E. and Toman, M.A. (1996) 'The Value of Health Benefits from Ambient Air Quality Improvements in Central and Eastern Europe', *Environmental and Resource Economics*, 7(4): 307–32.

Kumar, S.K. and Hotchkiss, D. (1988) *Consequences of Deforestation for Women's Time Allocation, Agricultural Production and Nutrition in the Hills of Nepal, IFPRI Research Report* No. 69, Washington, DC: International Food Policy Research Institute.

Kuznets, S. (1955) 'Economic Growth and Income Inequality', *American Economic Review*, 45(1): 1–28.

Lanjouw, P. (1997) 'Small-Scale Industry, Poverty and the Environment: A Case Study of Ecuador', *Research Project on Social and Environmental Consequences of Growth-Oriented Policies, Policy Research Department Working Paper* No. 18, Harrington, W. (1981) 'The Distribution of Recreational Benefits from Improved Water Quality: A Micro-Simulation', *Quality of the Environment Division, Discussion Paper* D-80, Washington, DC: World Bank.

Linde-Rahr, M. (1998) 'Rural Reforestation: Gender Effects on Private Investments in Vietnam', *Working Paper*, Goteborg: Department of Economics, Goteborg University.

Lopez, R. (1992) 'Environmental Degradation and Economic Openness in LDCs: The Poverty Linkage' *American Journal of Agricultural Economics*, 74: 1138–45.

Lopez, R. (1997) 'Where Development Can or Cannot Go: The Role of Poverty-Environment Linkages', *Proceedings of the Annual Bank Vonference on Development Economics, 1997*, Washington, DC: The World Bank.

Lopez, R. and Scoseria, C. (1996) 'Environmental Sustainability and Poverty in Belize: A Policy Paper', *Environment and Development Economics*, 1(3): 289–308.

Maddison, A. (1995) *Monitoring the World Economy 1820–1992*, Paris: OECD Publications.

Markandya, A. (1998) *The Indirect Costs and Benefits of Greenhouse Gas Limitations*, Handbook Reports, Risø: UNEP, Collaborating Centre on Energy and Environment.

Markandya, A. (2000) 'Poverty, Environment and Development', in A. Rose and L. Gabel (eds.) *Frontiers of Environmental Economics*, Cheltenham: Edward Elgar.

Markandya, A. and Dale, N. (2001) *Measuring Environmental Degradation: Developing Pressure Indicators for Europe*, Cheltenham: Edward Elgar.

Markandya, A. and Mason, P. 'Why Developing Countries Should Worry about 2050 and Beyond', *Journal of International Development*, 12: 601–12.

Mink, S.D. (1993) 'Poverty, Population and the Environment', *Environment Working Paper* No. 189, Washington, DC: The World Bank.

Mitchell, R.C. and Carson, R. T. (1986) *Valuing Drinking Water Risk Reduction Using the Contingent Valuation Method: A Methodological Study of Risks from THM and Girardia*. Report fot the US Environmental Protection Agency, Washington, DC: EPA.

Mortimore, M. (1989) 'The Causes, Nature and Rate of Soil Degradation in the Northern-most States of Nigeria and an Assessment of the Role of Fertilizer in Counteracting the Process of Degradation', *Environment Working Paper* No. 17, Washington, DC: The World Bank.

Nadal, A. (1999). Issue Study 1. *Maize in Mexico: Some Environmental Implications of the North America Free Trade Agreement (NAFTA)*, Montreal: Commission for Environmental Cooperation, 65–182.

Narain, U. (1998) 'Resource degradation, Inequality and Cooperation', *Working Paper*, Berkeley, CA: Department of Agricultural and Resource Economics, University of California.

OECD (1994) *The Distributive Effects of Economic Instruments for Environmental Policy*, Paris: OECD.

Patel, S.H., Pinkney, T. and Jaeger, W. (1995) 'Smallholder Wood Production and Population Pressure in East Africa: Evidence of an Environmental Kuznets Curve', *Land Economics*, 71(4): 516–30.

Pearce, D.W., Barbier, E.W. and Markandya, A. (1990) *Sustainable Development*, London: Earthscan.

Pingali, P., Bigot, H and Binswanger, P. (1987) *Agricultural Mechanization and the Evolution of Farming Systems in Sub-Saharan Africa*, Baltimore, MD: Johns Hopkins Press for the World Bank.

Resosudarmo, B.P and Thorbecke, E. (1996) 'The Impact of Environmental Policies on Household Incomes for Different Socio-economic Classes: The Case of Air Pollutants in Indonesia', *Ecological Economics*, 17: 83–94.

Sen, A. (1994) 'Population: Delusion and Reality', *New York Review of Books*, XLI(15): 62–71.

Smith, S. (1995) *'Green' Taxes and Charges: Policy and Practice in Britain and Germany*, London: The Institute of Fiscal Studies.

Southgate, D. (1988) 'The Economics of Land Degradation in the Third World', *Environment Working Paper* No. 2, Washington, DC; The World Bank.

Stern, D, Common, M. and Barbier, E. (1996) 'Economic Growth and Environmental Degradation: The Environmental Kuznets Curve and Sustainable Development', *World Development*, 24(7): 1151–60.

Stiglitz, J. (1998) 'Towards a New Paradigm for Development: Strategies, Policies and Processes', Prebisch Lecture, Geneva: UNCTAD.

Tietenberg, T. (1996) *Environmental and Natural Resource Economics*, New York: Harper Collins.

Tiffen, M., Mortimore, M. and Gichuki, F. (1994) *More People, Less Erosion, Environmental Recovery in Kenya*, New York: John Wiley and Sons.

Verbruggen, H., Kuik, O. and Benis M. (1995) *Environmental Regulations as Trade Barriers for Developing Countries*, CREED Working Paper No. 2, London: IIED.

World Bank (1992) *World Development Report*, New York: Oxford University Press.

World Bank (1997) 'Expanding the Measure of Wealth: Indicators of Sustainable Development', *ESD Studies and Monograph Series* No. 17, Washington, DC: The World Bank.

World Bank (2000a) *World Development Indicators*, Washington, DC: The World Bank.

World Commission on Environment and Development (1987) *Our Common Future* (The Brundtland Report), Oxford and New York: Oxford University Press.

6 Inequality and environmental policy[1]

E. Somanathan[2]

Introduction

Environmental problems occur as a side-effect of other activities. Economists have emphasized that they are a case of negative externalities. If they are left unchecked this is because the losers are different from those whose activities create the problems. This is not always the case. Sometimes the problem is created by those who suffer from it. An important example is indoor air pollution, which is very widespread in poor countries and occurs as a result of cooking with low-quality stoves or open fires using traditional fuel like wood, charcoal or agricultural wastes. The problem is left unchecked because the victims do not have the resources or technology to deal with it, and perhaps also because they do not understand the extent of the harmful effects on their health.

The traditional economic approach to such a problem is that as long as people understand the problem, it does not exist, since they choose to do nothing about it. The public-health approach to these issues is very different and reflects the belief that people often do not have the knowledge needed to make informed decisions. In this approach, attention is focused on what kind of education is necessary to deal with various health problems.

Inequality and the supply of pollution abatement

I will return to these issues as they occur also in the context of externalities and may, in fact, be magnified in their presence. Consider from now on only those polluting or environmentally degrading activities for which total benefits fall short of total costs in the sense that it would be impossible for the gainers to compensate losers and still be better off.

When the victims of such activities are aware of the cause of degradation, they will act to end it if they have the political power to do so. It follows that pollution will remain unabated when the net losers from the polluting activity have less political power than the net gainers. This implies that resource degradation and pollution will tend to take place in locations where the net losers from polluting activities lack the political power to stop them or abate their effects (Boyce 1994).

Who the net gainers are will depend a great deal on market structure in the polluting industries. If the industries are competitive, then the net gainers will mostly be consumers of the products of those industries. To the extent that the polluting industries generate rents, however, then producers will get a share of the net gains from pollution. They may not then face a significant problem of collective action in lobbying to protect these rents. This is even truer when government officials themselves are collecting the rents. Deforestation owing to logging of tropical hardwoods in Indonesia, Malaysia and the Philippines is an example of this. Leases for logging were given to timber companies with extensive government contacts, resulting in huge deforestation. Politically puny traditional residents of the forests had little or no chance of stopping them.

When is this conjunction of weak victims and powerful beneficiaries likely to be seen? When political power is concentrated and there are rents to be had in the polluting industries. The rents can be used to buy influence over government policy or government policy can be made to create rents. Sometimes it is difficult tell which came first, the chicken or the egg. The concentration of political power channels rents towards those who wield it, making it less likely that pollution will be abated. Authoritarian states tend to concentrate political power. They also have the convenient feature that protests and attempts to organize by anti-pollution activists can be crushed. Oil production and related pollution in Ogoni land in Nigeria is a much-publicized case in point.

What are the countervailing factors which favour abatement? The losers from pollution should also have some political power. This is more likely to be the case if there exists a reasonably large middle class. When the economy is diversified the economic interests of the upper classes are diffused through several industries. A significant section of them may be adversely affected by pollution without seeing sufficient economic gains from its existence to be net beneficiaries. This class can then put up resistance.

The poor, on the other hand, are least likely to be able to influence policy in their favour. They face the difficulties of having the least access to the relevant information, the least contacts with government officials, the least access to the news media, and the least resources to devote time to collective action. Of all these factors, the role of the media deserves further comment. The media is mostly driven by the concerns of its readers and viewers and, sometimes, by advertisers. Since, in poor countries, a significant section of the public is illiterate and cannot afford television, their concerns and problems affecting them attract the least attention in the media. Two consequences follow – they are then all the less likely to be informed about environmental problems concerning them, and, in addition, the state is under less pressure to address such problems. This feature of economic inequality producing political inequality is less pronounced in developed countries but still present simply because affluent people are a more important target for advertisers and, therefore, for the news media.

These considerations suggest that when the poor are the net losers from pollution, it is least likely to be abated. This implies that unabated pollution will be more severe in poor countries. Further arguments which strengthen this conclusion come from the observation that environmental problems are often not recognized as such without considerable research. The toxic effects of various pollutants are often not apparent. Identifying these problems, their health effects, and their causes may be a major research undertaking for which poor countries simply lack the infrastructure.

A related but distinct issue is the availability of impartial expert opinion. Consider the controversy over the building of various river development projects involving dams, the Narmada and Tehri projects in India, and the Three Gorges dam in China. Considerable research was needed to establish the likely environmental consequences of dam-building, with estimates of earthquake risks, siltation rates, and so forth being required. Neither country has much by way of a university system with impartial scientists with the necessary expertise. Instead, the news media in India were full of reports quoting either advocates or opponents of the projects. While some of these 'experts' did have expertise in the relevant disciplines, most were not impartial, since they were either partisans getting government funding to defend the projects or linked to non-government organizations opposed to the projects. The university system is simply not large enough and sufficiently resource-rich to generate the academic discourse necessary for the scientific process of peer review to weed out motivated claims. In these circumstances, it becomes difficult for the public to judge the truth of the matter and make an informed decision to support one side or the other. The result is the occasional panic, as happened during the plague that struck Surat in 1994. In fact, plague is treatable and far less dangerous than many other diseases to which Indians are exposed but which evoke little reaction. More frequently, however, the lack of reliable information on which to base a judgement works in favour of the polluters, since making changes to the status quo of pollution requires some costly collective action, which is not forthcoming on the basis of unreliable information.

Spatial implications of the theory

One implication of the theory of the supply of pollution abatement outlined above is that unabated pollution by the poor is likely to be of short range, affecting mainly the poor, while that by the rich is likely to be of long range and thereby affecting not themselves so much as less powerful people living further away. The principal examples of the former are air pollution from the cooking fires of the poor and degradation of local common property resources such as forests and pastures. Air pollution from cooking fires affects principally those cooking, and to a lesser extent others in the household as well as immediate neighbours. To some extent this reflects externalities within and between households. The gender division of labour and the lower status of women in patriarchal societies mean that while all members of the household benefit from the cooking, women and young children suffer disproportionately from its ill effects (Parikh *et al.* 1999).

An example of the rich polluting unabated at long range is carbon emissions and global warming. Most of the buildup of carbon dioxide in the atmosphere has originated in the rich countries. Until very recently, most studies of the threats of climate change have indicated that the mainly poor tropical countries are likely to be the worst sufferers while the rich temperate countries are likely to see fewer adverse effects and may even realize net gains from the climate change brought about by fossil fuel combustion.

Where pollution by the rich affects other rich and, therefore, powerful people, abatement happens faster. The abatement of halocarbons that threatened the ozone layer, and that would affect the rich temperate countries most, is an example. The Montreal Protocol and its successors have been very effective in reducing and even ending emissions of various halocarbons. It is true that the difference between these two cases can also be explained by appealing to costs. Abatement of halocarbons is a low-cost affair compared to abatement of pollution from as fundamental a part of the economy as its principal energy source. Nevertheless, the small sums spent on research on non-polluting energy sources suggest that the difference between these two cases is not one of abatement costs alone. For example, in 1997–98, the total public sector R & D spend on renewable energy and energy conservation in the USA, the EU and Japan, which together account for over 95 per cent of the energy research spend worldwide, was about US$ 1 billion (Dooley and Runci 1999). By way of comparison, the total R & D budget for 2002 for the US alone exceeded $100 billion, with $50 billion going to the Department of Defense, and $1.5 billion to counter-terrorism R & D (Koizumi and Turner 2002).

The theory discussed so far suggests that pollution by the poor will be abated if the rich are adversely affected by it. Two questions arise immediately. If this is true, then why is water pollution from untreated sewage so prevalent in poor countries in which the rich and powerful also live? Second, air pollution in Third World megalopolises is often largely from vehicles driven by the poor or lower middle class while the rich in these countries are concentrated in these cities. Why does this persist?

The answer to the first question is that the rich can to a large degree, though not perfectly, insulate themselves from water pollution by treating their domestic water themselves; this is what they do. A partial answer to the second question is that there are producer lobbies in poor countries which account for the persistence of polluting vehicles driven by the lower middle classes and poor. For example, in India, manufacturers who have invested heavily in two-stroke engine, two- and three-wheeled vehicles have prevented a ban on them. A similar observation applies to manufacturers of obsolete diesel engines for trucks and buses. The obsolete domestic industry grew up under trade barriers and is an obstacle to further progress. This is also true of the domestic oil refining industry which continues to produce low-quality diesel.

Poverty, bias, and the environmental Kuznets Curve

We have so far discussed two factors that affect pollution abatement. One, the informational issue, affects the demand for environmental quality, while the second, political structure, affects its supply. In addition, of course, income affects the demand for environmental quality positively. Income also affects incipient pollution, meaning the pollution that would occur if environmental costs were not taken into account at all. One may expect that this will be increasing in income in accordance with the well-known IPAT equation (Ehrlich and Holdren 1971) which says that environmental Impact = Population x Affluence x Technology. The logic of this is that increased economic output and technological capacity results in a greater use of natural resources and creation of waste in the course of production and consumption. Actual pollution or resource degradation is the result of incipient pollution being reduced as a consequence of environmental abatement expenditures, which depend on the demand for environmental quality and its supply which, in turn, depend on the factors indicated above.

The Environmental Kuznets Curve hypothesis is that actual pollution rises with per capita income and then falls as abatement increases in response to the demand for environmental quality. The theory discussed adds to this the notion that the supply of environmental quality will depend on the distribution of power. More democratic countries will abate more. This should strengthen the effect of income on abatement as per capita income and democracy are correlated. However, we can also test whether democracy matters – controlling income and its distribution. The latter control is necessary since, as pointed out by Scruggs (1998), inequality in incomes may lead to less pollution. The reason is that at higher income levels, there is a greater demand for environmental quality. Moreover, consumption may be less intensive in materials and more intensive in services which may result in less pollution per dollar of consumption.

The data on environmental indicators that are used in most cross-country studies are from the Global Environmental Monitoring System of the UN, started in 1977. These monitor selected air pollutants – sulphur dioxide concentrations, smoke, and heavy particles in 19–42 countries, and water pollution using measures of dissolved oxygen and fecal coliform bacteria in 58 countries. Monitoring is not nationally representative – air pollution data are from major cities which may not represent urban pollution in the various countries.

Torras and Boyce (1998) find that for low-income countries (among which there is considerable variation in inequality and democratic rights), inequality is associated with more of some pollutants and less of others. The reason may be that the effect of inequality on the composition of output is to reduce pollution while the political effect of inequality is to increase pollution. There is also the problem of the non-representative nature of the data mentioned earlier, as well as the fact that the data on income distribution are known to be very inaccurate.

Torras and Boyce find that the effect of democracy, as measured by their 'rights' variable, on pollution is more consistently negative at least for low-income countries. The probable reason for this is that it picks up only the political effect. Despite the various problems with the data, there is some support for the idea that a wider spread of political power reduces pollution.

It is important to note, however, that an uncritical use of the UN Global Environmental Monitoring System data can present a highly misleading picture. For example, most studies find an upward-sloping part of the Kuznets curve at low incomes, although the evidence for whether there is a downward-sloping part at higher incomes is mixed. But there is a selection bias in the nature of pollutants monitored. The two biggest health problems afflicting the poor in developing countries are water-borne diseases and respiratory infections, with the possible exception of AIDS in Africa. It is well established (Smith 2000), but unfortunately not yet well known, that indoor air pollution is a major cause of death in poor rural, and to a lesser extent, urban households in poor countries. But indoor air pollution monitoring has hardly begun anywhere in the world. To proxy for its effects, we examine a graph of the quantity of traditional fuel used per capita against per capita income in Figure 6.1 below.[3]

It is clear that traditional fuel use declines with income at low levels of per capita income and, therefore, so must exposure to indoor air pollution. The reason must be that households switch to cleaner fossil fuels as soon as they can afford to do so. This is probably not because they are aware of the lethal effects of smoke, but rather because it is a nuisance. The upturn in the graph for high income countries may be due to non-domestic uses of certain fuels and almost certainly does not reflect an increase in exposure to toxic indoor smoke.

However, as the environmental Kuznets curve literature generally shows, it is also true that exposure to urban outdoor air pollution increases with income at low levels of per capita income. The question then is: what is the net effect of increasing incomes on exposure to air pollution? One can get an idea of this by

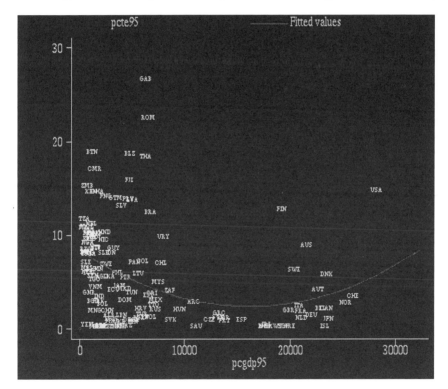

Figure 6.1 Per capita traditional energy consumption against income. (Source: graphed using 1995 energy data (billions of Joules per capita) from World Resources 1999. GDP data for 1995 are in US dollars adjusted for purchasing power parity from the *World Development Indicators* published by the World Bank.)

looking at data for India as Smith (2000) has done. Indian cities are among the most polluted in the world. Outdoor concentrations of PM_{10}, particulate matter smaller than 10 microns in diameter, range from 90–600 mg/m³ with a mean of 200 mg/m³. By contrast, the population-weighted mean for *indoor* concentrations is 700–800 mg/m³, more than three times as high. To put these figures in perspective, note that the (outdoor) mean for the USA is less than 30 mg/m³. Moreover, *exposures* to these high concentrations are greater for indoor air pollution since those in the kitchen are nearer to the source for long periods of time every day.

Since a switch from bio-fuels to gas results in indoor concentrations of fine particulate matter and other pollutants (carbon monoxide, polyaromatic hydrocarbons, volatile organic compounds) falling to negligible levels, it is clear that raising incomes enough to enable poor households to make this switch would result in a considerable decline in overall exposure, despite the expected rise in urban outdoor air pollution. Thus, we may conclude that as far as air pollution is concerned, the idea that pollution increases with income at low levels of income is false. The idea seems to have gained so much ground because most of those conducting measurements were simply not aware of, or ignored, the principal air pollution problem facing the poor in poor countries.

So much for air pollution. What about water pollution? As Figure 6.2 below shows, the proportion of those using water polluted by pathogens unambiguously increases with income.[4] Measures of chemical pollution as opposed to pollution by pathogens are not available as widely. Nevertheless, it is generally believed that their health effects are likely to be outweighed by the health effects of infection due to faecal pathogens, since the latter are far more frequent and have more immediate adverse effects (Gadgil 1998). Just as in the case of air pollution discussed above, it appears that the adverse health effects of water pollution decline with increases in income.

Thus, if one weights problems by some measure of their seriousness in terms of lost life-years and numbers of people affected, the biggest environmental problems globally appear to be those associated with poverty. This means that the environment actually improves with higher incomes, at least when one considers the move from low to middle incomes. This is the reverse of the Environmental Kuznets Curve. Low income is the central problem. All the same, better information about health effects might induce some poor households to switch to more expensive cleaner stoves even without subsidies and similarly, increase willingness to pay for sanitation and drinking water infrastructure. But a public information programme in the interest of the poor is not a high priority for governments for the reasons discussed above.

Status, consumption, and abatement

So far, we have worked with the standard assumption that environmental improvements or pollution abatement are necessarily costly. Someone has to give up consumption when they are made. This flows from the assumption that consumption is always a good thing. But there is a strand of literature in economics going back to Adam Smith (quoted in Ball *et al.* (2001), through Veblen (1899),

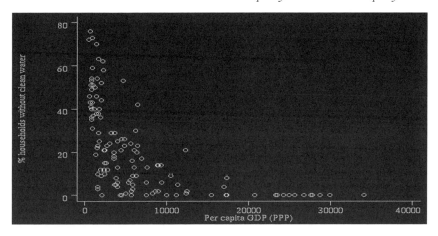

Figure 6.2 Exposure to unclean water against income. (Source: data on water are from the UNDP's Human Development Report 1999, while GDP data are from the World Bank's *World Development Indicators Data* for 1997.)

Duesenberry (1949), and Galbraith (1958), to modern treatments like Frank (1985), and Ng and Wang (1993), which points out that this need not be so. People care about their status relative to other people, and this may lead them to consume more of the type of goods that signal this status, than they would otherwise. One implication is that this will lead to underconsumption of public goods like environmental quality since such goods do not signal status. This is inefficient because, as long as everyone behaves this way, each person's ranking in the consumption of the 'status goods' is the same as it would have been if they had not taken their relative standing into account in making their consumption decision. Thus, the attempt to pursue status through consumption can be collectively futile.

It follows that social movements that attempt to discourage over-consumption, if they are successful in changing social norms, can lead to improvements in environmental quality at little or no real cost.[5] The campaign against wearing furs of endangered species and against the use of ivory are examples of successful movements. More generally, there has been a movement to discourage waste and improve conservation of energy. This is a much bigger effort and I am not aware of any studies that attempt to measure its impact. If successful, it would have implications not only for environmental quality, but also for the distribution of income, since it could lower world prices of fossil fuels to the benefit of those who consume too little of them. The dynamics of such social movements and changes in social norms is little understood, although there is a now growing literature in economics on social norms, conventions, and fashions, which utilizes evolutionary game theory as well as Bayesian decision theory.

Notes

1 This is a revised version of a lecture delivered at the University of Siena's International School for Economic Research's XVth summer workshop in June 2002.

2 Planning Unit, Indian Statistical Institute, Delhi. Email: som@isid.ac.in.
3 This variable includes industrial as well as domestic consumption of traditional fuels. So it is a very imperfect measure of what we are trying to capture – exposure to indoor air pollution from the use of polluting solid fuels in cooking. For example, Brazil's consumption of alcohol for transport is included as a traditional fuel. Moreover, the quality of the data are poor for some countries, since they are from estimates by the Food and Agriculture Organization rather than from measurements.
4 The definition of clean water in the *Human Development Report* is: piped water, a public tap, a borehole with a pump, a protected well, a protected spring or rainwater. It is a reasonable measure of water that is not likely to transmit infections (UNDP 1999).
5 A conventional economic instrument for dealing with the negative consumption externality, progressive taxation of consumption, is proposed by Frank (1999).

References

Ball, S.B., Eckel, C.C., Grossman, P. and Zame, W.R. (2001), 'Status in Markets', *Quarterly Journal of Economics*, 116(1): 161–88.

Boyce, J.K. (1994), 'Inequality as a Cause of Environmental Degradation', *Ecological Economics*, 11: 169–78.

Dooley, J.J. and Runci, P.J. (1999), 'Adopting a Long View to Energy R&D and Global Climate Change', Pacific Northwest National Laboratory, PNNL-12115.

Duesenberry, J.S. (1949) *Income, Saving, and the Theory of Consumer Behavior*, Cambridge, MA: Harvard University Press.

Ehrlich, P.R. and Holdren, J.P. (1971) 'Impact of population growth', *Science*, 171: 1212–17.

Frank, R.H. (1985) 'The Demand for Unobservable and Other Nonpositional Goods', *American Economic Review*, 75(1): 101–16.

Frank, R.H. (1999) *Luxury Fever: Money and Happiness in an Era of Excess*, Princeton, NJ: Princeton University Press.

Gadgil, A. (1998) 'Drinking Water in Developing Countries', *Annual Review of Energy and Environment*, 23: 253–86.

Galbraith, J.K. (1958) *The Affluent Society*, Boston, MA: Houghton Mifflin.

Koizumi, K. and Turner, P. (2002) *Congressional Action on Research and Development in the FY 2002 Budget*, Washington, DC: American Academy for the Advancement of Science.

Ng, Yew-Kwang and Wang, J. (1993) 'Relative Income, Aspiration, Environmental Quality, Individual and Political Myopia, Why May the Rat-Race for Material Growth be Welfare-reducing?', *Mathematical Social Sciences*, 26(1): 3–23.

Parikh, J., Smith, K. and Laxmi, V. (1999) 'Indoor Air Pollution: A Reflection on Gender Bias', *Economic and Political Weekly*, 34(9): 539–44.

Scruggs, L.A. (1998) 'Political and Economic Inequality and the Environment', *Ecological Economics*, 26(3): 259–75.

Smith, K.R. (2000) 'National Burden of Disease in India from Indoor Air Pollution', *Proceedings of the National Academy of Sciences of the USA*, 97(24): 13286–93.

Torras, M. and Boyce, J.K. (1998) 'Income, Inequality, and Pollution: A Reassessment of the Environmental Kuznets Curve', *Ecological Economics*, 25(2): 147–60.

United Nations Development Program (1999) *Human Development Report*, Washington, DC: UNDP.

Veblen, T. (1899) *The Theory of the Leisure Class*, New York: Macmillan.

World Bank (1999) *World Development Indicators*, Electronic Data file, Washington, DC: World Bank.

World Resources Institute (1999) *World Resources 1998–99*, Washington, DC: World Resources Institute.

Part III

Inequality and collective action towards the environment

7 Biodiversity as a local public good

Charles Perrings

Biodiversity as a public good

Biodiversity normally refers to the composition or mix of genes, species or ecosystems. Genetic diversity is a measure of the size and composition of the gene pool. Species diversity is a measure of the number of and differences between taxonomically distinct species. Intraspecific diversity is a measure of the variation within a taxonomically distinct species, e.g. varieties of rice. Ecosystem diversity is a measure of the differences between distinct ecosystems.

Since species can be differentiated in terms of their biochemistry, biogeography, ecology, genetics, morphology, physiology or the ecological role that they play in a particular community, there can be no one all-embracing measure of biodiversity. Genetic and species diversity are normally measured by indices that capture different aspects of the problem. The dominant indexes are the Simpson's index, $D = 1/\Sigma P_i 2$, (which captures the dominance of species); and the Shannon index, $B = -\Sigma P_i ln P_i$, (which captures the relative rarity of species) (Magurran 1988). It is natural to think of the elements P_i in such indices as equivalent to assets or stocks.

Such indices typically ignore differences between species in functional terms. Functional biodiversity is the combination of species required for a given function or process. Whereas the other measures of diversity capture differences in the genetic characteristics of species or the structural characteristics of ecosystems, functional diversity captures differences in the functions performed by species (the 'division of labour' in ecological systems). It is natural to think about functional biodiversity as a measure of the complementarity or substitutability between species as arguments in a production function. Attempts have been made to develop functional diversity indices (Brisby 1995).

Biodiversity conservation can be thought about as a joint public good. On the one hand it protects the gene pool – a global intergenerational public good (Sandler 1999). Conservation saves genetic information as a result of the depletion or extinction of some taxonomically distinct species. This comprises the genetic information now contained in the set of species on the planet, as well as the information that may be provided in the future through the genotypic evolution of those species. On the other hand, conservation of species threatened with local deletion or displacement protects a local public good – the capacity of the local

Table 7.1 Ecosystem functions and their uses

Regulation functions	Production functions	Carrier functions	Information functions
Providing support for economic activity and human welfare through: – protection against harmful cosmic influences – climate regulation – watershed protection and catchment – erosion prevention and soil protection – storage and recycling of industrial and human waste – storage and recycling of organic matter and mineral nutrients – maintenance of biological and genetic diversity – biological control – providing a migratory, nursery and feeding habitat	Providing basic resources, such as: – oxygen – food, drinking water and nutrition – water for industry, households, etc. – clothing and fabrics – building, construction and manufacturing materials – energy and fuel – minerals – medicinal resources – biochemical resources – genetic resources – ornamental resources	Providing space and a suitable substrate inter alia for: – habitation – agriculture, forestry, fishery, aquaculture – industry – engineering projects such as dams and roads – recreation – nature conservation	Providing aesthetic, cultural and scientific benefits through: – aesthetic information – spiritual and religious information – cultural and artistic inspiration – educational and scientific information – potential information

Source: Heywood, 1995.

system to deliver ecological services over a range of environmental and market conditions.

Biodiversity loss accordingly has two rather different consequences. The first is the irreversible loss of genetic information caused by the extinction of species. Loss of biodiversity in this sense may be measured by a change in the relevant index. The second is the exclusion or deletion of species populations from managed ecosystems. This may or may not mean that the excluded species is at risk of extinction. Once again there is a public good at stake – indeed a set of public goods. But these are local public goods. In addition to the food, fuel, fibres and medicinal products, ecosystems yield a range of important services. These include watershed protection and the mitigation of floods and droughts, waste assimilation, detoxification and decomposition, microclimatic stabilization, the purification of air and water, the generation and renewal of soil and its fertility, the pollination of crops and other vegetation, the control of agricultural pests and the dispersal of seeds and the transport of nutrients (Daily 1997). These services are provided over a range of spatial and temporal scales (see Table 7.1). Their conservation can be thought about as a local public good.

The structure of the public good

At both local and global levels, the public good nature of biodiversity conservation implies that, if left to the market, there will be too little conservation effort. There will be some conservation effort if biodiversity conservation is an impure public good, i.e. a public good yielding both privately capturable benefits as well as a set of non-exclusive and non-rival benefits to a wider community. In the absence of cooperation, the level of conservation effort will be determined by the privately capturable value of conservation.

Let V^i denote the welfare of the ith of n communities, which we may take to depend on consumption of a bundle of market goods, x^i, and a public good, biodiversity conservation, $Y = y^1, y^2, \ldots, y^n$. If there are m members of that community, the optimal commitment of resources to conservation by that community requires the solution to a public good problem in which and $V^i = V^i\left(U^i_1, \cdots, U^i_m\right)$ and $U^i_j = U^i_j(x, y^i_j, y^i_1, \ldots, y^i_m)$ for all $j = 1, \ldots, m$. Each of the m members of the ith community has an incentive to free-ride on the conservation efforts of other members of that community, and to neglect the benefit that their own conservation efforts confer on other members of the same community.

Formally, the problem faced by the ith community is of the general form:

$$\text{Max}_{xi, yi} V^i = V^i(x^i, y^i, Y)$$

That is, the ith community obtains benefits directly from its own conservation effort, y^i, and from the global benefits offered by its contribution to the global conservation effort, Y. The Barbier and Perrings (2001) problem for the ith community may be posed in the following way:

$$\text{Max}_{xi, ui} V^i(.) = V^i(x^i, y^i, C(Y, Z) \mid x^i + py^i = I^i)$$

where $C(Y, Z)$ is a conservation function, which is increasing in the size of the global public good (the level of biodiversity), Y, $C_Y > 0$, and the resources committed to conservation, Z, $C_Z > 0$. If all communities behave in a non-cooperative way, the welfare of the ith community is maximized where:

$$\frac{V^i_Y}{V^i_{x^i}} = p - \frac{V^i_C}{V^i_{x^i}} C_{y^i}$$

whereas the welfare of the global community requires that:

$$\frac{V^i_Y}{V^i_{x^i}} = p - \sum_i \frac{V^i_C}{V^i_{x^i}} C_Y$$

The extra terms in this reflect the conservation benefits that the ith community confers on others. If the 'cost' of conservation is denoted w, then the globally optimal level of conservation will satisfy:

$$\frac{V_{Y^i}^i}{V_{x^i}^i} = p - w\frac{C_Y}{Y_Z}$$

The problem is symmetrical at the global level. Each of the n members of the global community has a similar incentive to free ride on the conservation efforts of others, and to neglect the benefits its own conservation efforts confer on other members of the global community.

The extent of the free-rider problem depends on the technology of public good supply. This in turn depends on the nature of the public good itself. All of the following cases may be found:

Pure public good case (simple sum)	$\max_{x,y_i} U^i = U^i(x, y^1 + y^2 + \dots + y^n)$
Pure public good case (best shot)	$\max_{x,y_i} U^i = U^i(x, \mathrm{Max}(y^1, y^2, \dots, y^n))$
Pure public good case (weakest link)	$\max_{x,y_i} U^i = U^i(x, \mathrm{Min}(y^1, y^2, \dots, y^n))$
Impure public good case	$\max_{x,y_i} U^i = U^i(x, y^i, y^1, y^2, \dots, y^n)$
Local public good case (club good)	$\max_{x,y_i} U^i = U^i(x, y^i, S)\ S = \text{club size}$

Take the example of the control of biological invasions: a 'weakest-link' public good. A national quarantine policy to protect against invasive pathogens reduces the risk to all people in the country concerned. The benefits of quarantine are neither 'rival' nor 'exclusive'. If one person benefits from the protection offered by a quarantine policy it does not affect the cost of quarantine. Nor does it reduce the benefits of quarantine to others. But the level of protection offered to the whole community depends on the level of protection supplied by the least effective quarantine facility. If one quarantine facility fails in its responsibility to identify and exclude an invasive pathogen, all are at risk. The fact that all other quarantine facilities may do so is irrelevant. Ex situ genetic conservation measures, by contrast, are 'best shot' public goods. In this case free-riding imposes no costs on society.

The functional benefits of biodiversity conservation

The sustainability of any state (or development path) depends on the properties of the stability domain corresponding to that state (or path within the state). It depends on the resilience of the system in that state. Sustainability is a measure of the capacity of a stochastic system to function over a range of environmental conditions without flipping to a more degraded state, i.e. without losing resilience (Arrow *et al.* 1995). Resilience may be measured by the size of disturbance that can be absorbed before a system flips to another state (Holling 1973).

Biodiversity supports resilience and ecosystem functioning. Experimental grasslands research has shown that productivity increases with plant biodiversity.

The main limiting nutrient, oil mineral nitrogen, is used more effectively over a range of environmental conditions the greater the diversity of species (Tilman and Downing 1994). The implication is that biodiversity protects the ability of a system to absorb stress or shocks without losing productive potential.

Resilience to variation in environmental conditions requires species capable of supporting key functions as conditions vary. Deletion of species important under some conditions will have little effect if there are other species capable of stepping in as substitutes as conditions change. Species that are 'redundant' under one set of environmental conditions may be critically important under other environmental conditions (Holling *et al.* 1995). Note that 'redundancy' is a measure of the substitutability of ecological resources. This says that a species that is not preferred to a substitute species under one state of nature may be preferred to that substitute species under another state of nature.

There are many ways in which to model the impact of biodiversity. To keep things simple we may assume a single stock extraction problem, in which the extracted resource exhibits density dependent (logistic) growth. The impact of biodiversity on production of the resource may be defined by the function:

$$\frac{dx}{dt} = rx(t)\left(1 - \frac{x(t)}{K(B(t))}\right) - h(t)$$

where r is a growth rate, $x(t)$ is biomass of the resource (say a particular population) at time t, K is carrying capacity and $B(t)$ is the biodiversity index at time t. The final term, $h(t)$, is harvest at time t. Ecologically, biodiversity protects the resilience of ecosystems, where resilience is measured by the ability to absorb stress or shocks without losing productive potential. Dalmazzone (2000) has illustrated this as in Figure 7.1.

Consider the example of agroecosystems. Plant and animal breeding programmes have narrowed the genetic base of agriculture to the point where more than 90 per cent of global food supply derives from only 11 species –wheat, rice, corn, oats, tomato, potato, cattle, sheep, pigs, chickens and ducks.

At a local level, one effect of this is that agroecosystems have become more susceptible to shocks or changes in environmental conditions. The adoption of crops with a narrow genetic base increases average yields, but it also tends to increase the variance of yields (Conway 1993). The public good at stake in the simplification of agroecosystems is their capacity to maintain productivity over a range of conditions. Preliminary estimates of the relation between crop genetic diversity and arable systems and the variance of farm incomes in both developed countries (Gatto 2001) and developing countries (Prakash and Pearce 2001) confirms that the loss of crop genetic diversity increases the variance of farm incomes.

The cost of the local loss of land races and wild relatives is the opportunity forgone to use the genetic material to breed or engineer desirable traits in crops that may be cultivated world-wide. Most cultivated crop varieties and many livestock strains already contain genetic material from wild relatives, landraces or traditional livestock strains. Indeed, it has been estimated that at least half of the increase in

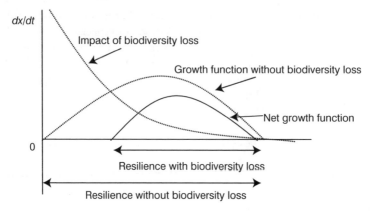

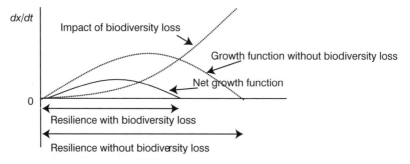

Figure 7.1 Impact of biodiversity loss on resilience

agricultural productivity this century is directly attributable to artificial selection, recombination and intraspecific gene transfer procedures. For example:

- Mexican beans have been used to improve resistance to the Mexican bean weevil which destroys or damages as much as 25 per cent of stored beans in Africa and 15 per cent in South America;
- Traditional wheat varieties from Turkey have been used to improve genetic resistance to a range of diseases in the USA;
- Indian land races have been used to strengthen resistance to grassy stunt virus in rice; Ethiopian barley has been used to combat yellow dwarf virus in Californian crops. (Heywood 1995)

Biodiversity in the production function

Biodiversity underpins the production of goods and services over a range of environmental conditions. In ecological terms, it ensures that the ecosystems supporting the production of goods and services are resilient, where resilience is measured by the capacity of a system to retain productivity following disturbance (Levin *et al.* 1998). In economic terms, biodiversity is equivalent to a portfolio of assets, and community conservation effort is equivalent to investment in that portfolio (Swanson 1992). The level of community conservation effort (investment in biodiversity) will depend on both the mean yield of the portfolio, and the covariance in yields.

In principle, the valuation of conservation efforts in support of local public goods requires specification of a 'production function' describing the relationship between the conserved species and the relevant ecological services (Mäler 1974). Specifically, if Q is the marketed output of an economic activity, and if it depends both on a range of marketed inputs, $x = x_1,\ldots,x_n$ (capital, labour, materials, etc.), and on natural resource, R, that itself depends on the set of species, $\mathbf{s} = s_1,\ldots,s_m$, then we can write the production function:

$$Q = Q(x_1,\ldots,x_n, R(s_1,\ldots,s_m))$$

If P denotes the value of Q, then the value of the ith species, s_i, is the value of the marginal impact of that species: $PdQ/dR\ dR/ds_i$. If a change in the abundance of the ith species also affects the abundance of other species in the community, then the value of the ith species, s_i, is $PdQ/dR(dR/ds_i + dR/d\mathbf{s}\ d\mathbf{s}/ds_i)$. That is, it includes both the direct and indirect impacts of a change in the abundance of s_i. In practice, relatively few studies are based on identification of the functional relationship between species and the provision of ecological services.

Consider an example from fisheries by Kasulo (2001). In a Gordon-Schaefer model, environmental factors can affect fish biomass:

- through the carrying capacity, K;
- through the intrinsic growth rate, r;
- through K and r together; and
- through catch.

Let water pollution affect total fish biomass through its impact on K and r together. The growth function for fish biomass takes the form:

$$\dot{X} = rX(1 - eW - X/K) - qEX$$

where W is the environmental quality variable, and e is a parameter that gives the amount by which a unit change in the environmental variable depresses the natural growth rate of fish biomass.

Let biodiversity affect the effectiveness of fishing effort:

$$Y = qBEX$$

where B is the bioeconomic diversity index.

When $B = 1$ the production function reduces to the form generally applied in single species fishery models. $B = 1$ implies that there is only one valuable harvested species. $B > 1$ implies there is more than one economically valuable harvested species. $B < 1$ implies the effectiveness of fishing effort declines due to the cost of sorting, clearing by-catch, the use of multiple gears and so on.

The growth and sustainable yield functions now become:

$$\dot{X} = rX(1 - eW - X / K) - qBEX.$$

and:

$$Y = qKBE(1 - eW - qBE/r)$$
p = the unit price of catch,
c = the unit cost of effort,
δ = the discount rate,

the open access steady state level of effort is given by:

$$E_{OA} = r(1 - eW - c/pqBK)/qB$$

and the corresponding stock level is:

$$X_{OA} = K(1 - eW - qBE_{OA}/r)$$

The profit maximizing steady state level of effort is:

$$\theta = \delta + r(1 - eW)$$

$$E_o = \frac{qB\xi \pm \left[((qB\xi)^2 - 8\phi q^2 B^2 \theta(\phi r(1 - eW) - c))\right]^{\frac{1}{2}}}{4\phi q^2 B^2}$$

$$\theta = \delta + r(1 - eW)$$
$$\phi = pqBK / r$$
$$\xi = \phi(\theta + 2r(1 - eW)) - c$$
$$\theta = \delta + r(1 - eW)$$
$$\phi = pqBK / r$$
$$\xi = \phi(\theta + 2r(1 - eW)) - c$$

The corresponding stock level is:

$$X_O = c(\delta r(1 - eW) - qBE_O)/(pqB(\delta + r(1 - eW) - 2qBE_O)$$

The MSY effort and stock levels for comparison are:

$$E_{MSY} = r(1 - eW)2qB$$

and:

$$X_{MSY} = K(1 - eW)/2$$

If an increase in biodiversity reduces the effectiveness of fishing effort then, in a multispecies fishery, the maximum sustainable yield level of stock size is not affected by changes in biodiversity but the effort required to catch the MSY increases (decreases) as fish diversity increases (decreases). In open access and profit maximizing fisheries, an increase (decrease) in fish biodiversity implies an increase (decrease) in stock size. However, the impact on the open access and profit maximizing levels of effort depends on the level of biodiversity. For small numbers of species an increase (decrease) in fish biodiversity implies an increase (decrease) in effort levels. As the number of species rises, the effect on effort levels reverses, and an increase (decrease) in fish biodiversity implies a decrease (increase) in effort:

$$\frac{dX_{MSY}}{dB} = 0, \frac{dE_{MSY}}{dB} < 0$$

$$\frac{dX_{OA}}{dB} < 0, \frac{dE_{OA}}{dB} \gtrless 0$$

$$\frac{dX_{O}}{dB} < 0, \frac{dE_{O}}{dB} \gtrless 0$$

This model has been estimated by Kasulo for one fishery in Lake Malawi. To estimate the parameters r, q, and K method, first define an equation for catch per unit effort (U). Since $Y = qBEX$ it follows that $Y/BE = qX = U$, and hence that $X = U/q$. The population growth function can therefore be expressed in terms of U. That is:

$$\dot{X} = rX(1 - X/K - eW) - qBEX$$

may be written in the form:

$$\dot{U} = rU\left(1 - \frac{U}{qK} - eW\right) - qBEU$$

or

$$\frac{\dot{U}}{U} = r - qE - \frac{r}{qK}U$$

Adding time subscripts and integrating from t to $(t+1)$ yields:

$$\ln\left(\frac{U_{st+1}}{U_{st}}\right) = r - qE_t - \frac{r}{qK}U_t - reW_t$$

where U_t is catch per unit effort at time t. Fishing effort, E_t, is total effort per year. The same applies to Y, the catch rate, so that U_t is the annual catch per unit effort.

Table 7.2 Regression results

R	Q	r/qK	re	R2	F Statistic	DW Statistic
1.3591	−0.0000019	27.4507	−1.4422	0.742	16.3267	1.7542
(3.3330)	(−4.232)	(2.3140)	(−4.434)			

Note: Figures in parentheses are t-statistics

If U_{st}, catch per unit effort at the beginning of year t, is approximately equal to the annual catch per unit effort for the preceding year, so that $U_{st} \cong U_{t-1}$, and $U_{st+1} \cong U_t$, we have:

$$\ln\left(\frac{U_t}{U_{t-1}}\right) = r - qE_t - \frac{r}{qK}U_t - reW_t + \varepsilon_t$$

Using a two-year moving average the estimated equation becomes:

$$\ln\hat{X}_t = r - q\hat{E}_t^* - \frac{r}{qK}\hat{U}_t^* - reW_t^* + \varepsilon_t$$

Using Malawian data relating to the period 1976–98, Kasulo found the results shown in Table 7.2

If the measure of diversity is weighted by the economic value (market value in this case) of species, the model turns out to have considerable predictive ability. The bioeconomic diversity measure captures the effect of a change both in the relative abundance of marketed species, and a change in the relative prices of those species.

If an increase in bioeconomic diversity reduces the effectiveness of fishing effort, as we assume in this chapter, the pressure on stocks is greater at all levels of biodiversity in open access than it is in profit maximizing regimes. In both regimes, effort levels first increase and then decrease as the bioeconomic diversity of catch falls.

However, in a profit maximizing regime both catch and the productivity of fishing effort is highest when the bioeconomic diversity index is 1 – there is a single marketed species. By contrast, in an open access regime the catch size reaches a maximum at a relatively low value of B. That is, open access catches are maximized at higher levels of bioeconomic diversity than in profit maximizing regimes.

The maximum harvest is similar in each case. The stock size corresponding to that harvest is slightly lower in the open access than the profit maximizing case, but the diversity of the catch is much higher. This accords with the general evidence on freshwater fisheries, where traditional open access regimes have typically been less selective in the set of harvested species than is the case in commercial fisheries, which tend to be highly selective.

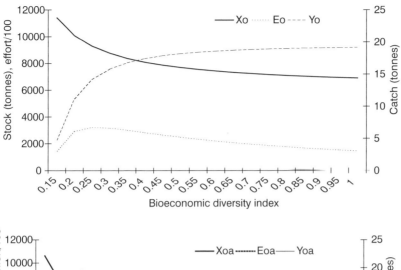

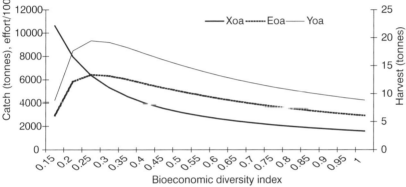

Figure 7.2 Stock and catch size as a function of bioeconomic diversity

Case study: cooperative production and intraspecific crop genetic diversity in Italian agroecosystems[1]

The measure of diversity in this case refers to the diversity of cultivars for the main type of wheat grown in Southern Italy, durum wheat. Conservation of that diversity is modelled as an impure public good with exclusion, i.e. as a club good. The club is an agricultural cooperative. Greater diversity is hypothesized to benefit cooperative members through the long run average payout they receive. At the same time it also increases the coordination costs of the cooperative, and hence the cost of cooperative membership. Farmers derive benefits from sale of the output from their own holdings, y^i, and from the price impact of their cropping decisions on the diversity of cultivars in the whole cooperative. The public good, Y, is measured by a diversity index, $G(Y)$. The payout to farmers depends on both the diversity index and the size of the cooperative, s. That is $p = p(G(Y), s)$ with $dp/dG < 0$, $dp/ds > 0$. The cost of the cooperative to the ith farmer, c^i, depends on both the costs of producing y^i and the size of the cooperative. That is $c^i = c(y^i, s)$ with $dc/dy^i > 0$, $dc/ds > 0$. Production of y^i depends on the set of inputs $x_1^i, \ldots, x_n^i$.

The profit function for the *i*th farmer accordingly has the following general form:

$$\pi^i = \pi^i\left(x^i, y^i, G(Y), s\right)$$

in which y^i is the *i*th contribution to the public good Y, which is measured by $G(Y)$; x^i is a vector of inputs to the production of y^i and s is the size of the cooperative. The size of the cooperative membership confers benefits in terms of market power, lobbying capacity and risk spreading, but also increases coordination, monitoring and knowledge dissemination costs.

The intraspecific diversity measure is based on both the number and abundance of cultivars. It is a Simpson's index:

$$G(Y) = \sum_i \left(\frac{y^i(1-y^i)}{Y(1-Y)} \right)$$

The problem for farmers is to maximize profits over their planning horizon through choice of input combinations, output level and composition. Presenting this as a static problem for simplicity, it is:

$$\text{Max}_{x^i}\, \pi^i = p\left(G(Y), s\right) y^i\left(x^i\right) - c\left(y^i(x^i), s\right)$$

The first order conditions for this problem require that:

$$p + p_{y^i}\, y^i = c_{y^i}$$

If the output of the *i*th farmer has no impact on the payout to that farmer the farmer will produce up to the point where marginal cost equals the price of output. If output of the *i*th farmer improves the payoff to that farmer, they will increase output up to the point at which marginal cost equals the price of output plus the marginal impact of output on the price.

Now consider the problem from the perspective of the cooperative. The cooperative is assumed to have a coordinating function. It aims to maximize profits to its members, i.e.:

$$\text{Max}_{y^i} \sum_i \pi^i = p(G(Y), s) \sum_i y^i(x^i) - \sum_i c(y^i(x^i), s)$$

The first order necessary conditions for maximization of this function include:

$$p + p_{y^i}\left[y^i + \sum_{j \neq i} y^j \right] = c_{y^i}$$

That is, from the perspective of the cooperative it is optimal for the individual farmer to produce up to the point where marginal cost is equal to the price of the product plus the impact of that farmer's decision on the payoff to all members of the cooperative. It is also optimal to expand membership up to the point where the marginal cost of membership is equal to the marginal benefit measured in terms of the payoff to members.

If the terms $\sum_{j \neq i} y^i$ are positive, then a cooperative with the power to coordinate production will lead to higher levels of crop genetic diversity than will the independent decisions of farmers, whether operating independently or in a cooperative. If the cooperative does not have the power to coordinate decisions, these benefits will be ignored by individual farmers. In this case the independent decisions of cooperative members will still lead to higher levels of crop genetic diversity than the independent decisions of private farmers. But the level of crop genetic diversity will be lower than if the cooperative has the power to coordinate decisions.

A test of this hypothesis using data from the Objective 1 regions of Southern Italy yielded the estimated results shown in Table 7.3.

Intraspecific diversity and the density of cooperatives both have a positive impact on the mean value of output of durum wheat, and this impact is significant at the five per cent and one per cent levels respectively (since the diversity index is smaller the higher the level of intraspecific diversity, the negative sign of the coefficient implies that biodiversity is positively related to the value of output).

Policy implications of local public goods

Finally, let me sketch some of the policy implications of biodiversity conservation as a local public good.

Protected area strategy. Large protected reserves in areas of high biodiversity will undoubtedly remain part of an international strategy for the conservation of biodiversity. But large protected areas alone will not solve the problem of biodiversity loss at either the local or the global level. There is a strong case for a complementary system of many small-protected areas. Not only can these more effectively capture variation along environmental gradients in comparison with a

Table 7.3 The effect of intraspecific crop genetic diversity on yields in Southern Italy

Variable	Coefficient	Std errors	t ratios	p values
Intraspecific diversity	$-.1962002798$	$.96675106E^{-01}$	2.029	.0468
Fertilizer	.1873173909	$.52966878E^{-01}$	3.537	.0008
Gasoline	$.2302583199E^{-02}$	$.91047169E^{-03}$	2.529	.0140
Machinery HP	$-.1374786228$	$.25582977E^{-01}$	-5.374	0000
Agric surface	1.521556281	.19767747	7.697	0000
Cooperatives	2.094632031	.28589662	7.327	0000
Employment	$.8222436787E^{-02}$	$.12230042E^{-02}$	6.723	0000
Island dummy	.3117894544	$.72230504E^{-01}$	4.317	0000
Constant	1.285010280	.46310082	2.775	0000

few larger refugia, they can also better meet local conservation needs in agriculture, forestry and fisheries. Such a dispersed system matches the conservation practices of traditional societies. Reports from the north-eastern hill states of India, for example, suggest that the overall area conserved as sacred groves or ponds was no less than the 10 per cent proposed at Caracas, but the composition of protected areas was far more dispersed. A decentralized and more participatory conservation strategy would better serve the conservation needs of modern communities (Perrings and Gadgil 2002).

To protect a few large islands of high globally significant diversity, surrounded by oceans of homogenized, low-diversity landscapes does not ensure sustainable and equitable use of biodiversity. What is needed is a two-pronged approach. Protection of the global public good requires protection of biodiversity in a dispersed system of refugia of appropriate size. Protection of the local public good requires protection of the 'optimal' level of biodiversity in production forests, aquatic bodies and pastoral and arable ecosystems. This may best be achieved by co-locating protection and production areas.

Markets in the external benefits of local biodiversity conservation. Because there are local external benefits to protection, there is scope for the development of markets involving the co-location of protected and production areas. Where the benefits of biodiversity conservation accrue to local communities, the costs of protection may be met from enhanced production revenues. That is, the main financial mechanisms might be related to local price and tax structures. Take the example of watershed protection. While local communities derive considerable benefits from local watershed protection, it is often the case that the main beneficiaries are downstream users who are protected from floods and who enjoy access to greater flows of higher-quality water than would be the case without protection. The watershed value of forests should be reflected in water or irrigation prices. This might be addressed directly by the inclusion of a watershed protection levy or fee. The revenue generated by the watershed protection fees should then accrue to the community authority charged with forest protection. In countries such as Costa Rica, El Salvador, Sri Lanka, Vietnam and Laos, which rely heavily on hydropower, the same watershed protection function might be priced through electricity tariffs.

Institutional reform. The EU applies the principle of subsidiarity to the governance of environmental resources. The principle implies that environmental problems should be addressed at a scale that maps onto the geographical distribution of environmental effects. In the case of environmental public goods, this implies that the jurisdiction of the authority charged with the regulation/provision of those public goods should span the spatial and temporal spread of effects.

At the international level, responsibility for the conservation of genetic diversity currently rests with a range of UN Agencies – UNEP, FAO, WTO, WIPO, UNESCO and with the relevant multilateral environmental agreements, principally the Convention on Biological Diversity (CBD) and the International Treaty for Plant Genetic Resources for Food and Agriculture. At the moment there are real impediments to the equitable sharing of international benefits. The incremental cost principle of the Global Environmental Facility (GEF) implies that countries should be compensated for their contribution to the international public good. But, the structure of global markets and the rules governing international trade and investment mean that transactions falling outside of GEF funded projects carry no guarantee of the equitable sharing of benefits. The solution is not necessarily to restrict those markets. Indeed, there is scope for the further development of markets in the external benefits of local biodiversity conservation. But if local communities are to be compensated for conservation efforts in agroecosystems that yield global benefits, then the remit of the GEF needs to be appropriately extended. The vision behind a World Environmental Organization/Global Environmental Organization (WEO/GEO) is of a mechanism to internalize global environmental externalities. Pending its establishment, the developing countries have a strong interest in and an even stronger argument for the extension of the GEF.

This implies a reappraisal of funding priorities. The historic emphasis on protection of refugia has begun to be relaxed already in recognition of the fact that many off-reserve conservation and development projects increase biodiversity protection within reserves as a side benefit. A financially strengthened GEF might serve both the CBD and the International Undertaking of the FAO by directly addressing the incremental costs of biodiversity conservation in agroecosystems. The main beneficiaries in this case would be small farmers, as custodians of agricultural biodiversity This would be consistent both with the recognition of farmers' rights in the International Treaty for Plant Genetic Resources for Food and Agriculture and the reference to equitable benefit sharing in the CBD. More importantly, it would reflect the genuine concern of those in developing countries that the loss of species in local production systems, and especially the loss of intraspecific crop-genetic diversity, has been systematically undervalued in the global conservation strategy.

Note

1 See di Falco and Perrings, 2002.

References

Arrow, K., Bolin, B., Costanza, R., Dasgupta, P., Folke, C., Holling, C.S., Jansson, B.O., Levin, S., Maler, K.G., Perrings, C. and Pimentel, D. (1995) 'Economic growth, carrying capacity, and the environment', *Science* 268: 520–1.
Barrett, S. (1994), 'The biodiversity supergame', *Environmental and Resource Economics* 4(1): 111–22.
Brisby, F.A. (1995) 'Characterization of biodiversity', in V.H. Heywood (ed.), *Global Biodiversity Assessment*, Cambridge: Cambridge University Press.
Cervigni, R. (2001) *Biodiversity in the Balance*, Cheltenham: Edward Elgar.
Conway, G.R. (1993) 'Sustainable agriculture: the trade-offs with productivity, stability and equitability', in E.B. Barbier (ed.), *Economics and Ecology: New Frontiers and Sustainable Development*, London: Chapman and Hall.
Daily, G. (ed.) (1997) *Nature's Services: Societal Dependence on Natural Systems*, Washington, DC: Island Press.

Dalmazzone, S. (2000) 'Economic activity and the resilience of ecological systems: complexity, non-linearities and uncertainty in economic-ecological modelling', DPhil dissertation, University of York.

Di Falco, S. and Perrings, C. (2002) 'Cooperative production and intraspecific genetic diversity in Italian agroecosystems', Paper presented at the Bioecon Workshop, Rome.

Gatto, E. (2001) 'Biological Diversity, Stability and Productivity of Agroecosystems: A Panel Data Analysis', York: Environment Department, University of York.

Heywood, V. (ed. 1995) *Global Biodiversity Assessment*, Cambridge: Cambridge University Press.

Holling, C.S. (1973) 'Resilience and stability of ecological systems', *Annual Review of Ecology and Systematics*, 4: 1–23.

Holling, C.S., Schindler, D.W., Walker, B.H. and Roughgarden, J. (1995) 'Biodiversity in the functioning of ecosystems: an ecological synthesis', in C. Perrings, C. Folke, C.S. Holling, B.O. Jansson, K.G. Mäler (eds) *Biological Diversity: Economic and Ecological Issues*, Cambridge: Cambridge University Press.

Kasulo, V. (2001) 'Bioeconomic management of aquatic ecosystems for the conservation and sustainable utilitsation of biodiversity', PhD dissertation, University of York, York.

Levin, S.A., Barrett, S., Aniyar, S., Baumol, W., Bliss, C., Bolin, B., Dasgupta, P., Ehrlich, P., Folke, C., Gren, I.M., Holling, C.S., Jansson, A.M., Jansson, B.O., Mifler, K.G., Martin, D., Perrings, C. and Sheshinski, E. (1998) 'Resilience in natural and socio-economic systems', *Environment and Development Economics* 3(2): 222–34.

Magurran, A.E. (1988) *Ecological Diversity and its Measurement*, London: Croom Helm.

Mäler, K.G. (1974) *Environmental Economics: A Theoretical Enquiry*, Oxford: Blackwell.

Pearce, D.W. and Moran, D. (1994) *The Economic Value of Biodiversity*, London: Earthscan.

Perrings, C. (1995) 'Biodiversity conservation as insurance', in T. Swanson (ed.), *Economics and Ecology of Biodiversity Decline*, Cambridge: Cambridge University Press.

Perrings, C. (2001) 'The economics of biodiversity loss and agricultural development in low income countries', in D.R. Lee and C.B. Barret (eds) *Tradeoffs or Synergies? Agricultural Intensification, Economic Development and the Environment*, Wallingford: CAB International.

Perrings, C. and Gadgil, M. (2002) 'Sustainable and equitable use of biodiversity: protecting the global and local public good', Working Paper CEDE/02-002, York: CEDE.

Perrings, C., Folke, C. and Mäler, K.G. (1992) 'The ecology andeconomics of biodiversity loss: the research agenda', *Ambio* 21(3): 201–11.

Prakash, T.N. and Pearce, D.W. (2001) *Resilience as a Measure of Environmental Sustainability: The Case of Karnataka Agriculture*, London: Department of Economics, University College London.

Sandler, T. (1997) *Global Challenges*, Cambridge: Cambridge University Press.

Sandler, T. (1999) 'Intergenerational public goods: strategies, efficiency and institutions', in I. Kaul, I. Grunberg and M.A. Stern (eds) *Global Public Goods*, Oxford: Oxford University Press for UNDP.

Swanson, T. (1992) 'Economics of a biodiversity convention', *Ambio*, 21(3): 250–7.

Swanson, T. (ed.) (1995) *The Economics and Ecology of Biodiversity Decline*, Cambridge: Cambridge University Press.

Tilman, D. and Downing, J.A. (1994) 'Biodiversity and stability in grasslands', *Nature* 367: 363–5.

8 Collective action on the commons

The role of inequality

Jean-Marie Baland

The 'canonical' model of collective action

Many problems of collective action can be represented with the help of a simple model, where agents draw unequal benefits from the resource in proportion to their endowments in the relevant productive asset (fisheries, irrigation scheme, anti-erosive barriers, etc.). Consider a situation under which each agent decides the level of his own contribution to a common good. The common good is produced by aggregating the individual contributions, according to the following production function:

$$G = G\left(\Sigma_j g_j\right)$$

where G represents the aggregate level of the common good, and g_i represents the individual contribution of agent i.

We furthermore assume that each agent i chooses the level of g_i which maximizes his utility, U_i, given the amounts contributed by the other agents:

$$U_i = U\left(\alpha_i G\left(\Sigma g_j\right), c_i\right)$$

with $c_i = w_i - g_i, g_i \geq 0$.

where w_i represents the individual income of agent i, c_i the quantity of private good he consumes, and α_i his share in the common good.

This is one of the simplest formulations of the problem. It is very flexible, and can be used to accommodate a variety of different 'common property resources' problems.

Example 1: farmers, endowed with different land assets, voluntarily decide their individual level of involvement and effort into the maintenance of a collective irrigation scheme that covers their land. The benefits they expect from the scheme are proportional to their land endowment α_i.

Example 2: in a fishery, each fisherman chooses to exercise care and follow good practices to protect juvenile species, or to preserve spawning areas. Doing so increases future catches, and benefits, in proportion to one's fishing potential.

Example 3: consider a forest user group, the members of which have to spend time and effort to protect and improve the collective forest. The effort they individually contribute to the activities of the group is a function of their perceived benefits from doing so, and can differ between individuals.

Example 4: the pure public-good case, where agents voluntarily contribute to the production of a public good. In this case, one can assume $\alpha_i = \alpha_j$ for all i, j.

Example 5: preservation of the local resource requires local coordination and regulation. Time and effort spent on collective action by each villager depend on the expected benefits from the regulation scheme.

The role of inequality in the canonical model

The problem above directly allows for two types of inequality, income inequality, w_i, and share inequality, α_i.

We first analyze the impact of income transfers on collective action (Bergstrom *et al.* 1986).

Key intuition: consider a 'full budget approach', where the level of common good provided by the other agents, G_{-i}, directly enters into the budget constraint of agent *i*:

budget constraint of agent *i* is: $c_i + g_i = w_i$,
which can be rewritten as $c_i + G_i = w_i + G_{-i}$.

Result: transfer \$1 from agent *j* to agent *i*.

Suppose agent *j* reduces his contribution by exactly \$1, agent *i*'s new budget constraint can now be written as: $c_i + G_i = w_i + \$1 + (G_{-i} - \$1)$.

Which is identical to the pre-transfer constraint – he does not change his consumption decision and his contribution increases by exactly \$1.

Similarly, agent *j*'s best reply is to reduce his contribution by exactly \$1.

Result 1 (neutrality theorem): the equilibrium aggregate level of the contribution is unaffected by (small) transfers between contributing agents.

Result 2: a transfer from non-contributors to contributors increases the level of the public good produced (normal good).

Proviso: agents do not have identical preferences. Income transfers here are not directly related to inequality.

Think of poor consumers with a 'strong' preference for the public good.

Transfers of shares (assume same preferences, same income).

Result 3: agents with higher shares contribute more.

Result 4: the largest quantity of common good is produced if one agent concentrates all the shares, so that he internalizes all the benefits (Olson).

(1) Result 3 seems to be consistent with a lot of empirical evidence, which suggests that larger users of the resource (big landowners, fishermen owning many boats and nets, etc.) tend to contribute more.

(2) Except for the case of extreme inequality, this does not imply that increasing inequality increases aggregate provision. The latter basically depends on

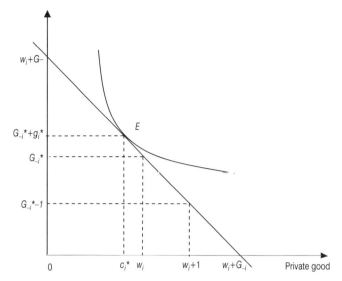

Figure 8.1 Consumer choice with voluntary provision to a public good

whether, in the reaction functions, contributions are concave or convex in the individual share (and some other conditions)

In Figure 8.1, one can see that the concavity of the relationship between individual contributions and individual share implies that greater equality in the distribution of shares increases the level of the common good: the contribution of an agent with an 'average' share is always greater than the average of the contributions.

The linearity of the objective function

We now introduce a slight modification of the initial objective function. We consider a linear objective function, so that each agent i maximizes:

$$U_i = \alpha_i G\left(\Sigma g_j\right) - g_i$$

with $g_i \geq 0$.

Such an objective function may appear as a more appropriate formalization under some circumstances, for instance, when agents are producers who maximize profits and have to invest in a common resource, which increases their private output. (It requires no imperfections on the output and the input market.)

The FOC to this problem is:

$$\alpha_i \frac{\partial G\left(\Sigma g_j\right)}{\partial g_i} - 1 \leq 0 \quad \text{and} \quad g_i \geq 0.$$

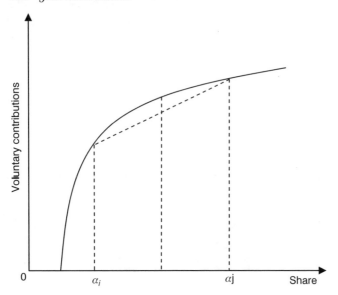

Figure 8.2 Share distribution and the level of common good

The solution to this problem is simply that the agent with the largest share is alone to contribute a positive amount, all the other agents 'free-riding' on his contribution.

Result 5: with a linear objective, the agent with the largest share is alone to contribute. His contribution increases with his share, à la Olson.

One can adapt the above model in various ways, for instance by imposing constraints on how much each agent can contribute. Richer results can then be obtained, with such small 'realistic' changes. Thus, Dayton-Johnson and Bardhan (2002) propose a model of a fishery, in which each fisherman has a given fishing capacity, say, c_1 and c_2. Each fisherman has to decide how much fish to catch in the first period, knowing that what is left at the end of the first period grows at a positive rate in the second period, so that efficiency requires that no fishing takes place in the first period. The time horizon stops at the second period. Both fishermen exhaust the second period stock of fish.

Constraint: no fisherman can catch more fish than his capacity.

Definition of the shares: in the second period, both fishermen, they share the stock in the proportion of their relative capacity. The share of fisherman 1 is thus $c_1/(c_1 + c_2)$.

The question is how much of the first period fish stock each fisherman decides to leave (or to catch).

Result: the preservation of the resource may be the lowest for intermediate levels of inequality, and highest for very small and very high levels of inequality. For high levels of inequality, preservation is only partial, with the smaller fisherman free-riding on the conservation efforts of the larger one.

The production technology of the collective good

We have so far assumed a very simple concave technology which transforms aggregate contributions into individual benefits. This raises three sets of issues:

(a)   the relationship between the level of common good and private benefits to the contributors;
(b)   the aggregation of individual contributions;
(c)   the concavity of the production process.

(a) We have assumed that individuals draw benefits in the collective good in proportion to their shares, thought as reflecting their initial endowments of some private good/asset/wealth. Other assumptions need to be investigated. Thus, Bardhan *et al.* (2000) do not put any restrictions about the precise nature of the relationship between the private asset and the individual benefits, so that they investigate the implications of the following benefit function:

$$U_i = f\left(a_i, G(\Sigma g_i)\right) - g_i$$
with $g_i \geq 0$.

Once again, the results obtained are very sensitive to the particular technological assumptions made, but there is no monotonic relationship between inequality and the provision of the collective good (or the efficiency of the Nash equilibrium).

(b) Another restrictive assumption in the present setting is that individual contributions simply add up to constitute the total input to the production of the common good. While this often makes sense when agents contribute money or labour time to the purchase or the building of a collective good, the assumption that individual contributions are perfect substitutes to one another is not always the best approach in other settings. Moreover, it tends to bias the results in favour of inequality, since what matters then is the total amount contributed, which increases with the share of the largest agent. By contrast, if all contributions are strict complements, more common good is produced when shares are equally distributed (Hirshleifer 1983; see also Bliss and Nalebuff 1984, and Cornes 1993).

In many joint projects, agents contribute levels of efforts and different skills, which are only partially substitutable. In this setting, what is the distribution of shares that maximizes the social surplus? This is the question raised by Baland *et al.* (2002). In an economy of *n* agents, each agent chooses his level of effort, g_i, to maximize:

$$U_i = \alpha_i \left[\sum_{j=1}^{n} g_j^{1-\sigma} \right]^{\frac{\alpha}{1-\sigma}} - g_i$$

where σ is the inverse of the elasticity of substitution (varies from 0 to infinity) and α is the decreasing returns parameter (< 1).

The question is: what is the distribution of α_j which maximizes ΣU_j?

The answer is that, for high enough degrees of complementarity, perfect equality in the distribution of shares maximizes the social surplus, hence generalizing the result obtained by Hirshleifer (1983). For low enough degrees of complementarity, the results are surprising (Figure 8.3).

(c) The production function G (.) may not be concave, because of setup costs, or threshold phenomena. Relaxing this assumption has also strong implications on the nature of the results obtained (see also Baland and Platteau 1997a and b).

Example (Gaspart *et al.* 1998): aggregate contributions must reach a critical level for the public good to yield any benefit; agents decide to contribute an amount g_i to the building of a common infrastructure, such that $G(\Sigma_j g_j) = 1$ if $\Sigma_j g_j$ is greater or equal to a constant C, and $G = 0$ otherwise.

If no share is large enough for a single agent to produce alone, there is a Nash equilibrium under which no agent contributes – there is coordination failure as only a limited number of contributions are needed; there are many Nash equilibria under which the common good is produced, where some agents may contribute more or less depending on the others' contributions. No precise predictions are possible, even though agents with larger shares will tend to appear more frequently in the possible equilibria, and their equilibrium contributions will, on average, be more important.

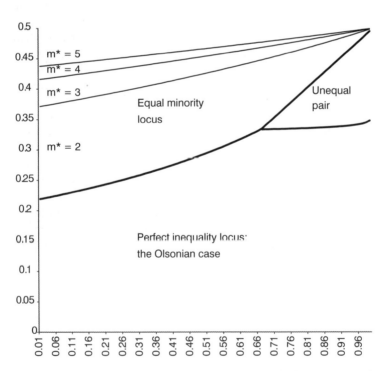

Figure 8.3 The optimal distribution of shares when contributions are not perfect substitutes

Some future directions

- Static equilibrium, in usually a one-shot game. It is worth investigating the role inequality plays when games are repeated a larger number of times (e.g. as in Bendor and Mookherjee 1987).
- We focused on decentralized provision to a 'common good'. Still, many collective action problems take the form of a regulatory authority, user group formation and influence on the regulated outcomes. Little is known about the 'technology' of collective action, in the sense of a collective regulatory scheme (see e.g. Banerjee *et al.* 2001).

References

Baland, J.M. and Platteau, J.P. (1997a) 'Coordination Problems in Local-Level Resource Management', *Journal of Development Economics*, 53, 197–210.

Baland, J.M. and Platteau, J.P. (1997b) 'Wealth Inequality and Efficiency in the Commons, Part I: The Unregulated Case', *Oxford Economic Papers*, 49(4): 451–82.

Baland, J.M., Dagnelie, O. and Ray, D. (2002) 'Inequality and Efficiency in Joint Projects', mimeo, University of Namur.

Banerjee, A., Mookherjee, D., Munshi, K. and Ray, D. (2001) 'Inequality, Control Rights and Efficiency: A Study of Sugar Cooperatives in Western Maharashtra', *Journal of Political Economy*, 109; 138–90.

Bardhan, P., Ghatak, M. and Karaianov, A. (2000) 'Inequality and Collective Action Problems', mimeo, University of California, Berkeley.

Bergstrom, T., Blume, S. and Varian, H. (1986) 'On the Private Provision of Public Goods', *Journal of Public Economics*, 29: 25–49.

Bliss, C. and Nalebuff, B. (1984) 'Dragon Slaying and Ballroom Dancing: The Private Supply of a Public Good', *Journal of Public Economics*, 25: 1–12.

Cornes, R. (1993) 'Dike Maintenance and Other Stories: Some Neglected Types of Public Goods', *Quarterly Journal of Economics*, 108: 259–71.

Dayton-Johnson, J. and Bardhan, P. (2002) 'Inequality and Conservation on the Local Commons: A Theoretical Exercise', *Economic Journal* (forthcoming).

Gaspart, F., Jabbar, M., Melard, C. and Platteau, J.P. (1998) 'Participation in the Construction of a Local Public Good with Indivisibilities: An Application to Watershed Development in Ethiopia', *Journal of African Economies*, 7(2): 157–84.

Hirshleifer, J. (1983) 'From Weakest Link to Best Shot: The Voluntary Provision of public Goods', *Public Choice*, 41: 371–86.

9 Overcoming asymmetries in the commons with sub-optimal strategies

An experimental exploration in the field[1]

Juan-Camilo Cardenas[2]

Asymmetries of opportunities, asymmetries of costs and benefits from the commons

Rural households satisfy their needs by interacting not only with markets, neighbours, and the state, but also with ecosystems. Households produce private goods for the market and for self-consumption by deciding daily over their use of land, labour and other inputs, by choosing technologies and by extracting resources from local commons such as mangroves, watersheds, forests or fisheries. These decisions have effects on their individual and group well-being by imposing externalities in time and space depending on the rates of use of such ecosystems.

Their income and well-being depend, therefore, not only on the allocation of their own assets but also on ecological goods and services that flow from the local commons they all use. This joint access to the commons creates problems of collective action among the users who face incentives for overexploitation, and where conservation measures are costly. These goods and services flowing from the local commons include not only excludable and rival goods like fibre, food or fodder, but also other public-good types such as water quality, biodiversity services like nutrient recycling and erosion control, as well as leisure, religious and cultural values.

These group externalities can be affected by heterogeneities within the group in various ways, which is the focus of this chapter. One of the ways in which such heterogeneities or asymmetries can be studied is by using experimental economics methods in order to understand more thoroughly the response by economic agents to different structures of individual and group incentives.

Wealth and other private opportunities can determine in various ways how people interact with local commons and how they interact with other commons users. On the other hand wealth determines private alternatives for the household, and therefore the need for exploiting a resource for which there is joint access. Marginal returns on private alternatives increase with assets such as education, land, livestock or equipment. Meanwhile, marginal returns on local commons depend on the individual extraction of resources from the commons, but also from the flow of other goods and services which decreases with aggregate extraction. Wealth and inequality can affect the institutional setting, e.g. the rights one has to use a resource, or the set of rules and norms that govern how a group manages and uses the commons; for instance, the level of enforcement of those rules, either endogenous or externally enforced and monitored, can vary depending on the wealth of the violator.

Wealth-related differences within the group of ecosystem users may influence in various and simultaneous ways the individual user's benefits and costs of exploiting the commons. As Baland and Platteau (1996: 80) argue:

> the case of heterogeneity may cover a wide variety of different situations which need to be carefully specified. Indeed, the meaning behind the notion of interest has to be clarified in order to be able to predict which type of resource user (the rich or the poor) is more likely to contribute.

Using the Olson model, but introducing more specificity to its characteristics, Sandler (1992) suggested that the effect of heterogeneity can go both ways, and that it might be also the case that the large can exploit the small in certain collective action situations.

Wealth might also affect preferences not directly related to the extraction of the commons, but regarding social relations with others, particularly when users attempt to deal with the collective action dilemmas associated with such joint use. The problem of bargaining over an optimal level of degradation when power among negotiating parties is discussed and formalized by Boyce (1994 and 2001).

Other types of asymmetries are relevant to this discussion. Location of the users, with respect to the resource, can introduce difficulties in solving the collective action dilemma. In irrigation systems, for instance, headenders and tailenders share the externality derived from maintaining the system, or from the aggregate flow of water. However, their location imposes different costs on each. Such asymmetry provides an advantage to those located closer to the head of the canal while increasing proportionally more the costs of over-extraction or under-maintenance on those at the end of the canal.[3]

The evidence to be presented in this chapter shows certain patterns regarding the relations between wealth inequalities and the sustainable use of the commons. The results expand the evidence on the negative effects that wealth inequality may have in the possibility of conservation of the commons. Further, the results may contradict those arguing that poverty in itself hinders collective action in the conservation of natural resources, and instead may be more compatible with the positions by Wade (1984) or Boserup (1965) regarding the capacity of agricultural societies to adapt and respond to constraints in resources availability via institutional or technological change. The results could therefore help to separate how poverty and wealth inequality play different roles, sometimes reinforcing, other cases opposing, in the decision-making behind group social dilemmas and incomplete contracts. The policy implications are central as increasingly public policies are moving towards poverty reduction and away from changes in the distributional structures.

A quick overview of the literature

An obligatory reference on the role that wealth differences may play in groups facing a collective action dilemma is Olson's (1965) proposition that when privileged agents within a group benefit proportionally more from the provision of the public goods generated by the collective action, they will contribute to its provision proportionally more, and that the rest of the group will therefore free-ride on such provision. Such proposition was qualified later, among others, by Sandler (1992) who in fact argues that the direction of the relation between heterogeneity of agents and collective action can go either way, depending on the specific parameters and form assumed for the production function of the public good. Another important point of reference in the role that inequality can play in the provision of public goods is the more formal development of Olson's proposition by Bergstrom *et al.* (1986). They study how the private income level of the individuals contributing to a public good affects aggregate contributions, yielding a similar conclusion to Olson, namely, that the wealthier will over-contribute to the public good while those with lower income levels will free-ride by not contributing.

There are however important distinctions to be made between pure public good and common-pool resource social dilemmas. These key distinctions may play a role in explaining how wealth and wealth differences affect the individuals' levels of cooperation in such social dilemmas, eventually in different ways.[4] As Ostrom *et al.* (1994) clarify, while the characteristic of rather costly exclusion of beneficiaries may be shared with public good dilemmas, commons dilemmas share the attribute of high levels of subtractibility with private goods. Units extracted by a user are no longer available for others in the group, therefore creating a set of incentives for free-riding which will vary on the aggregate level of use. Further extracted units may have different opportunity costs for some of the users, with respect to their other alternatives outside the use of the commons, therefore making the picture more complex. As I will discuss later using theoretical models, the decision to extract will, therefore, depend on these opportunity costs which may be asymmetric within the group.

More recent surveys on the role of heterogeneity and inequality in fact show the inconclusiveness of the literature on this matter. Varughese and Ostrom (2001) and Bardhan and Dayton-Johnson (2002) list a vast series of factors associated with heterogeneity and inequality, involved in commons dilemmas.

In a very synthetic and illustrative exercise, Agrawal (2002) makes a comparative analysis of three influential works that were published in the last decade on the issue of natural resource management and rural sectors: Wade's (1994) *Village Republics*, Ostrom's (1990) *Governing the Commons*, and a more recent book *Halting Degradation of Natural Resources* by Baland and Platteau (1996). Agrawal identified a taxonomy of factors suggested by these authors to affect commons use and sustainability. In all three cases there are elements related to our present discussion, but those involving poverty, wealth and inequality are rather inconclusive. On the one hand most authors identify higher dependence on the commons as a key factor for the users group to device self-governed institutions to avoid the tragedy. On the other hand, heterogeneity seems to work in different but simultaneous ways. While more heterogeneous endowments seem to be associated with a more sustainable commons management, interests, norms, identities and allocation of gains seem to contribute more to solving the dilemma when more homogenous and fair. In particular, the emergence of wealthier and innovative group members might be the key to the emergence of leaders that guide and promote the collective action (Baland and Platteau 1996). It is difficult to predict the net effect because in the field both mechanisms could operate simultaneously, namely, the greater contributions by the privileged subgroup, and unfair distribution of rights, allocation rules and outcomes.

Regarding heterogeneities in particular, Bardhan and Dayton-Johnson propose a comprehensive taxonomy of at least six types of heterogeneities based on a survey of theoretical and empirical works. The types of heterogeneity suggested by them are *income, wealth, exit options, location with respect to the benefits of the collective good, ethnic and social heterogeneities, and asymmetries in the rules choosing system*. In various recent works, Baland and Platteau (1996, 1997, and 1998) develop game theoretical models that explore how some of these factors may explain empirical evidence on an adverse effect of inequality in the management of common resources.

Much of the arguments for supporting the hypothesis that inequality may worsen the failures emerging from the commons dilemma emerge from the asymmetries in the information that the users have of the others' behaviour, and the difficulty of monitoring and enforcing contracts (self-governed or externally enforced) that restrict the overuse of the commons to avoid the tragedy. Bardhan *et al.* (2000) provide a more generalized explanation of why incomplete contracts and unequal rules in the opportunities of agents will generate socially inefficient outcomes, including a case for the use of local commons. Their argument is based on the proposition that once contracts become costly to enforce because of asymmetric information:

the distribution of wealth may affect allocative efficiency by its impact on:

- residual claimancy over income streams and hence incentives for both an agent's own actions and the agent's monitoring of the actions of others;
- exit options in bargaining situations;
- the relative capacities of actors to exploit common resources;
- the capacity to punish those who deviate from cooperative solutions; and
- the pattern of both risk aversion and the subjective cost of capital in the population.

These factors can easily be identified within the structure of a commons dilemma, and the structure of incentives, rules, norms and restrictions for the users group. I will discuss some of these below in order to provide a theoretical prediction to compare with the experimental evidence later on.

A simple model and experimental design of the commons

Assume a group of households surrounding an area (the commons[5]) with a certain set of attributes that provide ecological goods and services to society. Some of these households may have private control over certain assets such as livestock or land. Some may extract resources from the commons such as firewood or water from it, but they might also be affected like the rest of the village by the level of erosion, sedimentation, water pollution or biodiversity levels directly related to the aggregate extraction of resources from the natural area being exploited by these households.

Household's utility function

Define $U_i(x_i, \Sigma x_j)$ as the level of utility for user i, with $i \in (1, n)$ and $j = 1...n$, derived from the allocation of total effort e_i (e.g. total household labour) between private alternatives $(e_i - x_i)$ and individual extraction (x_i) of resources from the commons. Individual extraction x_i generates direct benefits to the household, but on the other hand individual allocation of effort into private alternatives $(e_i - x_i)$ will also increase i's well-being.

Aggregate allocation (Sx_j) of effort by the group of households into extracting the commons will generate a negative externality to i and the rest of the households. If benefits to i are increasing in i's effort extracting the commons as well as in i's effort into her own private alternatives, and decreasing in aggregate extraction, we can define then:

$$U_i = U_i(x_i, \Sigma x_j) = U_i\left[f(x_i) + g(\Sigma x_j) + w_i(e - x_i) \right] \tag{9.1}$$

In summary, in this model individuals maximize the net benefits from the different types of benefits they derive from extracting the commons, which are increasing in x_i (direct use value) and decreasing in Σx_j (indirect and non-use values), and from other sources based on private alternatives, which are increasing in $(e - x_i)$. These incentives create a typical group externality dilemma where individual and group incentives are not aligned. The central question, however, is how asymmetries of wealth can affect such a dilemma.

Using this simple model, we can think then of different types of inequalities that can affect the incentives for the individuals. Suppose that within a group there are differences in the individual wealth of players, where some players H have higher wealth than other L players. We can identify therefore different ways that such asymmetries enter into Equation 9.1. Let me mention the most common that are observed in the field.

Asymmetric marginal returns on extraction effort $\left[f_H(x_i) \neq f_L(x_i) \right]$.
Wealth can allow some agents to own equipment that increases the catch per unit of effort (e.g. larger or better nets, motor boats and chain saws).

Asymmetric marginal damages from over-extraction $[g_H(\Sigma x_i) \neq g_L(\Sigma x_i)]$.
Wealth can also provide H individuals with assets or advantages to locate their household far from the more vulnerable places subject to floods, sedimentation and erosion, all caused by over-extraction, or to provide privately the public goods they need (e.g. water pumping).

Asymmetric endowments of effort $[e_H \neq e_L]$.
With wealth, households can hire labour which increases their endowment of effort to extract more of the resource, in the cases where the optimization conditions are binding on such factors.

Asymmetric private options $[W_H \neq W_L]$
With private wealth people have access to higher education, to land and credit, all of which can increase the private marginal return on their labour allocated to private options, which they compare to the marginal return on the commons option.

Asymmetric utility functions, and other-regarding[6] preferences $[U_H(x_i, \Sigma x_i) \neq U_L(x_i, \Sigma x_i)]$.
In this case there might be other non-pecuniary factors playing a role in the decision making, such as inequity aversion (Falk *et al.* 2002). Trust in the rest of the group – a key driver of collective action – can vary for an individual i with the fraction of H and L players in the rest of the group.

The particular sets of experiments reported here explore some of these asymmetries, in particular the case of 'asymmetric private options' and 'asymmetric utility functions and other-regarding preferences'.

An economic experiment in the field

The basic components of the experiments conducted in the field are as follows. Fifteen sessions of eight people (i.e. 120 participants were recruited to be part of the experiments[7]), for 20 rounds, were conducted during the summer of 1998 in three rural villages of Colombia. In all three cases the villagers faced a similar dilemma – a forested area from which several products were extracted and from which other types of ecological services were generated for the community.

Through a simple decision-making exercise, eight participants in each group had to make repeated individual economic decisions that had salient economic incentives (in kind and cash) and with the kind of externalities in these group dilemmas. The average earnings, about two minimum-wage days of work, at the end of the sessions compensated for their time participating in the experiment and in a community workshop held at the end in each village.

Based on Equation 9.1, we constructed an incentives system which creates the environment for the economic decision-making exercise for the participants in the experiment. Recall x_i denotes the individual level of effort into extracting the resources. We define the direct use value function, based on benefits from extraction as $f(x_i) = \gamma x_i - \frac{1}{2} \phi (x_i)^2$, where γ and ϕ are strictly positive and are chosen in part to guarantee $f(x_i) > 0$, for $x_i \in (0, e)$. The strict concavity of $f(x_i)$ indicates diminishing marginal private returns to effort extracting resources. In the case of the indirect and non-use benefits that result from the aggregate level of extraction, we define $g(\Sigma x_j) = q^0 - \frac{1}{2} (\Sigma x_j)^2$, where b is a quadratic function of the aggregate amount of time individuals in the community spend collecting firewood; q^0 is interpreted to be the maximum level of non-use benefits when the natural area is in its ecological climax. The concavity of g is based on the assumption that at low levels of aggregate extraction the ecosystem is able to provide most of its ecological benefits but after a certain level of extraction these capabilities begin to diminish at increasing rates. And lastly, we can assume that the marginal return on the private alternative is a linear function, at a constant rate of w_i times the amount of effort not allocated into extracting resources from the commons. The parameter w_i will be used to introduce one particular type of heterogeneity within a group. By assigning some in the group a better private alternative (i.e. a higher w_i) and assigning the others a much worse option (lower w_i), we can compare with a baseline case where all players face the same payoffs structure, i.e. a w_i parameter equal for all.

Thus, we can express the utility function for our players as:

$$U_i(x_i, \Sigma x_j) = U_i[q^0 - \frac{1}{2} (\Sigma x_j)^2 + \gamma x_i - \frac{1}{2} \phi(x_i)^2 + w_i \times (e_i - x_i)] \qquad (9.2)$$

For each individual i, and for all j users of the commons.

Social versus individual efficiency in the use of the commons

One of the simplest cases is when all households face the same utility function and have the same marginal returns from their private and collective alternatives. From Equation 9.2 we can therefore express the joint welfare function as:

$$W(x) = n[q^0 - \frac{1}{2} (nx)^2 + \gamma x - \frac{1}{2} \phi(x)^2 + w_i \times (e - x)]. \qquad (9.3)$$

The first-order condition for the maximization of $W(x)$ requires that $-xn^2 + \gamma - \phi x - w = 0$. Solving for x, the optimal individual level of extraction should be $x^{so} = \gamma - w)/(\phi + n^2)$, which basically equates the marginal rate of gains from the private alternative to the sum of the marginal gains from extracting the commons and perceiving the other non-consumptive goods and services from extraction.

However, achieving such a socially efficient outcome will require certain institutions if the individuals do not coordinate their actions. Due to the structure of the payoffs function, there is a group externality and a conflict between individual and collective use of the commons. Each individual benefits from increasing its extraction, but suffers the costs of aggregate extraction for which it has only partial control, in the baseline case where we assume the absence of institutions correcting the externalities. If for the moment we assume again symmetry in the payoffs structures of the n individuals, and symmetry in the assumptions about the behaviour of the individuals, we can derive the optimizing decision x^* by each player as a best response function of the others' expected behaviour, and of the parameters in Equation 9.1. The symmetric Nash[8] equilibrium where each individual, by choosing x, maximizes the utility function shown in Equation 9.1, requires that:

$$x^{nash} = (\gamma - w)/(\phi + n) \tag{9.4}$$

Clearly $x^{nash} = (\gamma - w)/(\phi + n) > x^{so} = (\gamma - w)/(\phi + n^2)$ as long as $\gamma > w$ which we will assume for purposes of simplicity.[9] Given that the individual payoffs function is increasing in x_i, at equilibrium, these n individuals will find themselves in a commons dilemma where individual and group interests are in conflict. For any specified number of households, n, and for any level q^0 of ecological services for an unexploited commons, the distance in aggregate payoffs between the two benchmarks depends on the marginal returns from extracting resources (determined by γ and ϕ), and on the marginal rate on the private alternatives, w.

In the particular case of the private alternative, w, clearly higher exit options should under this model induce a reduction in the individual extraction of the commons and – at equilibrium – a socially superior outcome given that the reduction in gains for less resource extracted is more than compensated by the increase in the outside option, and also by the increase in ecological benefits from a lower aggregate extraction. This would clearly suggest, for policy purposes and under the assumptions given here for the rationality and incompleteness of the contracts among the individuals, that improving the private alternatives of the commons users such as higher returns on land or labour, better crops prices, subsidies for education, and the like, should reduce the pressure over natural resources over which there is joint access and lack of institutions.[10]

However, recall that the symmetric Nash equilibrium that supports these conclusions assumes that the individuals cannot devise any institution to correct the failures generated by the social dilemma. Rather they are following their non-cooperative Nash best responses given the assumption that everyone else in the user group will do so. Once external agents or self-governance institutions emerge that attempt to align the individual and collective goals, these predictions would just provide a set of benchmarks but not necessarily a prediction of actual behaviour.

Conducting the experiments[11]

In brief, during our experiments each participant had to decide in each round the number of months (from zero to eight) that she would allocate to extract resources from a jointly used forest. For a group of eight players we would collect the eight private decisions, add the total effort for the group, announce it in public and let each player check her earnings from a payoffs table (see note 11) by reading the column (player's decision) and the row (the sum of the months by the rest of the group). The earnings in the table are for one round, and each cell representing earnings in Colombian pesos at a rate of 1300Col\$=1US\$. Each session would take between 17–20 rounds.

The net earnings from such decision were based exactly on the payoffs function in Equation 9.2. It is clear what the dilemma is. By increasing the level of extraction (months in the forest) one increases earnings, but those earnings decrease with the total group's extraction, giving rise to the group externality. For the symmetric case, when all eight players had the same payoffs table (see note 11), we chose the parameters of the payoffs structure such that if every player choose one month in the forest, for a maximum of eight, the group would achieve the social optimum solution where group earnings would be maximized and where the group would be at a Pareto optimal point. And if each player chose six months, they would find themselves in the symmetric Nash equilibrium at about 24 per cent of the social efficiency. From the S table it is clear that when everyone else chooses $x = 6$, there are no incentives to deviate one's months in the forest.

For 10 of the 15 groups we constructed groups of eight players all of which had the same payoffs (S) table, while for the other five groups the eight players had a heterogeneous assignment of the payoffs tables as follows. For each of the (HL) groups, and in a random and public procedure, two of the eight players received an H table while the other six received an L table.[12] The values used for the w_i parameter were 20, 30 and 60 for the L, S and H tables respectively. In this way the average for the marginal return on the private option remained equal in both the symmetric and asymmetric cases, at 30 points.

The Nash equilibrium for this asymmetric (HL) game would predict that those players with the L tables should allocate their entire eight months in the forest, and therefore those with H tables should not use the forest (i.e. choose zero months) since their best alternative is much better at such point. In the same manner, the social optimum solution to this asymmetric game would require that the six L players chose $x = 1$ month while the two H players chose not to allocate effort into the forest.[13]

The summary of the predicted benchmarks for the Nash outcome and the social optimum case are included in the following Table 9.1. for both the symmetric game where all eight players had the same payoffs table, and for the asymmetric game where two players had the H table and six had the L table.

Notice that at the group level the earnings for the two benchmarks are comparable (the Nash solution represents about 24–26 per cent of the earnings at the social optimum), although the individual earnings for the two benchmarks differed substantially.

Each of the sessions was run in two stages. In the first stage players would make repeated decisions for about eight rounds and then the monitor announced that the first stage ended and that a second stage was going to start with a different rule, group communication in between rounds in this case. Then they would make repeated decisions for another eight to 10 rounds. The last round in each stage was never announced in advance to avoid possible problems of people changing their strategy in the last round. Under this experimental design we could observe individual choices for the symmetric and asymmetric payoffs function, and also we could observe how groups would deal, after face-to-face communication, with such asymmetries in the cases of the HL groups and compare them to the S groups.

Two major predictions can be used as benchmarks to compare to the observed behaviour. First, under the first stage players should approach the Nash prediction in Table 9.1, and in particular, the L players should choose the highest levels of

Table 9.1 Experimental benchmarks based on the payoff tables (see note 11)

Two benchmarks for equilibria in the commons game		Symmetric game (all 8 players)	Asymmetric game	
			Two H	Six L
Social optimal solution	Individual decision (X^{opt})	$X_s^{opt} = 1$	$X_H^{opt} = 0$	$X_L^{opt} = 1$
(GroupMax strategy)	Yields ($) per round per player	$Y_s^{opt} = \$645$	$Y_H^{opt} = \$801$	$Y_L^{opt} = \$602$
	Group yields	$SUMY_s^{opt} = \$5,160$	$SUMY_{HL}^{opt} = \$5,214$	
Nash solution (IndivMax strategy)	Individual decision (X^{nash})	$X_s^{nash} = 6$	$X_H^{nash} = 0$	$X_L^{nash} = 8$
	Yields ($) per round per player	$Y_s^{nash} = \$155$	$Y_H^{nash} = \$117$	$Y_L^{nash} = \$191$
	Group yields	$SUMY_s^{nash} = \$1,240$	$SUMY_{HL}^{nash} = \$1,380$	

effort, and the H players the lowest. For the second stage the conventional prediction of the selfish homo-economicus player would be that communication, being not binding, should have no effect on behaviour given that the group conversations were free and open and also because we did not allow them to make any threat or promise of transferring earnings after the session. Therefore, any commitment or agreement made during the group discussion would not be binding as their decisions would still be kept confidential and private by the experimenter. Such hypothesis has been labelled as the 'cheap talk' but has no strong evidence to support it. As mentioned in previous studies (Ledyard 1995, and Ostrom *et al.* 1994) face-to-face communication has proved to be a powerful mechanism for inducing more cooperative behaviour.

A summary of the experimental results

Table 9.2 shows the summary (means) for the decisions and outcomes during the two stages, for the different payoff tables. Given that players shifted their decisions in different ways within stages, the means were calculated also for the first three and last three rounds of each stage, as shown in the four columns of the table. The variables compared are the average choice variable, X (months in the forest), Y$ (average round earnings), and SUMY$, the average of group earnings for the two types of groups (HL and S).

In general all types of players showed average behaviours that did not fit well in the model of self-regarding payoffs maximizing players. The differences in the second stage were even greater. However, the differences across types (S, L, H tables) seem to show the different incentives derived from the private alternative.

Table 9.2 Average choices and outcomes for the symmetric (S) groups and the asymmetric (HL) groups before and after communication. Columns represent rounds periods (1–3), (6–8), (11–13), (17–19)

		Periods during games			
		Before communication		After communication	
Variable	Table	A1 = (1–3)	A2 = (6–8)	B1 = (11–13)	B2 = (17–19)
X	H	3.667	2.462	2.100	2.467
	L	4.767	4.128	3.278	3.044
	S	4.388	4.388	3.783	3.616
Y$ (earnings)	H	$406.63	$522.08	$618.80	$634.37
	L	$347.71	$447.86	$503.44	$498.39
	S	$368.17	$371.41	$444.47	$460.14
SUMY$ (group)	HL	$2,900	$3,731	$4,258	$4,259
	S	$2,945	$2,971	$3,556	$3,681

Thanks to the introduction of the face-to-face communication, all groups, symmetric and asymmetric, improved their earnings. Consistent with previous experimental evidence (Ostrom *et al.* 1994, and Ledyard 1995) such a device improves cooperation even if it is not binding; and also consistent with such evidence, the variation within groups and across groups is wide and unexplainable from the structure of payoffs.

For the case of the 10 groups under the symmetric payoffs, the improvement was only partial.[14] However the wide variation in behaviour at individual and group levels deserved a deeper exploration of the video and audio tapes available from those experiments. Some groups were able to devise more effective agreements than others during the experiment, and the level of compliance with the agreements seemed to be related to the composition of the group, as reported elsewhere (Cardenas 2003 and 2002). For those groups, we could explain individual and group cooperation as a function of the social distance to the others in the group, and also as a function of the actual wealth by the participants in the experiment. Recall that these eight subjects knew each other, as they lived in the same village and shared the same commons in reality. In brief, players who were more familiar with resource extraction and more dependent on its use cooperated more in the experiment. Also, using data from their actual wealth, we observed that poorer and more homogenous groups devised and followed an agreement that was more effective in increasing earnings.

Asymmetric payoffs: different exit options

This chapter, however, deals with the problem faced by the asymmetric groups before and after communication was allowed. As argued before, exit options should affect choices, and in fact this is how much of the theoretical literature has dealt with the problem of inequality. Asymmetric payoffs create different incentives to contribute to the public good or refrain from doing so. Olson's argument of the privileged group goes along these lines, that if a privileged member of the group individually benefits from providing the public good, she might provide it despite the free-riding of the others in the group. That is, if the marginal returns from contributing to the collective action are higher for some, they are more likely to cooperate.[15] However there is another side to this problem. It might be the case that the marginal return from not contributing is also asymmetric, that is, that the opportunity cost of allocating effort into the private next best alternative is different for some in the group. In other words, that some may depend more on the commons because their marginal return on their private alternative is much lower due to wealth effects. Ostrom *et al.* (1994) explore in their experiments a heterogeneous payoff structure, but based on an asymmetric endowment of tokens to be allocated to the private or collective market. In their design they allowed some players in the group to allocate greater levels of tokens to either fund (private or collective), but they did not explore the case of some players deriving higher returns on the tokens in the private market as we did here.

Let us focus now on the behaviour and outcomes for the asymmetric payoffs groups. Notice from the Table 9.2 above that these asymmetric (HL) groups achieved higher earnings than the symmetric case, even if we compare the end of the first non-cooperative stage. In another paper (Cardenas *et al.* 2002) we discuss in detail the incentives behind this asymmetric structure and why these HL groups seemed to perform better than the symmetric one. There we explain how a combination of a lower dependence on the others' extraction by the H players, and a much higher dependence on collective action by the L players, induced a lower group level of extraction, which was reinforced during the second stage, although it was mostly by the cooperation by the six L players since the two H players maintained their strategy closer to the Nash prediction. Such behaviour is summarized in Figure 9.1. Chan *et al.* (1996) have shown similar results from a pure public goods experiment. Although comparisons in the incentives structures have to be made with care, they also found that when they introduced asymmetric income distributions within groups, aggregate contributions increased, but because of a higher contribution by those endowed with lower income levels, contrary to the Bergstrom *et al.* (1986) game-theoretical model predicting that unequal income would increase the private provision of the public good.

Nevertheless, the higher performance of the asymmetric groups also showed a wide variation across the five groups, and deserves a further exploration of the data. Once again, reviewing the audio and video tapes from these groups provided a key source for understanding the success and variation for these groups.

Shared norms versus optimal solutions: strategies to solve the asymmetries through self-governance

One of the ways in which cooperation emerges and results in higher social outcomes in group dilemmas is by developing shared norms by resource users (Ostrom 1990 and 1998, and Ostrom *et al.* 1994). Throughout these experiments different norms or agreements emerged clearly during the communication rounds. Most agreements

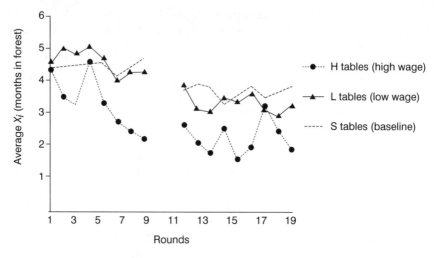

Figure 9.1 Average 'months in the forest' for the symmetric (S) groups and for the asymmetric (HL) groups (from Cardenas *et al.* (2002))

were aimed at defining what the best decision should be for each player. The specificity of the agreement varied, from a general statement of 'reducing the months in the forest' to stating clearly exactly what every player should choose from the table. Obviously the symmetric (S) groups found that the social optimal solution was achieved at $X = 1$ much faster and more frequently than the asymmetric groups.

When reviewing the videotape data from the discussions, we could see that the asymmetric (HL) groups found it more difficult to agree on what a better X decision should be for the group and earnings. Much of the time allowed for communication was spent understanding the incentives, with low success in many cases. In several groups one can observe confusion on what a change in one's months in the forest do to individual earnings or to the group outcome. Further, when realizing that the different tables implied different incentives and returns from cooperating or from defecting, it became more difficult to agree on a group maximizing strategy. It is easy to notice from the tables that for many rows the best responses for H and L players go in opposite directions, despite the fact that earnings in general increase if all players choose lower levels of effort or months in the forest. This created some confusion among group players when discussing the possible agreements to increase earnings. Such confusion might explain the variance in group efficiencies across the asymmetric groups as shown in Table 9.3.

As mentioned before, even at the first stage the divergent paths by H and L players allowed the group efficiency to increase as the Nash best response by H players was to decrease their months in the forest when the group level was at higher levels. Then at the second stage, the groups attempted various strategies when allowed to communicate. The communication was used to induce a shared norm about what the group should achieve and how to do it.

Table 9.3 Average group efficiency by periods for five asymmetric groups

	Average group efficiency			
	No communication		Communication	
Asymmetric Group	Rounds (1–3)	Rounds (6–8)	Rounds (11–13)	Rounds (17–19)
1	37.26%	80.58%	70.24%	63.70%
2	70.54%	73.51%	86.60%	88.17%
3	42.90%	77.17%	84.59%	84.46%
4	68.32%	76.49%	69.38%	84.93%
5	59.03%	53.59%	97.54%	87.17%
Mean	55.61%	72.27%	81.67%	81.69%

The question, then, is how developing a shared norm in each group affected the outcome. We know from Table 9.1 that for the asymmetric case, the optimal solution needs a mixed strategy of $X_H = 0$ and $X_L = 1$ or 2. We will call this the 'differentiated strategy' (or Differ-X). However we could see in the tapes that some groups did not attempt such strategy, and, instead, tried an easier norm of just 'reducing X'. We will label this as the 'equal strategy' or Equal-X.

A simple way to test what kind of shared norm emerged during the communication rounds for each group would be to look for a statistical difference in the average X between H and L players. Such tests are shown in the following Table 9.4. The p-values in the table show if there is a statistical difference in average choices by H and L players within each of the five groups for the first (B1) and last (B2) three rounds in each stage, as well as for the entire set of rounds in the second stage (B). The p-values that resulted were small enough (i.e. reject the null hypothesis that the averages are equal) to show the cases in which there was a statistical difference in choices between H and L players, i.e. the groups that attempted a 'differentiated X' strategy. When the p-values were large enough we conclude that H and L players were choosing months in the forest that were statistically similar.

To achieve the maximum group earnings solution this strategy would be sub-optimal, but it was a much easier norm to agree on, and it could be much easier to follow and control by the group during the communication rounds. The next step then is to compare the outcomes for the two strategies, Differ-X and Equal-X. The lower part of Table 9.4 shows the average earnings for the two sub-groups, and the graph below (Figure 9.2) shows the average earnings for the two strategies. Clearly the sub-optimal strategy of a shared and simple rule of doing the same allowed those three groups to achieve higher earnings. Further, the figure shows how the 'Differ-X strategy' groups in fact achieved efficiency levels quite close to the symmetric baseline case.

Conclusions

Self-governance requires the development and sustainment of certain norms to induce a cooperative behaviour that overcomes the problem of collective action.

Table 9.4 Non-parametric tests for differences in choices within groups between H and L players

Tests for 'shared rules' (equal versus proportional appropriation)

Comparing X choices between payoffs tables (H L)

p-values (Wilcoxon–Mann–Whitney test)		After communication			
		B1 (11–13)	B2 (17–22)	B (11–22)	Result
Test: (H versus L)	Group 1	0.126	0.025	0.001	=> Different X
by groups	Group 2	0.919	0.916	0.377	=> Equal X
	Group 3	0.306	1.000	0.440	=> Equal X
	Group 4	0.100	0.096	0.001	=> Different X
	Group 5	0.199	0.231	0.212	=> Equal X
Test: Y$ Group earnings	Differ-X	$3,640	$3,875	$3,757	
	Equal-X	$4,670	$4,515	$4,593	
	p-value (t-test):	0.001	0.13	0.001	

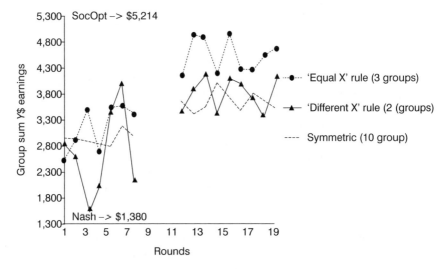

Figure 9.2 Average group earnings for two strategies: 'differentiated vs equal X strategies'

Communication within groups is a powerful tool to achieve this, among others, because it helps the members to agree on group-oriented strategies. Hackett *et al.* (1994) studied the effect of communication in solving commons dilemmas by introducing heterogeneity in the initial endowment to be allocated in the private and public goods investments under a Common Property Resource (CPR) experimental design. They found that despite heterogeneity, communication remained effective in inducing cooperation. However, homogeneity made the development of rules simpler and easier to endorse and enforce. Their findings also suggest that the complexity introduced by heterogeneity leads to confusion and difficulties on maintaining the agreements discussed in the communication stage:

> Face-to-face communication is a powerful tool. It is handicapped significantly, however, in situations in which group members are unable to develop or sustain the social capital necessary for enduring commitments. (1996: 123)

The difficulty to create or sustain an agreement based on a 'differentiated X strategy' in our experiments is one of these cases. Such strategy makes it more difficult to create group identity if we compare to the case with a homogenous level of effort which yielded higher group earnings

In these experiments we could observe, or create, enough variation in the levels of wealth and inequality, and observe possible statistical relations with the environmental outcome, namely, the conservation or over-exploitation of a commons. Some of these inequalities can be expressed through the asymmetries in the private options for the members as in the experiments reported here. In other cases even under symmetric payoffs from using the commons, other types of non-material asymmetries (e.g. cultural or in social distance) can restrict cooperation as reported in Cardenas (2003 and 2002).

Some lessons emerge from these experiments. Lower exit options, measured by the marginal value from effort not allocated into exploiting the commons, induced greater cooperation within a group given the higher dependence of income on the conservation and use of the commons. Those with lower exit options were willing and able to cooperate more in solving the dilemma after communication was allowed. In the case of these asymmetric payoff experiments, the 'poverty' was assigned randomly to six of the players. But recall also that in the case of the 10 symmetric groups, higher cooperation was observed for the groups whose members were in reality poorer or that owned fewer assets.

The asymmetries in the HL groups were approached in different ways by the groups. However, the greater gains from cooperation happened for the groups that attempted a simpler – although sub-optimal – strategy of a shared norm of all doing the same, i.e. an equal-x decision for H and L players.

The results might contribute to some debates on the role of poverty and inequality when solving collective action and group dilemmas as in many environmental problems. Poverty in itself is not a limitation to cooperation in the commons. Further, poorer but homogenous groups seem to be willing to cooperate in order to increase their collectively generated individual benefits, even if at personal cost. This however does not invalidate the necessity for addressing problems of poverty and lack of freedoms (Sen 1999) which affect other issues of well-being including, eventually, the use and management of natural resources. The only claim from these results is that blaming the poor and not other institutions that create poverty and mismanagement of commons might deviate the attention away from structural problems, such as inequality.

Inequality, however, does seem to affect cooperation. Heterogeneous groups can find it more difficult to cooperate if, for instance, there are wealth distances in the group that limit the possibility of getting group communication to be effective to build trust, cooperation and a commonly shared goal. Even if all agents depend equally on the commons, inequality and wealth distance within a group can limit cooperation, at least for the case when groups were allowed to communicate and devise a self-governance solution.

Public policy regarding the agricultural sector in much of the developing world has reduced attempts to change directly the distribution of wealth towards more equal institutions. Greater attention is being paid to progressive policies focused on the poorest, and on the creation of safety-nets. Such strategy surely can change the equality of opportunities and freedoms of rural people, particularly for the share of their income depending on transactions based on complete markets. However, there is still an important share of their well-being and income that depends on solving collective action dilemmas such as in the case of resources from the commons (e.g. food, energy and water); further, there are other cases where contracts are incomplete (e.g. rural credit) that are still relevant and critical to well-being in the agricultural sector. In these cases inequality in general can have a significant and negative effect in solving the failures, and therefore the focus on public policies that are aimed at the distribution of wealth should continue, in this case over efficiency grounds besides equity and justice.

The results presented here suggest that the ratio of income sources coming from collective to individual activities does not necessarily explain the emergence of collective action in cases of overuse of the rural commons. Although poverty increases the marginal relative value of a unit of the resource extracted from the commons, the poor can also compensate their less advantageous private alternatives with more effective community institutions to reduce the losses from the collective action dilemma. Through more effective, adaptive, local and self-governed institutions, they reduce the social losses when confronting the free-riding behaviour within their group. However, when inequality is present in the group, other types of difficulties emerge for making these self-governance mechanisms effective and then the gains from cooperation are reduced giving way to the losses from lack of opportunities.

Notes

1   This chapter emerged from a lecture presented at the XV workshop of the ISER International School of Economic Research, 'Environment, Inequality and Collective Action', Siena, Italy, 16–23 June 2002. My gratitude to the participants and commentators. This research has been possible thanks to a Research and Writing Grant from the John D. and Catherine T. MacArthur Foundation, and support from the School of Environmental and Rural Studies at Javeriana University.

2   Profesor Facultad de Economia – CEDE, Universidad de Los Andes, Bogota, Colombia.

3   Bardhan and Dayton-Johnson (2002) survey some of these issues in detail. Lam (1998) discusses the particular problem of headenders and tailenders for a set of irrigation systems in Nepal.

4   The two types of dilemmas show similarities in the sense that the individual action in one game is the mirror image of the other, i.e. extracting in the commons versus contributing to a public good. In both cases there is a conflict between the individual and the group interests generated by the incentives where each individual sees her payoffs increased by her own extracting (not

contributing or free-riding) but the group's payoffs decrease with aggregate extraction (aggregate free-riding). The main differences between the two types of dilemmas, however, emerge from having different structures of the marginal per capita ratio between the public good and the private alternative (MPCR). A careful inspection of the payoff structures of public good and common-pool resources will show that most public goods structures involve a constant MPCR while the commons involve MPCR that are variable on the aggregate level of cooperation in the collective action.

5 'Commons' will not be assumed here only as a common property resource, but in a more general way as a resource area for which there is joint use by a group, and partial leves of excludability and of sustractibility (Ostrom *et al.* 1994). Thus, state owned natural parks may fall within this definition, particularly if exclusion rules are very costly to enforce. Also, natural areas that provide congestible public good benefits to households in the form of non-extractive benefits will coincide with the definition used here.

6 By other-regarding preferences, I refer to a component in the utility function of an individual that involves the well-being or outcome of another individual. Altruism, envy or spite can be sources of other-regarding preferences (Bowles 2004).

7 In each of the three villages the invitation was made to all adults older than 15 years of age, with basic knowledge of numbers being able to add, subtract and read numbers. We avoided having two people from the same household in the same group. Each session lasted about three hours between explaining the instructions of the game, the experiment itself, and the response to a set of questions in a questionnaire including demographic, economic and personal data.

8 By 'Nash' prediction or solution I will assume the prediction of the homo-economicus model where the player maximizes her own material payoffs, i.e. the pure self-regarding preferences model.

9 For $\gamma < w$, we would be assuming that the marginal return on the first unit of effort into extraction is less than the marginal return on a unit in the exit option which would make the commons not an option.

10 One could also make the argument that such improvement in household human and manmade capital could also improve the marginal returns on the individual extraction of the commons via changes in the parameters γ and ϕ. One clear example is better fishing or logging equipment that could increase the quantity of resources extracted per unit of labour.

11 The complete set of instructions which were read to the participants can be downloaded from: http://www.prof.uniandes.edu.co/~jccarden or from the author at jccarden@uniandes.edu.co

12 They were told that those with the H tables would receive in average higher returns while those with L tables would receive lower points. All tables were posted in a large poster and visible to everyone. Also, during the examples or practice rounds the monitors used both tables to illustrate the differences.

13 Notice that in this benchmark H players also choose x = 0. The reason for this is that they again benefit more from their private alternative – depend less on the commons – while the L players depend mostly on the group's cooperation conserving the commons.

14 Similar experiments in the lab with students, reported in Ostrom *et al.* (1994), show a much higher improvement in cooperation after communication. There is no other evidence of similar experiments in the field to make a comparison.

15 Sandler (1992) develops the Olsonian propositions in detail and shows that depending on the production function for the public good, such claim may or may not hold.

References

Agrawal, A. (2002) 'Common resources and institutional sustainability', in E. Ostrom, T. Dietz, N. Dolsak, P.C. Stern, S. Stovich and E.U. Weber (eds), *The Drama of the Commons*, National Research Council, Washington, DC: National Academies Press.

Baland, J.M. and Platteau, J.P. (1996) *Halting Degradation of Natural Resources: Is there a Role for Rural Communities?*, New York: Oxford University Press.

Baland, J.M and Platteau, J.P. (1997) 'Wealth inequality and efficiency in the commons: the unregulated case', in *Oxford Economic Papers*, 49: 451–82.

Baland, J.M. and Platteau, J.P. (1998) 'Wealth inequality and efficiency in the commons: the regulated case', in *Oxford Economic Papers*, 50: 1–22.

Bardhan, P., Bowles, S. and Gintis, H. (2000) 'Wealth inequality, wealth constraints, and economic performance', in A.B. Atkinson and F. Bourguignon (eds) *Handbook on Income Distribution, Volume 1*, North Holland: Elsevier.

Bardhan, P. and Dayton-Johnson, J. (2002) 'Unequal irrigators: heterogeneity and commons management in large-scale multivariate research', in E. Ostrom, T. Dietz, N. Dolsak, P.C. Stern, S. Stovich, and E.U. Weber (eds) *The Drama of the Commons*, National Research Council, Washington, DC: National Academies Press.

Bergstrom, T, Blume, L. and Varian, H. (1986) 'On the private provision of public goods', *Journal of Public Economics*, 29: 25–49.

Boserup, E. (1965) *The Conditions of Agricultural Growth: The Economics of Agrarian Change under Population Pressur*, Republished 1993, London: Earthscan Publications.

Bowles, Samuel (2004) *Microeconomics: Behavior, Institutions and Evolution*, Princeton, NJ: Princeton University Press.

Boyce, J. (2001) 'Power inequalities and the political economy of environmental protection', Paper prepared for the Conference on Inequality, Collective Action, and Environmental Sustainability, Santa Fe Institute, September 2001.

Boyce, J.K. (1994) 'Inequality as cause of environmental degradation', *Journal of Ecological Economics*, 11: 169–78.

Cardenas, J.C. (2003) 'Real wealth and experimental cooperation: evidence from field experiments', *Journal of Development Economics*, 70: 263–89.

Cardenas, J.C. (2002) 'Wealth inequality and overexploitation of the commons: field experiments in Colombia', Working Paper Series, Santa Fe Institute.

Cardenas, J.C., Stranlund, J.K. and Willis, C.E. (2002) 'Economic Inequality and Burden-Sharing in the Provision of Local Environmental Quality', in *Ecological Economics*, 40(3): 379–95.

Chan, K., Mestelman, S., Moir, R. and Muller, R.A. (1996) 'The voluntary provision of public goods under varying income distributions', *Canadian Journal of Economics*, XXIX(1): 54–69.

Falk, A., Fehr, E. and Fischbacher, U. (2002) 'Appropriating the commons: a theoretical explanation', in E. Ostrom, T. Dietz, N. Dolsak, P.C. Stern, S. Stovich, and E.U. Weber (eds) *The Drama of the Commons*, National Research Council, Washington, DC: National Academies Press.

Hackett, S., Schlager, E. and Walker, J. (1994) 'The role of communication on resolving commons dilemmas: experimental evidence with heterogeneous appropriators', *Journal of Environmental Economics and Management* 27(2) (September): 99–126.

Lam, W.F. (1998) *Governing Irrigation Systems in Nepal: Institutions, Infrastructure, and Collective Action*, Oakland, CA: ICS Press.

Ledyard, J.O. (1995) 'Public goods: a survey of experimental research', in J.H. Kagel and A.E. Roth (eds) *Handbook of Experimental Economics*, Princeton, NJ: Princeton University Press.

Olson, M. (1965) *The Logic of Collective Action: Public Goods and the Theory of Groups*, Cambridge, MA: Harvard University Press.

Ostrom, E. (1990) *Governing the Commons: The Evolution of Institutions for Collective Action*, Cambridge and New York: Cambridge University Press.

Ostrom, E., Gardner, R. and Walker, J. (1994) *Rules, Games and Common-Pool Resources*, Ann Arbor, MI: University of Michigan Press.

Ostrom, E. (1998) 'A behavioral approach to the rational choice theory of collective action', *American Political Science Review*, 92(1) (March):1–22.

Sandler, T. (1992) *Collective action: Theory and Applications*, Ann Arbor, MI: University of Michigan Press.

Sen, A. (1999) *Development as Freedom*, New York: Knopf.

Varughese, G. and Ostrom, E. (2001) 'The contested role of heterogeneity in collective action: some evidence from community forestry in Nepal', in *World Development*, 29(5): 747–65.

Wade, R. (1994) *Village Republics: Economic Conditions for Collective Action in South India*, San Francisco, CA: ICS Press.

Part IV

Institutions, inequalities and the environment

10 Environment and global public goods

Graciela Chichilnisky[1]

A human-dominated Earth

Human beings – or their close genetic relatives – have lived on Earth for several million years. Yet only recently has human activity reached levels at which it can affect fundamental natural processes – such as the concentration of gases in the atmosphere, the planet's water mass and the complex web of species that constitute life on earth. Scientists find that the most environmental damage has occurred in the last 60 years. Why? What happened 60 years ago? What is the origin of today's global environmental problems – and what can be done to resolve them?

In the last 50 years the human species has consolidated its dominance of the planet, while at the same time embarking in an unprecedented and rapid form of economic development known as industrialization. This chapter offers a historical perspective of the economic causes behind the global environmental problems we face today, and of the economic solutions that can be anticipated.

Our global environmental problems originate from the tremendous industrial growth in the world economy since World War II. Industrialization is voracious in the use of natural resources. Economic growth during this period was fuelled by abundant and inexpensive raw materials, most of which were exported by poor countries and imported by industrial countries. In the last 50 years international trade grew three times faster than the countries themselves – and with it grew the international demand for energy derived from fossil fuels, and the demand for other natural resources such as wood, which are extracted from developing countries' forests.

International trade in resources is directly implicated in the global environmental problems we face today. Most of the natural resources we use worldwide are extracted from developing countries, where they are held usually in conditions of common property or free-access property, and end up being consumed in the rich industrial countries. In a divided world economy in which poor countries trade with rich nations, natural resources are treated as common or free-access property, which distorts the market behaviour. Resources are extracted from developing nations and sold internationally at low prices because they are treated as common property. Low resource prices lead to poverty at home, and to over-consumption in the rich nations that import them. Most of the planet's carbon emissions come from oil that is burned in rich nations. The USA, for example, imports most of its oil from developing nations – and it is the largest oil consumer in the world originating 26 per cent of the planet's carbon emissions. We now know that carbon emissions could change the global climate and become catastrophic for the survival of the human species.

Even though international markets are at the root of the problem, nevertheless, this chapter suggests that international markets could also be instrumental in finding solutions. Global resource markets play a key role in the problem – and a solution may be found in markets involving global public goods, such as markets for trading the rights to release emissions into the atmosphere. A word of caution is needed here. Emission markets, which trade the 'rights to use the planet's atmosphere', are in reality trading global public goods, and as such are very different from the markets that economists have known for centuries. Global emission markets are totally new – these markets were introduced by the author in the Kyoto Protocol that was created in 1997 by the United Nations Framework Convention on Climate Change (UNFCCC), see Chichilnisky 1996 and Chichilnisky and Heal 2001. The Kyoto Protocol was finally ratified in January 2005, becoming international law.

Markets for emission trading are key to the global environment – and global equity issues are important for the efficient functioning of these global markets. A resolution of the global environmental problems that concern us today depends therefore upon achieving a measure of equity in the global economy. While conventionally opposed to each other, the notions of *equity* and *efficiency* now converge in a world economy that is increasingly dominated by goods and services based on environmental resources and on knowledge – both of which are global public goods.

International scope

Global environmental problems require a new form of international cooperation. Such problems include the impact of CFCs on the ozone layer of the atmosphere, the loss of the planet's biodiversity, and the problem of acid rain and the international transport of sulphur dioxide, SO_2. Ozone depletion was successfully tackled by the international community through the Montreal Protocol of 1987, which restricted the use of CFCs in industrial products. With respect to greenhouse gas emissions, in 1996, the Intergovernmental Panel on Climate Change (IPCC) reported that human induced emissions of carbon and other greenhouse gases have a 'discernible effect on climate'.

While there is still uncertainty about the scientific evidence on climate change, the risk of climate change is now known to be real, and potentially catastrophic. The greenhouse effect is a typical example of a problem where international cooperation is required. No single country can tackle this problem on its own.

How does the greenhouse effect work? Figure 10.1 illustrates the situation.

Greenhouse gases form a 'blanket' which traps energy within the atmosphere, thus warming the Earth. The source and composition of greenhouse gases is represented in Figure 10.2, which shows that human activity is the main source – and this is human activity for economic purposes.

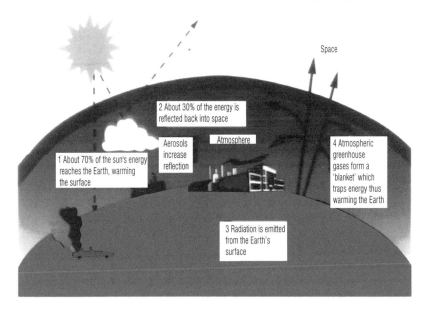

Figure 10.1 How the greenhouse effect works (Source: Chichilnisky 2001: 5)

Most of the destruction of the earth's ecosystems is driven by economic incentives. Forests, where most known biodiversity resides, are cleared for the extraction of natural resources (such as oil and wood products) or for growing cash crops and grazing livestock. These are mostly sold for export markets. Climate change is driven by the use of energy which increases with industrialization – and energy in the world is mostly produced by burning fossil fuels – leading directly to higher emissions of greenhouse gases. Greenhouse gas emissions in turn drive the risk of climate change. Biodiversity destruction is led by the destruction of habitat in forests – for economic purposes. And CFC emissions that damage the ozone layer originate from industrial products.

Yet while the causes of global environmental problems are economic, the effects are physical or biological. Because the effects are physical, the economists underestimate them – and since the causes are economic, physical scientists cannot find solutions. Climate change therefore requires thinking and acting across social and physical disciplines. This is a major challenge.

Population and the global environment

Many believe that global environmental problems emanate from the enormous growth of human population on the planet. The phrase 'the population bomb', created by Paul Elrich more than 25 years ago, symbolizes this perspective. The view has been erroneously used to imply that the developing countries – whose populations grow on the whole faster than industrial nations – are the main source of danger to the global environment.

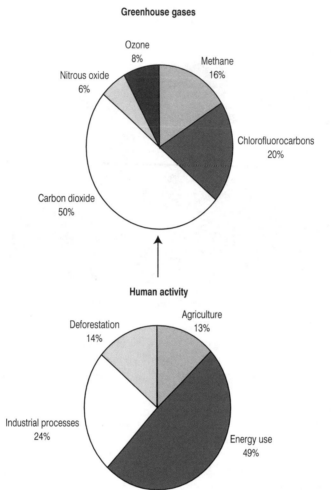

Greenhouse gases

Ozone
8%

Methane
16%

Nitrous oxide
6%

Chlorofluorocarbons
20%

Carbon dioxide
50%

Human activity

Agriculture
13%

Deforestation
14%

Industrial processes
24%

Energy use
49%

Figure 10.2   Sources and composition of greenhouse gases (Source: Chichilnisky 2001: 6)

The view is not without merit – global environmental issues are related to the human dominance of the planet. If there were no humans, the problem would cease to exist. However the implications that have been drawn from this view are incorrect because they presuppose a linear response from the cause to the effect – it presupposes that the regions with more humans are the ones responsible for most of the problems. This is incorrect. Developing nations have indeed higher rates of population growth on the whole. However, it is now widely known that developing nations – and the regions of the world with the lowest population growth – are not the main cause of global environmental damage. Indeed the regions with higher population growth contribute far less to the global environmental problems than those with lower population growth. This is because it is industrialization that causes the environmental problems we have today – not population pressures by themselves. And the areas that industrialize faster are also those with lower population growth. Therefore lower population growth is associated with the largest environmental impact and damage. This is true for biodiversity loss, for carbon emissions and also for CFC emissions, all of which emanate principally from industrial nations, as illustrated in Figure 10.3, which presents current and projected annual emissions of carbon to the atmosphere from fossil fuels in selected countries and regions – and their rates of population growth. The figure shows that there is a negative association between population growth and emissions. The higher the emissions the lower the population growth, and reciprocally the higher the population growth the lower the emissions. Of course, in the future, most emissions could originate in developing countries as they industrialize – because industrialization is resource intensive. This shows once again how separating the world's nations into developing and industrialized can be helpful in understanding the environmental problems we face today. Elrich's predictions of run away population growth in the planet have been proven incorrect. Currently the United Nations has adjusted its population growth predictions so that the planet has now a rate of growth nearing replacement levels. This means that the human populations are becoming stable throughout the world.

More precisely, with respect to the global environment, the population connection that is usually drawn is incorrect. Table 10.1 presents data providing the share of world carbon dioxide emissions, population, and GDP for industrial and less developed countries. It shows that historically and currently economic output is the major determinant of carbon emissions. Indeed, industrial countries emit 60–70 per cent of all emissions, and have 23 per cent of the population. Reciprocally, developing countries have 77 per cent of the world's population and emit 30–40 per cent of all emissions. In terms of GDP, 84 per cent of the world's GDP is in industrial nations and 16 per cent in developing nations. There is a direct positive relation between GDP and emissions – and a direct negative relationship between emissions and population.

Sustainable development and basic needs

In 1974, to address these issues, I introduced a way to measure economic progress that is different from GDP – the concept of development based on the 'satisfaction of basic needs'. Basic needs development does not measure GDP as the foundation of economic progress – but rather, as its name indicates, it measures the satisfaction of basic needs by the population to indicate economic progress. This concept was introduced so that economic development patterns would be consistent with environmental constraints, and this was studied in five continents, empirically and mathematically, within the Bariloche Model (Herrera *et al.*, 1974 and 1976). This led directly in 1987 to the Brundtland Report, which introduced the concept of sustainable development in the Earth Summit in Rio de Janeiro, Brazil. Sustainable development is based on the satisfaction of basic needs. But the Brundtland report

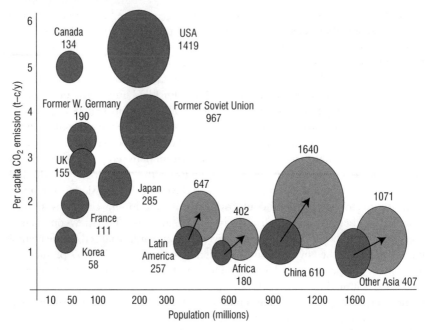

Figure 10.3   Current and projected annual emissions of carbon (Source: Chichilnisky 2001: 9)

Table 10.1 CO_2 emissions

Countries	Cumulative	Current	Population	GNP
Industrial	70%	60%	23%	84%
Less developed	30%	40%	77%	16%

Source: Author's calculations based on World Bank data

links the basic needs of the present and those of the future – the definition proposed here for sustainable development is 'development that meets the needs of the present without compromising the ability of future generations to meet their own needs' (WCED 1987).

Scientists find that most of the damage to biodiversity and the atmosphere has occurred in the last 50 years. Why? What happened 50 years ago?

Emissions of greenhouse gases and biodiversity destruction are connected to the rapid pace of industrialization since World War II. Here is a brief historical background.

After World War II, following the destruction of Germany and Japan, the US share of the world economy was 40 per cent. Today the USA is back to 25 per cent of the world economy, as it was before the war.

Following World War II, the US pattern of economic development became a global benchmark. This is a pattern of development based on rapid industrialization, led by a deep and extensive use of natural resources – a frontier approach to economics. Global institutions were created, and their metrics for economic progress reinforced this vision of resource-intensive economic development:

- The World Bank.
- The International Monetary Fund.
- The United Nations.
- NATO.
- The current system of national accounts.

The American dream went global and the Bretton Woods Institutions created by Lord Maynard Keynes played an important role in making this possible. Keynes viewed the role of the Bretton Woods Institutions as replacing wars by trade – using the differences among nations as a source of gains from trade rather than military strife. His dream succeeded beyond anyone's expectations and in the 60 years since the end of World War II international trade grew four times more than the world economy.

North and South

The rapid increase in emissions of carbon dioxide of the last 50 years was due to the burning of fossil fuels linked to intensive energy use for production of goods and services in industrial nations. The globalization of the world economy since World War II has intensified a pattern of resource use by which developing nations extract most natural resources, exporting them to industrialized nations at prices that are often below replacement costs. Through the international market, industrial nations, which house less than 20 per cent of the world's population:

- Consume most forest products (pulp, wood).
- Consume most products produced through the clearing of forests (cash crops such as cotton, livestock including beef and veal).
- Consume most mineral products (copper, aluminum, and fossil fuels such as petroleum). The industrial countries are geographically located, on the whole, in the Northern hemisphere of the planet, and are therefore often referred to as the North. Table 10.2 and Figure 10.4 provide data on such consumption from the World Resources Institute based on the Food and Agriculture Organization (FAO) of the United Nations. As it can be seen, the North's economy represents the main driving force in global environmental problems.
- Have produced and continue to produce 60–70 per cent of the world's CO_2 emissions.[2]
- Emit most CFCs which have been responsible for damage to the ozone layer of the planet.

Figure 10.5 shows that most emissions of greenhouse gases originate in energy use and production (including the production of electricity) – and 84 per cent of

Table 10.2 Consumption of mineral products

Fossil Fuel Consumption (gigajoules/person)

Classification	1961–65	1966–70	1971–75	1975–80	1981–85	1985–90
Industrialized	115.82	142.53	165.70	1895.2	153.81	160.06
Developing	7.37	8.26	10.34	12.91	14.53	17.26

Source: Analysis by World Resources Institute (1993) based on data from United Nations Statistical Division (UNSTAT). *UN Energy Tape* (UNSTAT, New York, 1992).

Aluminium Consumption (metric tons/100 people)

Classification	1961–65	1966–70	1971–75	1975–80	1981–85	1985–90
Industrialized	5.99	9.00	11.65	13.50	12.56	14.13
Developing	0.13	0.23	0.37	0.51	0.58	0.69

Sources: Analysis by World Resources Institute (1993) based on data from:
1. World Bureau of Metal Statistics, *World Metal Statistics Yearbook 1992* (World Bureau of Metal Statistics, Ware, UK, 1992).
2. Metalgesellschaft Aktiengesellschaft, *Metalstatistik 1961–71* and *Metalstatistik 1970–80* (Metalgesellschaft AG, Frankfurt, 1972 and 1981).

Copper Consumption (metric tons/100 people)

Classification	1961–65	1966–70	1971–75	1975–80	1981–85	1985–90
Industrialized	6.17	7.00	7.45	7.90	7.50	8.05
Developing	0.17	0.17	0.29	0.34	0.38	0.48

Sources: Analysis by World Resources Institute (1993) based on data from:
1. World Bureau of Metal Statistics, *World Metal Statistics Yearbook 1992* (World Bureau of Metal Statistics, Ware, UK, 1992).
2. Metalgesellschaft Aktiengesellschaft, *Metalstatistik 1961–71* and *Metalstatistik 1970–80* (Metalgesellschaft AG, Frankfurt, 1972 and 1981).

Beef and Veal Consumption (kilograms/person)

Classification	1961–65	1966–70	1971–75	1975–80	1981–85	1985–90
Industrialized	24.53	27.37	28.58	29.65	27.69	27.17
Developing	3.98	4.06	3.84	4.21	4.05	4.29

Sources: Analysis by World Resources Institute (1993) based on data from Food and Agriculture Organization of the United Nations (FAO), *Agrostat PC*, on diskette (FAO, Rome, 1992).

Cotton Consumption (kilograms/person)

Classification	1961–65	1966–70	1971–75	1975–80	1981–85	1985–90
Industrialized	6.91	5.32	5.30	4.70	4.77	5.35
Developing	1.93	2.29	2.40	2.29	2.75	2.60

Sources: Analysis by World Resources Institute (1993) based on data from Food and Agriculture Organization of the United Nations (FAO), *Agrostat PC*, on diskette (FAO, Rome, 1992).

World Trade Matrices, 1990 a

Mineral fuels (d)

	Imports			
Exports	OECD	Developing	Transition	Total
OECD	91,392	11,233	1,106	103,732
Developing	159,721	39,850	2,320	201,891
Transition	20,833	2,499	6,301	29,634
Total	271,946	53,583	9,727	335,257

Manufactures (e)

	Imports			
Exports	OECD	Developing	Transition	Total
OECD	1,587,007	377,995	41,668	1,997,690
Developing	278,812	143,390	5,069	428,172
Transition	26,936	12,600	33,709	73,244
Total	1,883,775	533,984	81,366	2,499,105

the world production is located today in industrial nations. At the same time, in the developing countries – which are geographically located on the whole in the Southern hemisphere of the planet – there is currently an intensive and extensive destruction of ecosystems for agricultural production and for mineral extraction, mostly directed towards export markets.

As shown in Figure 10.6 most remaining forests in the world are still in the developing countries where tropical deforestation is occurring most rapidly today. This reflects the fact that the industrial countries have already exhausted most of their own forests in their own process of industrialization and it follows that most environmental resources in the planet are currently in the South – forests and biodiversity are examples. The South emits fewer greenhouse gases into the planet's atmosphere – roughly 30 per cent of the world's total – even though it has about 80 per cent of the world's population.

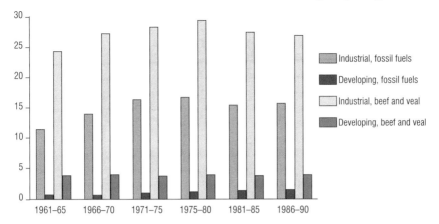

Figure 10.4 Industrial and developing country consumption of fossil fuels (10 ×gigajoules p.c.) and beef and veal (kilograms p.c.) (Source: Chichilnisky 2001: 38)

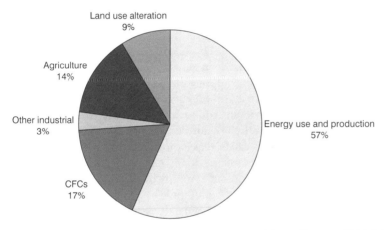

Figure 10.5 Where emissions of greenhouse gases originate (Source: Chichilnisky 2001: 25)

Even though the South has the most remaining forests and biodiversity, and has produced less damage to the global environment, it is, however, most vulnerable to the effects of environmental damage, such as climate change, on its:

- food production;
- living conditions;
- impact of increase in sea level.

The North therefore produces the most risks, but the South bears them more. The origins of today's environmental dilemmas involve the historical coupling of two different worlds through the international market – the industrialized and the

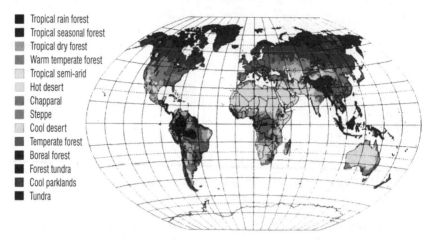

Figure 10.6 Holdridge life zone classification (Source: Leemans and Prentice, 1990)

developing regions of the world that we described as the North and the South Trade with Common Property Resource. The matrix drawn in Figure 10.7 gives a geometrical representation of world trade in mineral fuels in 1990. This illustrates a persistent pattern of trade in resources during the last 50 years between industrial and developing nations. The figure illustrates international trade in mineral fuels in 1990 – confirming that the developing countries are the main exporters of fuels – which they export mostly to the OECD countries. This fits the pattern of North–South trade already discussed in which developing countries are those mostly extracting and exporting natural resources – in this case, mineral fuels – the same resources which are imported and consumed mostly by the industrial countries.

What explains this pattern of North–South trade in resources? One possibility is that there is a geographical coincidence, that the developing nations of the world mostly in the Southern hemisphere are rich in natural resources such as mineral fuels. Coincidentally, perhaps, the South has a comparative or absolute advantage in natural resources. This explanation would view the pattern of trade simply as a manifestation of countries' respective advantages at work – as traditional trade theory of international trade would predict.

The facts however do not fit a conventional view of comparative or absolute advantages. While Middle Eastern countries indeed have abundant oil reserves Saudi Arabia and Kuwait have the largest known reserves in the world – the big consumers such as the USA do not import their oil mostly from the Middle East, but rather from a variety of sources including prominently South America. And many of the countries the USA imports oil from – such as Mexico and Ecuador – have shallow oil resources that are widely expected to be depleted soon. Nevertheless they export oil to the USA, a nation that has one of the largest reserves of unconventional oil sources in the world (e.g. tar sands). What could be an alternative explanation of this trade pattern?

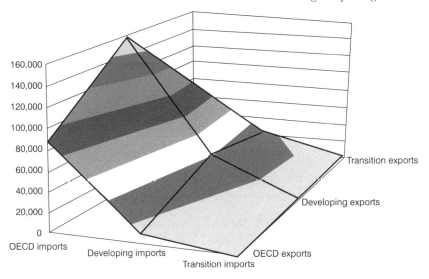

Figure 10.7 World trade matrix. mineral fuels, 1990, ($ million) (Source: Chichilnisky 2001: 40)

This pattern of North–South trade can be explained in substantial measure by a historical difference between agricultural and industrial societies, a difference in the property rights regimes for resources which prevail in these two types of nations. The existence of a link between trade patterns and property rights in resources was proposed in the early 1990s (Chichilnisky 1991 and 1994) and has gained acceptance ever since.

In developing nations natural resources are typically held as common property, for example oil deposits are often government property, or else they are held as 'open access' property – extracted on a 'first come, first served' basis as fish, wood and other forest products. The industrial revolution was generally preceded by the privatization of resources – such as the 'enclosures movement' in the UK, which privatized the commons. This difference in property rights regimes has been shown to lead, through the international market, to a pattern of trade such as the one we observe between the North and the South. It explains the historical pattern by which countries in the South export resources to the North even though these countries may not be resource-rich and even though the industrial countries may be richer in resources themselves. The facts are that developing countries hold most resources as common property (or open access) while in industrial economies these are usually held as private property (Dasgupta 2000).

In a world where agricultural societies trade with industrial societies (the North–South world, described here), international markets magnify the 'tragedy of the commons', the over-extraction of natural resources that typically occurs under common property or open access regimes. The resulting agricultural output is mostly sold in international markets (pulp, wood, cash crops and livestock) (Chichilnisky 1994).[3] In sum, natural resource exports, and the world's use of natural resources, exceed what would be optimal if private property conditions prevailed, and the attendant prices in the global markets are also below what would prevail with private property rights. International markets – even if they work competitively – fail to reach an optimal solution. International trade is therefore skewed, leading to resource exports from countries that do not have a comparative advantage in resources – and resource imports in countries that do. Indeed the historical coupling of the North and the South through the international market leads directly to over-extraction of resources in the world, to resources prices that are lower than replacement costs, and also to over-consumption of these resources in the industrial countries that import them.

Differences in property rights regimes between agricultural and industrial societies – the North and the South – explain therefore:

- The South's over-extraction of natural resources for the international markets.
- Why the South sells natural resources below replacement costs.
- Why emphasizing resource exports does not necessarily benefit developing countries.
- Why there is a false impression of resource abundance and comparative advantage leading to a global version of the 'tragedy of the commons'.
- Why the North over-consumes resources – and the South over-extracts them.
- Why the earth's resources are undervalued in international markets.
- Why lower wages and thus poverty persists in resource exporting nations.
- How the economies and the people in developing nations are also undervalued in economic terms.

Figure 10.8 illustrates two different supply curves for resources in a domestic economy of the South – and illustrates the problem of over-extraction and under-pricing of resources. One supply curve (the steeper one) is derived from the standard conditions of efficient supply behaviour in private property economies. At each price in the vertical axis the quantity supplied is measured in the horizontal axis, and this is that quantity at which prices equal marginal costs of extraction, therefore ensuring that the market has a Pareto efficient solution under private property regimes. This curve, however, is not the one that prevails when there are no private property rights, it does not prevail for example under 'common property' or 'open access' for resources. Using a game theoretical approach introduced in Dasgupta (2000) to explain through a Nash equilibrium the supply of the resource provided under common property or open access regimes, we show in Chichilnisky (1994) that the supply curve that prevails under common property is 'flatter' than the private property supply curve.

This means (as shown in Figure 10.8) that at each price the country will supply more resources than it would do under private property regimes. The implications of using a flatter supply curve for resources detonate throughout the entire system and establish that: (1) more will be exported than is optimal, and (2) that exports will be at lower prices than is appropriate (namely under private property). Gains

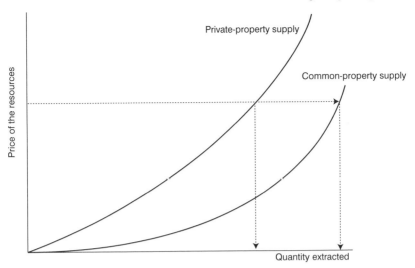

Figure 10.8 At every price, the supply of resources is larger with common property regimes than it is with private property. This gives a false impression of resource abundance or 'comparative advantage' in exporting resources in developing nations, which hold resources typically as common property. (Source: Chichilnisky 2001: 48)

from trade fail to materialize under these conditions, and the theory of comparative advantage is in question and often fails as well.

Through this process, resource-intensive trade leads to an increasingly divided North–South world.

Property rights – the global commons

The problematic North–South trade patterns just discussed could be improved by accelerating the privatization of natural resources in developing countries. History suggests that in any case, this would probably occur naturally in those countries that are undergoing a transformation from agricultural to industrial societies. The suggestion would therefore be to accelerate a process that occurs naturally as their economies evolve.

Privatizing resources in developing countries, however, may be impractical in any reasonable time-scale. The world is trying to reach a solution to the overuse of natural resources now in order to prevent biodiversity destruction and climate change – both of which are potentially catastrophic and irreversible events. Privatizing land – for example land reforms policies in South Africa and South America – has proven to be very contentious and difficult to implement. It quickly degenerates into political issues of a scope that seems difficult to overcome in the short term.

It is clear, however, that the lack of private property on resources, which are inputs to production, leads to the overuse of the planet's atmosphere, that is the 'sink' in which outputs are deposited. Over-consumption of petroleum as an input leads, for example, to the overuse of the atmosphere as a 'sink' for the greenhouse gases that are part of the output. We saw that resources are held as common property in developing nations – but the planet's atmosphere is held as 'free-access' property in the entire world. Perhaps rather than privatizing on the input side, one can privatize on the output side. This means privatizing the world's use of the global commons rather than privatizing the developing countries' use of resources. One would expect somewhat less contention from allocating property rights to the use of the atmosphere, simply because these are property rights that have not yet been defined so the problem is still in a more fluid state.

The suggestion is therefore to privatize the global commons. Rather than privatizing forests and mineral deposits 'on the ground' we can privatize, for example, the rights to use the atmosphere of the planet as a carbon 'sink', and the use of biodiversity.

While this seems a far-fetched idea, it is exactly what happened in the 1997 Kyoto Protocol, which provided a table in its Appendix delimitating the rights to emit of Annex B countries – which are mostly the industrial nations. Chichilnisky and Heal (2001) reproduces the Kyoto Protocol. This table was an international attempt to determine the property rights for the various countries – in their use of the atmosphere of the planet as a 'sink' of greenhouse gases associated with burning of fossil fuels and other industrial activity. The Kyoto Protocol has not yet been ratified – mostly because of the opposition from the USA which voted for it originally but has not supported its ratification. Yet the provisions of the original treaty ensure that this year, with just one more nation voting in its favour, the Kyoto Protocol will become international law.

Global emissions markets: equity and efficiency

Property rights, in the use of the planet's atmosphere, are the first step. The Kyoto Protocol goes further, offering also a first step in the creation of global markets for trading such rights. These are called 'global emission markets', emerging for the first time in history. Emission markets by themselves are not new – they have a short but successful history. In the USA they were introduced by the Chicago Board of Trade to trade permits to emit SO_2. They were deemed to be very successful and cost-effective in the reduction in emissions of sulphur dioxide by power plants in the USA.

There are other examples of environmental markets (Chichilnisky and Heal 2000) but the Kyoto Protocol offered the first opportunity to trade a global public good – the use of the planet's atmosphere – in terms of trading the rights to emissions of greenhouse gases.

Once global emissions markets are created – and it is expected that some time will pass before they will be – the next question is how to ensure that they will be efficient. Successful markets require successful regulation – the most successful markets in the world are regulated not to restrict trade, but to ensure healthy competitive conditions. For example, the Securities Exchange Commission (SEC) in the USA is very active in promoting the sharing of information in securities markets and sternly penalizes 'insider trading' in which asymmetric information exists.

Efficiency of emissions markets however requires different conditions than efficiency of standard private markets. New economic findings establish that there is a deep connection between the distribution of property rights (rights to emit) and the efficient performance of markets with privately produced public goods – such as the use of the planet's atmosphere (cf. Chichilnisky and Heal 2001).

Global public goods

Efficiency in trading permits requires that more emission rights be given to the developing countries – just as provided in the Kyoto Protocol. Indeed, the Protocol places no constraints on the emissions rights of developing nations – all its restrictions are on Annex B countries which are industrialized. Therefore it implicitly provides more emission rights to the developing countries. But what is the connection between efficiency in emissions markets and the emission rights given to developing countries?

Conventional wisdom up to now has been that the distribution of property rights does not affect the efficiency of markets. Standard thinking is that equity and efficiency are independent from each other in competitive markets, and indeed often orthogonal to each other as well. What makes this situation different?

Indeed, the 'Coase theorem' has shown that equity and efficiency are unrelated in markets created to internalize externalities. The textbook case concerns property rights to pollute that are assigned to a factory producing soot that interferes with a laundry's right to produce clean clothes. The externality is the soot. One compares the rights of the factory to emit soot to the rights to clean air of the laundry itself. Coase showed that, in the end, whoever gets the rights to pollute or to clean air does not matter – as long as we assign property rights clearly and let the parties trade them, the market solution will be efficient. Of course, the assignation of rights does affect the welfare of the traders and therefore the equity of the situation, but it does not affect the efficiency of the market solution. This common wisdom is universally accepted, and it is correct. Then why does this not apply to our case? Why is equity in the assignment of carbon emission emissions rights connected with the efficiency of markets?

Global emission markets for CO_2 are different because they involve a global public good, namely the quality of the atmosphere of the planet as measured by its concentration of carbon dioxide. In Coase's case, the initial distribution of rights does not matter because he considers markets with private goods, goods that are 'rival' in consumption, such as soot.

Indeed, the soot that the factory deposits on the laundry's clean clothes is 'rival' – whatever soot is deposited in one shirt, it is not deposited on another shirt. The situation however is different in the case of carbon dioxide, which spreads very evenly and stably throughout the entire planet's atmosphere, requiring 60 years to decay. These are physical properties of carbon dioxide which do not depend on social organization. They make carbon dioxide concentration a global public good

– the result is that everyone in the planet is exposed to the same concentration of CO_2, in China as well as in South America, Europe or Australia The concentration of carbon in the atmosphere is one for all – it is a global public good. And markets that trade the rights to emit carbon are therefore markets trading a global public good. Carbon dioxide is in addition a very special public good, quite different from classical public goods that are produced by governments, such as roads and law. Carbon dioxide is produced by individuals as a by-product of private activities such as heating one's home or driving one's car.

Carbon emissions rights are therefore traded in markets for privately produced public goods. These are unusual markets, of a type that economists are not used to. However, these markets are increasingly important because they include also the trading of knowledge rights. Like carbon concentration, knowledge is a privately produced public good and one that is fast becoming the most important input of production in advanced societies. Markets with privately produced public goods are new and different but should not be considered exotic. They are possibly the most important type of markets in the new century.

Here is the main difference of markets with privately produced public goods, which alters fundamentally Coase's conclusions. Market efficiency now requires more conditions than in standard markets for private goods: (1) the usual conditions for efficiency are needed, namely that marginal costs should equal prices, and equal marginal rates of substitution among commodities are needed, but now in addition a new condition is required, (2) the Lindahl, Bowen, Samuelson conditions for efficiency with public goods is needed, which requires that the marginal rate of transformation equals the sum of the marginal rates of substitution among the traders. This latter condition derives from the public goods property of 'no rival' consumption – namely that in the end everyone consumes the same amount of the public good. As we said, in our case, this means that everyone in the world is exposed to the same concentration of carbon dioxide in the atmosphere of the planet. This is the reason for which additional efficiency conditions must be required in emissions markets which do not exist in markets with private goods. The additional conditions required for efficiency 'over-determine' the market equilibrium. Therefore while market solutions exist, they are not efficient in general. New policy tools are required to reach and implement efficient market solutions. It turns out that the distribution of property rights on the global public good across nations is the right tool and has the right dimensionality to solve this problem. Distributing properly these initial rights to emit allows one to reach solutions that clear the markets and are, simultaneously, efficient in the use of the global public good.

This, in a nutshell, explains the tight relation between efficiency and equity in markets for global public goods.

Equity is an important consideration for developing nations in the climate negotiations. Industrial countries have emphasized, instead, market mechanisms and economic efficiency as their own priority. The unexpected connection that we discussed between equity and efficiency is therefore a potential overlap between the two regions' priorities and interests – the interests of the North and of the

South. Since North–South conflicts of interests have led to debate and delays in ratifying and implementing the Kyoto Protocol, an overlap in interests of the North and of the South is welcome. However, the connection between equity and efficiency that emerges here is new in economic terms, and is still not completely understood yet. More economic work remains to be done, academic as well as diplomatic and political. Properly interpreted and implemented, however, the Kyoto Protocol may signal the way to a sustainable future.

Notes

1 This chapter is based on a series of lectures that the author gave at the International School for Economic Research (ISER) University of Siena, Pontignano, Italy, in the Summer of 2002, as well as three public lectures – The Pegram Lectures – presented by the author at the Brookhaven National Laboratories in Long Island, New York, USA (Chichilnisky 2001). Articles and books on which this chapter is based are also Chichilnisky and Heal 1991, 1993 and 2001, and Chichilnisky 1995, 1996 and 1997. See also www.chichilnisky.com

2 See 'The Kyoto Protocol and the Carbon Cycle', G. Chichilnisky: Pegram Lectures, Brookhaven National Laboratories, L.I.2001, included in www.chichilnisky.com

3 See reference to Barbier in Chichilnisky 1994.

References

Chichilnisky, G. (1991) 'Property rights and the dynamics of trade in renewable resources', in C. Carraro (ed.), *Trade, Innovation and the Environment*, Dordrecht: Kluwer.

Chichilnisky, G. (1993) 'Property rights and the dynamics of renewable resources', in *Structural Change and Economic Dynamics*, 4: 219–48.

Chichilnisky, G. (1994) 'North–south trade and the global environment', *American Economic Review*, Vol. 84: 851–74.

Chichilnisky, G. (1995) 'The economic value of the earth resources', *Trends in Ecology and Evolution (TREE)*, 6: 135–40.

Chichilnisky, G. (1996) 'The greening of the Bretton Woods', *Financial Times*, 10 January.

Chichilnisky, G. (1997) 'Development and global finance: the case for an international bank on environmental settlements', *Discussion Series* No 10, New York: UNESCO and UNDP.

Chichilnisky, G. (2001) 'The Kyoto Protocol and the carbon cycle', *Pegram Lectures*, New York: Brookhaven National Laboratories.

Chichilnisky, G. and Heal, G. (1991) *Oil and the International Economy*, Oxford: Clarendon Press and Oxford University Press.

Chichilnisky, G. and Heal, G. (1993) 'Global environmental risks', *Journal of Economic Perspectives*, 7: 65–86.

Chichilnisky, G. and Heal, G. (2001) *Environmental Markets: Equity and Efficiency*, New York: Columbia University Press.

Dasgupta, P. (2000), *The Control of Resources*, Oxford: Oxford University Press.

Herrera, A., Chichilnisky, G. *et al.* (1976) 'Catastrophe and new society' Toronto: International Development Research Center (IDRC).

WCED (World Commission on Environment and Development) (1987) *Our Common Future*, Brundtland Report, Oxford and New York: Oxford University Press.

11 Economic institutions and governance of the commons

Daniel W. Bromley

What are institutions?

'Institutions are the means whereby going concerns – families, firms, villages, nation states – regularize and channel individual action and interaction' (Bromley 2006).[1] The study of institutions brings us into direct contact with the socially constructed norms, working rules and entitlements that shape and influence individual fields of action. Institutions create markets by creating the socially sanctioned legal space within which ownership of income streams might (and might not) be permitted. Markets, after all, are not about exchange of mere possession. Rather, markets are about exchange of ownership of future values arising from recognized legal control (ownership) of those values (Bromley 1999). Most economists seek to explain market behaviour in terms of prices, preferences, and the maximization of utility. However, utility is not a reason for action. Desires can function as explanations for action only if there are reasons for those desires. The human will in action, looking to the future, constitutes plausible reasons for choice and action. When applied to the realm of public policy, again the human will in action, looking to the future, offers clarity of thought about the reasons for particular institutions. And since institutions are the plausible reasons for actions, understanding reasons for particular institutions will get us close to clarity regarding the essence of institutions.

Understanding the institutional foundations of the economy poses a conceptual challenge for many economists. Contemporary economics has come to be defined as the study of self-interested individuals choosing among alternatives so as to maximize utility. In such choice-theoretic manifestations, institutions are treated as constraints on individual maximization algorithms. Therefore, it is common, even among those who study institutions, to regard them as constraints on individual action. For instance, one common definition insists that 'Institutions are the rules of the game in a society or, more formally, are the humanly devised *constraints* that shape human interaction' (North 1990: 3) (emphasis added). This treatment of institutions as constraints reveals something important about efforts within the 'new institutional' economics to fashion a theory of institutions, and of institutional change. Notice that if institutions are seen as constraints then the intellectual problem becomes one of trying to explain why these pernicious constraints exist in a democratic market economy. More seriously, this view of institutions seems to suggest that markets are natural human phenomena against which these 'humanly devised constraints' impose conditions that impede the otherwise beneficent properties of presumptively 'free markets.' We see a version of this when 'new institutionalists' such as North express puzzlement as to why political entrepreneurs do not emerge to drive out 'inefficient' institutions that merely serve redistributive purposes rather than the more 'natural' purpose of economic growth. Notice the teleology here – that the purpose of the nation state is to foster growth, and institutions ought to be crafted to promote that purpose.

Not only is this view value laden, it may be motivated more by the desire to protect the existing choice-theoretic models of contemporary economics – and in the process reify methodological individualism – than to gain a clear understanding of the meaning and role of institutions in an economy. Indeed, North has written:

> Defining institutions as the constraints that individuals impose on themselves makes the definition complementary to the choice theoretic approach of neoclassical economic theory. Building a theory of institutions on the foundation of individual choice is a step toward reconciling differences between economics and the other social sciences. The choice theoretic approach is essential because a logically consistent, potentially testable set of hypotheses must be built on a theory of human behavior. The strength of microeconomic theory is that it is constructed on the basis of assumptions about individual human behavior (even though I shall argue for a change in those assumptions). Institutions are a creation of human beings. They evolve and are altered by human beings; hence our theory must begin with the individual. At the same time, the constraints that institutions impose on individual choices are pervasive. Integrating individual choices with the constraints institutions impose on choice sets is a major step toward unifying social science research.
>
> (North 1990: 5)[2]

I very much doubt that the other social sciences seek a 'unification of social science research' based upon the precepts of contemporary neoclassical economics. More seriously, this flawed formulation misses the fact that institutions are at once both liberation and restraint of individual and group action. North's formulation also sabotages any hope of developing a coherent theory of institutional change. After all, if institutions are only constraints on individual action, how is it possible to explain the existence of institutions in a democracy? How can something that only constrains individuals possibly be approved through democratic processes? The usual answer is that those with the most 'power' are able to impose their will on others.[3] Notice that this view is circular, and that it encourages the 'villain theory' of economic institutions. Indeed, a variant of this villain theory already exists in economics – we call it 'rent seeking'.

More seriously, how is it possible to regard the prohibition of child labour as nothing but a constraint? Are not children liberated by such a rule? How is it possible to regard pollution control laws as a constraint? Are not the current victims of pollution liberated by new laws? In each case, new institutions simply modify choice sets – fields of action – for atomistic maximizing individuals (or firms). To regard institutions as simply constraints is to reveal an unsubstantiated affinity for the *status quo ante* – and then to reify the current situation by referring to it as 'the market'. If one lives in a market economy then the *status quo ante* – by being called 'the market' – gains a privileged position in any discussion of desired or necessary policy change. We see that *laissez faire* becomes just another word for protecting the *status quo ante* institutional setup in the interest of safeguarding those well served by that particular *status quo*.

A clear understanding of institutions requires that we see them as both liberating and restraining individuals. In fact, the proper way to regard institutions is that they define choice sets – fields of action – for members of a political entity (village, nation state). With a proper focus on institutions as constitutive of social and economic relations rather than simply as constraints on those relations, economists can usefully bring analytical attention to bear on these essential aspects of an economic system. This new perspective places emphasis on institutions as structural parameters in an economy rather than as mere constraints on some prior and allegedly natural entity called the 'market'. There is, after all, no such thing as 'the market'. There are, instead, arenas of exchange that are the product of conscious human creation. Any market is a social construct, and changes in the parameters of that construct – new institutional arrangements – are also human creations.

The study of economic institutions requires paying attention to three fundamental realms of human interaction – ethics, economics and jurisprudence. Ethics deals with the rules of conduct arising from conflict of interests, necessitated by scarcity, and enforced by the moral sanctions of collective opinion. Economics in the narrowest sense then deals with the rules of conduct arising from conflict of interests, necessitated by scarcity, and enforced by the collective economic sanctions (and definitions) of profit or loss. Notice that the economic problem is simply one of allowing for individual and group behaviours that are themselves constrained and liberated by the prior ethical and legal parameters of the community. This is made obvious when we recall that the very concepts of 'profit' and 'loss' are themselves social constructs. Profit is what is left over after all factors of production have received their proper compensation. But what is 'proper' compensation? The economist would respond that proper compensation is determined by the 'market'. But of course this is circular since 'the market' at any particular moment is itself a reflection of prior ethical and legal deliberations. There is no divine source to tell a community (a nation state) how to organize its market. Rather, that particular market simply emerged and evolved as the necessary and inevitable ethical and legal structure of the community evolved. Does the American market economy look like the Norwegian market economy? Does the Italian market economy look like the market economy in The Netherlands? Finally, jurisprudence deals with the rules of conduct arising from conflict of interests, necessitated by scarcity, and enforced by the organized sanctions of collective (and state sponsored) violence.

Notice that all institutions embody a combination of ethics, economics and jurisprudence. Institutions represent the application of ethics and jurisprudence to daily life. The particular nature and scope of institutions represent the ethical judgements of those in a position to determine the precise institutional arrangements to implement; democracy casts that ability rather more widely than do other political systems. And once those institutions are in place, individuals and groups engage in behaviours that are economic in nature, and that hold economic implications.

This leads us to the next question: from whence does this apparatus arise, and how does it persist? Obviously, institutions arise from the political community within which individuals and groups find themselves. A nation state is the political community that carries on a 'conversation' about exactly which institutional structures it ought to adopt. New institutions are manifestations of collective action in liberation and restraint of individual action. When I say collective action here I mean that new institutions are products of the processes and structures of governments which are – by definition – the facilitating and implementing arm of democratic nation states. Institutions are given form and content (and the potential for enforcement) by the agents of the state we call government.

It is essential to understand that in the economic realm the state is necessarily a party to every transaction. I say necessarily because it is the state that must agree which transactions shall be allowed. Drugs, child pornography, slavery and extortion are transactions that are not allowed in most societies. That is, members of the nation state assert, through their parliaments and courts, that these particular transactions shall not be permitted. Once particular transactions have been deemed by the collective to be acceptable, there remains the problem of state ratification of contracts and other aspects of transactions. After all, if contract disputes arise, where do the aggrieved parties go but to the nation's courts? Nation states cannot avoid being a party to every transaction. By agreeing to be a party to every transaction the state agrees that it always stands ready to consider the interests of all citizens – but especially those engaged in 'legal' contracting. This reminds us that there are 'illegal' contracts between parties that the state will refuse to recognize and enforce. By agreeing to be the enforcement agent for private transactions, the state is declaring that it cares about the well-being of individuals who choose to enter into particular contracts.

The three classes of institutions

There is a sense in economics that institutions are universities, the central bank, or some government agency. This is both wrong and unhelpful to coherent analysis. Universities, central banks and government agencies are organizations, the purpose of which is to implement a specific set of activities collectively desired and ratified in their very creation. Universities congregate faculty and students for the purpose of research and teaching. The nature of this congregation is ascertained (defined) by the institutions that underlie the idea and practice of that particular organization. We see the same idea at work in thinking about other organizations. Organizations are simply defined and known by the rules of which they are constituted.

There are three classes of institutions: (1) norms and conventions, (2) working rules, and (3) entitlements.

Norms and conventions

Norms and conventions are widely accepted regularities in behaviour that bring order and predictability to human relationships. Norms and conventions are sometimes lumped together with other types of behavioural structures. In formal terms, we might agree that norms and conventions are regularities in human behaviour to which everyone prefers to conform on the expectation that all others will also conform. A norm or convention is a structured set of expectations about behaviour driven by shared and dominant preferences for the ultimate outcome.

The enforcement of norms and conventions tends to reside close to the individual. Young people are socialized into a pattern of living that, for the most part, entails the apprehension and adoption of family and community norms and conventions. The inculcation of such behavioural expectations, and their enforcement, resides in the family and its logical extensions. This is not to deny the importance of norms that work at the larger level of social interaction throughout our adult lives. But the norms we learn when young are largely enforced by our own codes of conduct as we mature. Indeed social misfits, while not necessarily criminals, are those who have rejected some of the norms and conventions that the rest of us regard as our social (and possibly personal) obligations. We see, therefore, that norms and conventions must be distinguished from the class of institutions for which there exist formal (codified) enforcement mechanisms. These are the latter two types of institutions.

Working rules

We now encounter a class of institutions that emerge from conscious social action and that entail a formal structure of rules and sanctions. In this second class of institutions we encounter rules that carry the expectation, indeed threat, of legal sanction. These rules must now be understood in their more formal – that is, legal – clothing. Because institutions are collective rules that define socially acceptable individual and group behaviour, they are sets of legally sanctioned dual expectations. The concept of an institution is always one of correlates (of dualities). Institutions are the working rules that indicate what:

> ... individuals must or must not do (compulsion or duty), what they may do without interference from other individuals (privilege or liberty), what they can do with the aid of collective power (capacity or right), and what they cannot expect the collective power to do in their behalf (incapacity or liability).
> (Bromley 1989a: 43)

Notice immediately mention of the collective power. It is here that working rules are differentiated from norms and conventions. Imagine two individuals, Alpha and Beta. Since legal relations are also group specific, we may imagine Alpha to be a person (an individual) and Beta to be all other persons. The four fundamental legal relations are shown in Table 11.1.

Table 11.1 The legal correlates

	Alpha ←	→ Beta
Static correlates	Right ←	→ Duty
	Privilege ←	→ No right
Dynamic correlates	Power ←	→ Liability
	Immunity ←	→ No power

Source: Bromley, 1989a

A right means that Alpha has a state-sanctioned (and enforced) assurance that Beta will behave in a certain way toward Alpha. Specifically, a right means that Alpha may expect that Beta will not act against Alpha's interests, and if that should happen, Alpha can seek relief from the collective power of the state. A duty means that Beta must behave in a specific way with respect to Alpha. This means that Beta may not act contrary to Alpha's interests. Notice that the dual of Alpha's legal position is Beta's legal position; Alpha has the right, Beta has the duty.

The second correlate is that of privilege and no right. If Alpha has privilege with respect to Beta then she (Alpha) is free to act without regard for the implications that may befall Beta from that action. For instance, Alpha is free to discharge toxic pollutants into a river in which Beta seeks to catch fish. Beta, by standing in a position of no right to Alpha's privilege, is unable to gain relief from this instance of cost shifting. If Beta should seek relief he would be told that there is 'no law' against Alpha's actions. Beta has no rights. We see that situations of privilege and no right define what the economist calls an externality.

Turning to the dynamic aspect, to have power is to have the ability to force another individual into a new legal situation against his or her will. If Alpha has power then she may put Beta in a new legal situation not of Beta's choosing. And whence does this ability come? This capacity comes from the ability of Alpha to enlist the coercive power of some authority (the state, village leaders) to impose her will on Beta's field of action. The state (or the pertinent authority system) becomes an essential participant in the exercise of Alpha's power with respect to Beta. When Alpha has power, Beta suffers from a liability to the capacity of Alpha to force Beta into a new and unwanted legal situation. It is here that institutions expand the capacity of the individual. If Beta is not exposed to Alpha's attempt to create a new legal relation inimical to Beta's interests, then Beta enjoys immunity in the face of Alpha's efforts to put Beta in an unwanted legal position. And in the face of Beta's immunity we would say that Alpha has no power. To have no power means that Alpha is unable to put Beta in a new legal situation that is not to Beta's liking.

We can regard these four legal relations as being either active or passive. The right/duty and the power/liability relations are active in that they represent imperative relations subject to the authority of the state (or the appropriate authority system). On the other hand, the privilege/no right and immunity/no power relations are passive in that they are not subject to direct legal enforcement. Instead, these latter correlates define the limit of the state's legal activities. That is, they indicate types of behaviour in which the state has no interest. As we see in the case of privilege, the state declares that it is none of its concern if Alpha pollutes a river (and kills the fish) of interest to Beta.

In modern legal systems every right that Alpha has upon Beta is given effect by the obligation held by the state to compel Beta to abide by the duty incumbent on Beta. That is, to have a right is to know and to expect that the coercive power of the state will be continually brought to bear on those who bear a duty against your right. Indeed, there is more to the story. To have a right is to be able to compel the state to protect your interests. Notice that if Alpha has a right this is more than being a mere passive recipient of the state's direct support. Rather, the state agrees, when it grants a right to Alpha, to stand ready to defend Alpha's interests against the claims and incursions of others. That agreement is manifest in the state's coercion against those with a duty against Alpha's right. We say, in this respect, that the state is a party to every transaction.

Property relations[4]

Finally we come to the third level of institutional arrangements – those that concern income (or benefit) streams arising from control of particular valuable objects or circumstances. We call these particular institutional arrangements property relations. Property relations – along with what have come to be called civil rights – are perhaps the most fundamental social constructs among members of a political community. While civil rights laws are entitlements concerning the expected behaviours of all members of a polity towards each other, property relations concern collective assurance among members of the polity with respect to particular income (or benefit) streams.

To have a right with respect to a particular activity (say the right to free assembly or to free speech) is to have the capacity to compel the state to protect your ability to assemble or to speak. To have a right with respect to a stream of future economic benefits is to have the capacity to compel the state to protect your control over that income stream. More profoundly, to have a property right over some action or setting is to know that the state will indemnify from the public treasury your financial interests in that action or setting.

Property rights obtain their empirical content from the imposition by the state – or a comparable authority system – of a duty on all others to forbear from interference with the income stream accruing to the owner of the object or circumstances so protected. As we consider the analysis of property relations it is important to resist the temptation to cast these relations in dyadic terms – the owner against an all-powerful and meddling government. Clarity is possible only if we understand that property relations are not dyadic – a person against government. Rather, property relations must be seen as triadic. That is, property relations must be understood as social arrangements that define the relations among: (1) one person (or several persons) whom we will call the 'owner(s)', (2) an object or circumstance of value to the owners as well as to others, and (3) all other persons in the polity. When we consider property relations in this manner it allows us to comprehend the essence of property relations as foundational social institutions.

The empirical reality of property relations is that they situate all members of a polity in a particular position with respect to valuable assets and circumstances. The essence – the empirical content – of ownership is the socially sanctioned ability to exclude others. A copyright prevents others from benefiting at the expense of the creator. A patent gives temporary protection to the inventor. Private property in land and other related assets sanctions exclusion of others. Property rights dictate economic relations. If the gold fields of South Africa are owned by one large corporation then economic relations throughout the economy cannot help but be affected in a particular way. If the vast majority of the best agricultural land in a particular nation state is owned by a few large and aggressively dynastic families, then the social costs of landlessness and related social pathologies cannot be so easily dismissed. As Henry George put the matter:

> Place one hundred men on an island from which there is no escape, and whether you make one of those men the absolute owner of the other ninety-nine or the absolute owner of the soil of the island, will make no difference either to him or to them.
>
> (George 1955: 347)

It is this exclusionary attribute that renders property relations inevitably contentious economic and social relations. To be the owner of something of great economic value is to find oneself in a rather comfortable situation on two counts. First, as indicated above, to have a right (in this case a property right) is to have that wonderful capacity to compel the coercive power of the state to come to your aid in protecting your economic interests. Who would not like the capacity to order the state to come to your protection? I have characterized this situation as institutional change that expands individual action. When the state grants a property right it is, of necessity, also acknowledging a durable obligation on its part to defend the interests of those to whom the property right has been granted. Also, to own something of economic value in a market economy is put one in a position of a seller. In a market economy one always wants to be a seller rather than a buyer. But, as a seller, one wants to be in a position as a seller of more than just one's labour power. If one has only labour power to sell in a market economy one is at the mercy of those in need of buying labour power. If one owns not only labour power but other assets of significant economic value – land and other forms of capital – then one is twice a seller. Economic advantage in a market economy accrues to those with a diversified asset portfolio who stand in a position of seller rather than buyer.

Contention over property relations arises because historical access to some income stream – say the ability to avoid costly processing of industrial wastes by discharging them directly into a nearby river – will invariably be regarded by the beneficiary of this favourable situation as a right to that income stream (the avoided costs). This ability, a legal privilege, to discharge industrial wastes into a river represents no secure claim at all. In terms of the legal correlates, the industrial polluter is simply enjoying privilege; she is free to act without regard for the interests of others. This is a regime of no law with respect to waste disposal practices.

Property relations are more than codified institutional arrangements specifying who may use an object of value, who controls the use of that object, and who may receive the benefits from that object. Property relations, along with the other state-backed working rules and entitlements, are also the legally sanctioned capacity to impose costs on others. That is, the correlates of privilege for Alpha and no right for Beta define a situation in which Alpha is free to disregard costs imposed on Beta and the latter has no avenue for registering objections to this situation.

With an understanding of both institutions and property rights we can now approach the topic of property regimes.

Property regimes

My theme concerns governance of the 'commons' so it is imperative that we be clear about what, precisely, it is we are talking about. As Socrates insisted, the beginning of wisdom is to call things by their right name. It is now well established that the word commons has an unfortunate history of misuse in general, but especially is this so in economics. The early work in fishery economics started things off on the wrong foot when Scott Gordon called the open-access fishery a 'common property' resource (Gordon 1954). Since that time there has been a long and sad tradition of economists using legal concepts without taking the trouble to find out if their language bore any relation to reality, or to careful legal descriptions of that reality (Cole and Grossman 2002). But things really went off the rails with Garret Hardin's misnamed 'tragedy of the commons' (Hardin 1968). Hardin has since recanted, and expressed the wish that he had used the term 'unmanaged commons'. But even this reconsideration puts the focus on management, while the essence of property is not management but legal relations.

At a gross level, there are three general classes of property regimes over settings and circumstances (and objects) that warrant consideration. These are state property (*res civitas*), private property (*res privatus*), and common property (*res communes*).[5] Private property is reasonably familiar to us. State property is less familiar as a concept, but it is all around us. Only common property remains confusing. And it is confusing precisely because many of those who write about it seem curiously intent on resisting the small expense of minimal effort to be clear about what it is they study and write about.

The commons as governance regime

The conventional economics wisdom is that private property rights are a necessary condition for the generation of economic wealth; in land this means that private ownership of land is a necessary precursor to the realization of an economic surplus. Interest within economics in property rights has led to the recognition of the

Table 11.2 Property regimes

State property

The political community is the recognized owner of the asset. Individuals in the political community may benefit from the asset but must observe rules of the government agency responsible to the political community.

Examples: national forests and parks, military bases, government office buildings, the 200-mile Exclusive Economic Zone now accepted in commercial fishing.

Private property

Individual members of the political community have recognized rights to benefit from the asset, subject to legislative mediation and judicial review. Non-owners have duties to allow owners to behave as above.

Examples: fee-simple land and buildings.

Common property

A group of owners holds rights in common, including the right to exclude non-owners. Individual owners have specific rights and duties with respect to their ability to benefit from the asset, subject to legislative mediation and judicial review within the larger political community.

Examples: irrigation districts, condominiums, the Swiss and Italian high pastures.

Res nullius

No defined group of users or owners. The asset is available to anyone. The asset is an open-access resource.

Source: Bromley, 1989: 205

so-called 'property rights school' of thought, best represented by the writings of Alchian and Demsetz (1973), Cheung (1970), Demsetz (1967), and Furubotn and Pejovich (1972). This view has been challenged for its ideological predisposition towards individualism, and for thus crafting a theory consistent with those biases (Field 1989). I have also challenged this theory for its failure to understand that the socially efficient property regime is a function of the asset value over which the social construction of property must be imposed (Bromley 1989b). That is, investment and derived income may well be a function of the property regime, but the property regime may also turn out to be a function of the investments that have been made (Sjaastad and Bromley 1997 and 2000). We see that it is necessary to be very careful with presumptions of causality.

Common property has a bad name in contemporary economics because we have failed to accord it the same conceptual status that we accord to private (individual) property regimes. Recall that the core of economics is possessive individualism – all of our models, and all of our metaphors, start with the utility maximizing individual who can only gain utility by acquiring higher levels of income in order to enjoy higher levels of consumption. Because the individual is the sufficient unit of analysis in contemporary economic theory and practice, it is logically impossible for any other property regime to fit with standard maximizing models. This doctrine of methodological individualism remains one of the central value judgements of economics. For those who have been told that economics is value free, this realization may come as a bit of a surprise. As a value judgement, methodological individualism is no worse – and no better – than any number of other possible normative positions. The problem, however, is that most of contemporary economics proceeds as if methodological individualism were some divinely inspired truth about which there can be no further discussion. This is not the place for that discussion, but it is the place to explore how that normative presupposition biases and distorts conversations about – and analyses of – the role of land and property rights. The essential point here is that economic analysis of property rights and natural resources not be carried on at a level, and in a manner, that will lead the unsuspecting reader to miss the fatal circularity in this work. In other words, the very essence of economics must always remain the honest quest for the sufficient reasons for particular policy prescriptions, not the facile advocacy of such prescriptions because they are the inevitable entailments of atomistic models constructed for precisely that purpose. When atomized utility maximizing algorithms are conjured, in which income (or wealth) is the only thing giving of utility, we should not be at all surprised to 'discover' that tenure security increases income (or the utility of income) when tenure security enters such models as a factor that increases income. It could not possibly be otherwise. Do such models reveal to us what is best for economic policy in diverse economies? Or do such models merely justify what is best for the fictitious and quite autonomous utility-maximizing agent who is the subject of our atomistic models?

The fundamental issue, therefore, is not to conjure fictitious models demonstrating that individuals will attain the highest possible levels of utility (and/ or income) if only they had complete atomized control over – and absolute security with respect to – land and related assets. Such models are now commonplace and are distinctive by their comprehensive circularity; they 'prove' what their very structure prefigures them to prove. Rather, the only correct approach is to draw upon economic theory in an effort to see if there are ways and means to enhance individual and group well-being without the necessity of abandoning enduring cultural values concerning the place of the individual within a community of many individuals – family, village, local river valley or hillside. If we can do this, we can thereby show that economics is a valuable analytical aid to governments who seek development assistance on their terms, not ours. If we cannot (or will not) do this, we expose economics as nothing but applied engineering dressed up with monetary weights. Much of the literature on privatization of land – and land titling – fits the latter description rather than the former.

The key is for governments to assure the same level of external legitimacy for all property regimes – not just private property regimes (Larson and Bromley 1990). Once this has been assured, so that individuals do not have to self-enforce that which the collective authority of the state ought to protect, then we can expect to see the emergence and evolution of what we have called internal authority (Larson and Bromley 1990). The concept of internal authority addresses the ability of owners – freed from the need to stand guard, as it were, at the physical boundary of what they collectively own – to devote themselves to management rather than to vigilante duty against the illegitimate claims of predatory neighbours.

I will close with a few thoughts on how economists might think about institutions and institutional change.

Institutional change and volitional pragmatism

The interesting economic questions tend to focus not on institutions per se, but rather in the felt need, at any moment, to modify those institutions. It is here that notions of purpose and necessity inform the process whereby existing institutions are found deficient, and the search begins for new institutions. That is, existing ways of parameterizing domains of choice – individual fields of action – are found to lead to social outcomes that no longer command sufficient assent. It is here that we require an evolutionary model of institutional change. This model is found in the logic of volitional pragmatism.

We start with the idea of prospective volition – the human will in action, considering the present in terms of the future. That is, what actions must be taken now in order that the future shall not become worse than it is now? This vision sees reasons for action running from the future back to the present. This vision of the policy problem requires the concept of final cause:

> the 'final cause' of an occurrence is an event in the future for the sake of which the occurrence takes place (…) things are explained by the purposes they serve. When we ask 'why?' (…) we may mean either of two things. We may mean: 'What *purpose* did this event serve?' or we may mean: 'What earlier circumstances caused this event?' The answer to the former question is a teleological explanation or an explanation by final causes; the answer to the latter question is a mechanistic explanation.
>
> (Russell 1945: 67) (emphasis added)

If we regard final cause in human systems as synonymous with reason, I believe some clarity emerges. This alternative terminology also helps us to apprehend the somewhat novel idea that the explanation – the reason – for an action can be some outcome in the future. Are not all causes antecedent and all outcomes consequent? The answer is that only mechanical causes are antecedent to the outcome. Final causes – reasons – concern future states. Final causes – reasons – are those that entail belief and desire on the part of an agent who looks to the future and acts accordingly. We call this an act of prospective volition – the human will in action, considering possible outcomes in the future. Explanations by mechanical cause consider the future in terms of the present.

On the other hand, the human will in action – prospective volition – considers the present in terms of the future. Reasoning backwards is precisely the act of understanding the present in terms of the future, and deciding how we wish the future to unfold for us. Final cause – reason – is concerned precisely with this idea.

Of course individuals will create different imaginings about possible outcomes. This should not surprise us. As G.L.S. Shackle says, we have different imaginings because the available actions are novel events in our lives. We have not done that before, so why should it be supposed that each of us could have definitive data and similar imaginings concerning precisely what will transpire? In other words, 'An action which can still be chosen or rejected has no objective outcome' (Shackle 1961: 143).

Once there is an emergence of plausible created imaginings, we begin to approach the final stage of institutional change – policy formulation. Economies are in continual need of new created imaginings as new problems and new opportunities arise almost on a daily basis. Those who celebrate the dynamic properties of markets are telling us only half of the story. The real dynamism arises because the existing institutional arrangements are seen as the malleable architecture for adaptation. With this idea at hand, it is easy to see that this cacophony of created imaginings will evolve from just that – an inchoate cacophony – into a slowly coalescing and emerging consensus that begins to narrow the range of institutional alternatives and plausible imaginings.

When the process of sifting and winnowing through the various created imaginings reaches the point that several of them have come to dominate the collective conversation, the final component of institutional change comes into play. This final stage is the actual process whereby the norms, rules and entitlements are modified for the explicit purpose of implementing one of the emergent created imaginings. We may properly consider this emergent and now reigning imagining as the reason for the new institutional arrangements. That is, the emergent created imagining is the outcome in the future for the sake of which the new institutional arrangements must be implemented now. This dominant imagining comprises the sufficient reason for the new institutions. It explains the institutional change.

The process is repeated *ad infinitum* in a democratic market economy. There is a continual process of: (1) assessing existing settings and circumstances, (2) searching for causal connections between those outcomes and the institutional arrangements on which they are plausibly predicated, (3) searching for new created imaginings, (4) working out the political arrangements to discard the most outrageous imaginings, (5) searching for and articulating the plausible mappings between surviving created imaginings and the institutional arrangements that are their plausible explanations, and (6) undertaking collective action in the parliaments, the executive branch, and the courts to move the implicated institutional arrangements from their *status quo* configuration to a new and plausible configuration that will – on the newly accepted emergent imagining – generate the desired outcomes in the future.

We may notice that the essential problem here reduces to which of the competing accounts (stories) appear to be the most compelling. One way we often hear this expressed is to suggest that the more successful claimant is the one with the better facts. Economists are critical of such approaches, regarding them as nothing but rhetorical exercises shot through with values and normative propositions. But those of you who know your welfare economics at more than a superficial level, and who have read the works of Blackorby and Donaldson (1990), Boadway (1974 and 1976), Boadway and Bruce (1984), Chipman and Moore (1978), Gillroy (1992), Gorman (1955), Graaff (1957), Little (1950), Mishan (1969 and 1980), Samuels (1974 and 1989), Samuelson (1950) and Sen (1993) will know that the central normative propositions of consequentialist welfarism are fictions and without merit for understanding the socially preferred thing to do.

This means that economists need a new theory of public policy, and in the present context it means that we need a new way of thinking about alternative property regimes – especially what we like to call 'the commons'. I insist that policy is collective action in restraint, liberation and expansion of individual action. Public policy is, therefore, institutional change – the collective redefinition and restructuring of fields of action for individuals. My essential concern here is to offer ways and means to understand the process of institutional change. Indeed when one has acquired an understanding of something, it is possible to say that one has acquired an explanation of that thing now understood. In more formal terms, we can also say that one has acquired a theory of the thing that is now understood.

We must come to think of a theory as an internally consistent system of 'if, then' propositions that allows one to offer plausible and testable conjectures about particular events – why certain events occur (or have occurred), and why other events do not occur (or have not occurred). I suggest that a new theory must start with a new epistemology – abduction. The second component concerns a new way of representing the essential logic of human action. I suggest that the syllogism of practical inference represents this new way of understanding individual and collective action. Finally, we need a new way of thinking about the concepts of 'good', 'right' and 'truth'. I suggest that pragmatism represents the essential method that offers clarity in this regard. Taken together, abduction, practical inference and pragmatism combine to provide us with the essential foundation for advancing sufficient reasons for understanding – and therefore explaining – institutional change.

Abduction[6]

Abduction represents a search for plausible reasons for observed results. Unlike deduction, abduction is not concerned with advancing received truths about why things are as they are. The essential benefit to arise from this situation is that abduction liberates the economist from the standard disciplinary confinement that institutional change is either in the interest of efficiency or else it is merely redistributive. Notice that in deduction these two alleged 'reasons' serve to exhaust the set of explanations for institutional change. The deductive approach to public policy – captured by an epistemology that sees self-interest (and notions of efficiency) as the only possible reasons for all human action – is unable to offer reasons for institutional change that do not follow from its confining covering laws. This stunted dichotomy induces the economist to search for efficiency explanations of institutional change and when none can be found this approach leaves the economist no choice but to denounce the new policy as 'inefficient' or wrongheaded. More seriously, this dichotomy induces economists to move beyond explanation and to engage in advocacy of the idea that institutional change should be for the purpose of economic efficiency since we all 'know' that redistribution cannot possibly benefit the economy as a whole. Little good comes from this situation – and from this behaviour.

Abduction liberates the economist to create propositions about institutional change that constitute plausibly true accounts of the pertinent reasons for the changes under consideration. Allegations of self-interested bureaucrats and politicians, or grand narratives concerning economic efficiency, cannot possibly comprise such accounts. Self-interest, because it is ubiquitous, cannot possibly comprise a reason for institutional change – unless one is charmed by a 'theory' that says institutional change favours those with the ability to get their way. Similarly, economic efficiency, because it is merely a concept by postulation, cannot logically be a guide to institutional change. To say that the pursuit of economic efficiency is a reason for institutional change is to commit the teleological fallacy. But there is a more serious flaw in the deductive approach to institutional change. Advancing the pursuit of efficiency as a reason for institutional change entraps the economist into a futile search for affirmation – the absence of which comprises grounds not to challenge the dichotomous explanatory project of economics, but to ridicule and to reproach politicians for doing the 'wrong' thing.

Practical inference[7]

Possibly true descriptions of reasons for particular actions (decisions) bring us immediately to the concept of created imaginings. Since all proposed action regarding the future entails new circumstances beyond the experience of most, if not all, members of the decision-making body, individuals must create their own imaginings of the possible futures. These created imaginings comprise – indeed inform – the volitional premises of those contemplating particular actions. These volitional premises comprise the imagined desired outcomes that constitute the purpose for which a particular decision is contemplated.

With the created imaginings in hand, the next task is to mobilize the epistemic premises that provide the theoretical linkage between the volitional premise and the necessary action. It is here that specific knowledge from various fields of knowledge – including, often, traditional knowledge – will play a decisive role. What is known about the constellation of 'if, then' propositions pertinent to a particular set of imagined and desired future states? Who has the most plausible account?

Pragmatism[8]

We finally come to the task of consolidating the volitional and epistemic premises. This entails instrumental valuing – the pragmatic evaluation of truth. As the pragmatists would say, truth is a matter of collective judgement that serves to transform particular conceptual and empirical claims into warranted knowledge. That is, truth is a term we apply to that which it now seems plausible to believe. Truth is the compliment we pay to our settled deliberations.

We see that understanding institutions and institutional change via volitional pragmatism does not slam doors on possible hypotheses, nor does it prejudge institutional change as always in the interest of efficiency or else it is merely redistributive. Volitional pragmatism simply asks that the scientific enterprise approach the study of institutions and institutional change with an open and enabling epistemology. Abduction, prospective volition, and pragmatism provide that epistemology.

The search for a theory of institutional change has been hampered by the deductive bias prevalent in economics. The quest to make institutional change endogenous has been, ironically, an endeavour geared to render institutional change deterministic rather than apprehensible. As with standard economic stories of individual choice, the idea of endogenous institutional change is simply an endeavour that seeks to remove the human will in action from playing any role at all. In the received story ('theory'), institutions change – machine like – when it is efficient for them to change. And if they do not change then it is efficient that they not change. So far this can be seen as descriptive. But there is a prescriptive part as well – if it is efficient then they should change, and if it is not efficient then they should not change. Such a theory of institutional change is a tautology – and yet its normative presumptions continue to find resonance among many economists. The project to make institutional change endogenous in economic models suffers from the fatal flaw that endogenization brings events into a structured mechanical relation and this fact necessarily strips away any possibility of actual choice. Endogeneity is just another word for nothing left to choose.

A credible theory of institutional change requires, first, recognition that individuals undertake those actions for which they can, at the moment, marshal the most compelling reasons. This process conflates both the volitional and epistemic premises in a process of coming to grips with what we 'want' by coming to grips with what we can 'have'. Wanting is not some abstract lunging toward the infeasible. It is, instead, a process of reasoned construction of created imaginings that are informed by their very feasibility.

From this constructed realm of plausible futures, we then reflect on – and usually argue about – the various reasons why these plausible futures make more or less sense to us. We reason about what we want predicated on reasoning about what we can have.

Our daily life, embedded as it is in democratic market economies, is not about contingent wants. It is, instead, about coping with behaviours and outcomes that please us – or that fail to do so. When we are not pleased with those outcomes, we seek, through democratic structures and processes, relief. It is often tedious, and it can be contentious. But the process of seeking relief forces us – on all sides of suddenly contentious issues – to create imaginings about what constitutes relief. More importantly, we are forced to confront the reality of what constitutes plausible relief. The very act of accepting the adjective 'plausible' brings us, as individuals, or as members of decision-making bodies, in direct contact with the pragmatic evaluation of truth. That is, what is better than what we now have? What would move us in an agreeable direction? What will it take to move us? Is it worth it? What will others seek? Our individual and collective existence is defined by our epistemology. We are all volitional pragmatists. And a good thing, too.

Notes

1 See Bardhan (1989) for a treatment of institutions in the development context.
2 For criticism of North's approach see Field (1979 and 1981).
3 And that such impositions are harmful to the 'correct' ' purpose of institutions – which is to foster growth.
4 Other sources on property are Becker (1977), Bromley (1991), Christman (1994), Hallowell (1943), Hohfeld (1917), and Macpherson (1962 and 1978).
5 Some of the literature on common property is Bromley (1992a and 1992b), Bromley and Chapagain (1984), Ciriacy-Wantrup and Bishop (1975), Jodha (1986), Netting (1976), Rhoades and Thompson (1975), Runge (1981 and 1984), and Wade (1987).
6 Abduction was perfected by the American philosopher Charles Sanders Peirce. For a good description see Ducasse (1925).
7 For a treatment of practical inference see von Wright (1983).
8 For a treatment of pragmatism see Rorty (1979, 1982 and 1999).

References

Alchian, A., and Demsetz, H. (1973) 'The Property Rights Paradigm', *Journal of Economic History*, 13: 16–27.
Bardhan, P. (1989) 'Alternative Approaches to the Theory of Institutions in Economic Development', in P. Bardhan (ed.), *The Economic Theory of Agrarian Institutions*, Oxford: Oxford University Press.
Becker, L.C. (1977) *Property Rights*, London: Routledge and Kegan Paul.
Blackorby, C. and Donaldson, D. (1990) 'A Review Article: The Case Against The Use of the Sum of Compensating Variations in Cost-Benefit Analysis', *Canadian Economics Journal* 3(August): 471–94.
Boadway, R.W. (1974) 'The Welfare Foundations of Cost-Benefit Analysis', *Economic Journal* 84: 926–39.
Boadway, R.W. (1976) 'Integrating Equity and Efficiency in Applied Welfare Economics', *Quarterly Journal of Economics* 90: 541–56.
Boadway, R.W. and Bruce, N. (1984) *Welfare Economics*, Oxford: Blackwell.
Bromley, D.W. (1989a) *Economic Interests and Institutions: The Conceptual Foundations of Public Policy*, Oxford: Blackwell.
Bromley, D.W. (1989b) 'Property Relations and Economic Development: The Other Land Reform', *World Development* 17(6): 867–77.
Bromley, D.W. (1991) *Environment and Economy: Property Rights and Public Policy*, Oxford: Blackwell.
Bromley, D.W. (ed.) (1992a) *Making the Commons Work: Theory, Practice, and Policy*, San Francisco, CA: ICS Press.
Bromley, D.W. (1992b) 'The Commons, Common Property, and Environmental Policy', in *Environmental and Resource Economics*, 2: 1–17.

Bromley, D.W. (1999) 'Markets', in Philip O'Hara (ed.), *The Encyclopedia of Political Economy*, London: Routledge.

Bromley, D.W. (2006) *Sufficient Reason: Volitional Pragmatism and the Meaning of Economic Institutions*, Princeton, NJ: Princeton University Press.

Bromley, D.W. and Chapagain, D.P. (1984) 'The Village Against the Center: Resource Depletion in South Asia', *American Journal of Agricultural Economics*, 66: 868–73.

Cheung, S.N.S. (1970) 'The Structure of a Contract and the Theory of a NonExclusive Resource', *Journal of Law and Economics*, 13: 49–70.

Chipman, J.S. and Moore, J.C. (1978) 'The New Welfare Economics: 1939–1974', *International Economic Review* 19(3): 547–84.

Christman, J. (1994) *The Myth of Property*, Oxford: Oxford University Press.

Ciriac-Wantrup, S.V. and Bishop, R.C. (1975) 'Common Property as a Concept in Natural Resources Policy', *Natural Resources Journal*, 15: 713–27.

Cole, D. and Grossman, P. (2002) 'The Meaning of Property Rights: Law vs. Economics', *Land Economics*, 78(3): 313–30.

Demsetz, H. (1967) 'Toward a Theory of Property Rights', *American Economic Review*, 57: 47–59.

Ducasse, C.J. (1925) 'Explanation, Mechanism, and Teleology', *Journal of Philosophy* 22. 150–5.

Field, A.J. (1979) 'On the Explanation of Rules Using Rational Choice Models', *Journal of Economic Issues*, 13(1): 49–72.

Field, A.J. (1981) 'The Problem with Neoclassical Institutional Economics: A Critique with Special Reference to the North/Thomas Model of Pre-1500 Europe', *Explorations in Economic History*, 18: 174–90.

Field, B. (1989) 'The Evolution of Property Rights', *Kyklos*, 42(3): 319–45.

Furubotn, E. and Pejovich, S. (1972) 'Property Rights and Economic Theory: A Survey of Recent Literature', *Journal of Economic Literature*, 10(4): 1137–62.

George, H. (1955) *Progress and Poverty*, New York: Robert Schalkenbach Foundation.

Gillroy, J.M. (1992) 'The Ethical Poverty of Cost-Benefit Methods: Autonomy, Efficiency, and Public Policy Choice', *Policy Science*, 25: 83–102.

Gordon, H.S. (1954) 'The Economic Theory of a Common Property Resource: The Fishery', *Journal of Political Economy*, 62: 124–42.

Gorman, W.M. (1955) 'The Intransitivity of Certain Criteria Used in Welfare Economics', in *Oxford Economic Papers (new series)*, 7(1): 25–35.

Graaff, J. de V. (1957) *Theoretical Welfare Economics*, Cambridge: Cambridge University Press.

Hallowell, A.I. (1943) 'The Nature and Function of Property as a Social Institution', *Journal of Legal and Political Sociology*, 1: 115–38.

Hardin, G. (1968) 'The Tragedy of the Commons', *Science*, 162: 1243–8.

Hohfeld, W.N. (1917) 'Fundamental Legal Conceptions as Applied in Judicial Reasoning', *Yale Law Journal*, 26: 710–70.

Jodha, N.S. (1986) 'Common Property Resources and Rural Poor in Dry Regions of India', *Economic and Political Weekly*, 21: 1169–81.

Larson, B.A. and Bromley, D.W. (1990) 'Property Rights, Externalities, and Resource Degradation: Locating the Tragedy', *Journal of Development Economics*, 33(2): 235–62.

Little, I.M.D. (1950) *A Critique of Welfare Economics*, London: Oxford University Press.

Macpherson, C.B. (1962) *The Political Theory of Possessive Individualism*, Oxford: Oxford University Press.

Macpherson, C.B. (1978) *Property: Mainstream and Critical Positions*, Toronto, ON: University of Toronto Press.

Mishan, E.J. (1969) *Welfare Economics: An Assessment*, Amsterdam: North-Holland.

Mishan, E.J. (1980) 'How Valid Are Economic Evaluations of Allocative Changes?', in *Journal of Economic Issues*, 14: 143–61.

Netting, R. (1976) 'What Alpine Peasants Have in Common: Observations on Communal Tenure in a Swiss Village', in *Human Ecology*, 4: 135–46.

North, D.C. (1990) *Institutions, Institutional Change and Economic Performance*, Cambridge: Cambridge University Press.

Rhoades, R.E. and Thompson, S.J. (1975) 'Adaptive Strategies in Alpine Environments: Beyond Ecological Particularism', *American Ethnologist*, 2: 535–51.

Rorty, R. (1979) *Philosophy and the Mirror of Nature*, Princeton, NJ: Princeton University Press.

Rorty, R. (1982) *Consequences of Pragmatism*, Minneapolis, MD: University of Minnesota Press.

Rorty, R. (1999) *Philosophy and Social Hope*, London: Penguin Books.

Runge, C.F. (1981) 'Common Property Externalities: Isolation, Assurance, and Resource Depletion in a Traditional Grazing Context', *American Journal of Agricultural Economics*, 63: 595–607.

Runge, C.F. (1984) 'Institutions and the Free Rider: The Assurance Problem in Collective Action', *Journal of Politics*, 46: 154–81.

Russell, B. (1945) *A History of Western Philosophy*, New York: Simon and Schuster.

Samuels, W.J. (1974) 'The Coase Theorem and the Study of Law and Economics', *Natural Resources Journal*, 14: 1–33.

Samuels, W.J. (1989) 'The Legal-Economic Nexus', *George Washington Law Review*, 57(6): 1556–78.

Samuelson, P.A. (1950) 'Evaluation of Real National Income', *Oxford Economic Papers* (new series), 2(1): 1–29.

Sen, A. (1993) 'Markets and Freedoms: Achievements and Limitations of the Market Mechanism in Promoting Individual Freedoms', *Oxford Economic Papers*, 45: 519–41.

Shackle, G.L.S. (1961) *Decision, Order, and Time in Human Affairs*, Cambridge: Cambridge University Press.

Sjaastad, E. and Bromley, D.W. (1997) 'Indigenous Land Rights in Sub-Saharan Africa: Appropriation, Security and Investment Demand', *World Development*, 25(4): 549–62.

Sjaastad, E. and Bromley, D.W. (2000) 'The Prejudices of Property Rights: On Individualism, Specificity, and Security in Property Regimes', *Development Policy Review*, 18(4): 365–89.

von Wright, G.H. (1983) *Practical Reason*, Ithaca, NY: Cornell University Press.

Wade, R. (1987) 'The Management of Common Property Resources: Collective Action as an Alternative to Privatisation or State Regulation', *Cambridge Journal of Economics* 11: 95–106.

12 Decision-making under uncertainty and irreversibility

A rational approach to the precautionary principle

Marcello Basili[1] *and Maurizio Franzini*[2]

Introduction

New and particularly severe risks, also of a catastrophic nature, have made their appearance in the last few decades – from global warming to genetically modified food to political terrorism. Modern societies are engaged in a struggle to reduce risks which are, to a certain extent, the result of economic and technological progress. Unfortunately, this is not an easily achievable goal. Our knowledge in most cases is too limited to be of any help and the chances that to reduce some risks new ones are created are not negligible. Above all, the costs implied by a risk-abating strategy may be high and we apparently live in a world where the growing exposure to catastrophic risks is not matched by a parallel willingness to pay for their reduction.

For some decades now the Precaution Principle (PP) has been advocated as the right response to such new risks. The PP has been the subject of intense discussion both among scholars in different fields and policy makers. As a consequence, opinions about its relevance in policy making vary markedly. Some people think that the PP is a misguided concept for regulating human activities, since it induces innovation and technology-development aversion among human beings. On the other hand, many environmentalists and politicians see the PP as the only protection against the many human activities that may endanger public health and the environment. Such conflicting views are due, at least to some extent, to the lack of a well-defined and widely agreed definition of the principle.

To make the PP a reliable guide to policy making, two problems should be addressed – both of which have received only limited attention in the debate in this area. The first is to establish how the PP relates to individual rationality – is the principle in contrast to what we know about rationality or does it prescribe a type of behaviour that is rational under the given circumstances? The second problem is how to go from the individual to the collective level, making the PP a rational decision criterion also at society's level. This chapter analyses some aspects of both these problems. In particular, since the PP should be applied in situations characterized by uncertainty, irreversibility and catastrophic events, we shall clarify what rationality entails in such situations and suggest an interpretation of the PP as a specific rational behaviour.

We shall also explore some of the problems faced by the PP as an acceptable and viable criterion for collective decision-making. The origin of the problems is at least twofold – preferences and attitudes may be extremely diversified with respect to the risks to be run; moreover the negative effects of the risky actions can be very unequally distributed. As a consequence, it may be difficult both to reach a democratic decision and to implement it. In this respect, the institutional setting is of utmost importance for the PP to be effective. Our main concern is with the implementation problems, some of which will be analyzed on the basis of a Principal–Agent model, where the Principal abides by the PP but has to motivate the Agent – who will not bear the likely negative consequences of his choices – to carry out the 'right' action.

This chapter is organized as follows. In the next section we briefly reconstruct the origins of the PP and offer an account of the many references made to it in official documents both at national and international level. We then compare the two prevailing interpretations of the PP – the strong and the weak – and point out that both fail to clarify how the principle relates to rationality. The impact of the PP on the regulation of markets and the criticisms that this has aroused is the subject of the following section. Here we try to clarify what rational behaviour is in the presence of uncertainty and irreversibility, the two distinguishing features of the PP. In particular we make use of the notion of ambiguity and argue that it is the attitude to ambiguity that makes it possible to define the PP and reconcile it with rationality. Quasi-option values may be a good measure of precaution. Next we stress the distinctive elements of our interpretation also by comparing it to others which are rooted in rational decision-making. Next we focus on precautionary behaviour in the presence of Agency problems on the basis of a formal model. Finally, some conclusions are drawn.

The origin and the success of the precautionary principle

It is customary to trace the origins of the PP back to the *Vorsorgegsprinzip* that made its appearance in West Germany's legislation in the early 1970s.[3] But other contemporary experiences or even earlier applications of a PP-like principle cannot be ruled out. Löfstedt (2004) asserts that in those same years the Swedish Environmental Protection Act made use of an analogous concept while Morris (2000: 2) reminds us that, according to Mazur (1996), PP-like arguments have been used in the USA since the 1950s, by both conservatives – opposing the fluoridation of waters – and radicals – against nuclear power.

Indeed the PP seems to address a highly charged issue in the post-World War II boom years – how to face new and largely unknown collective risks endangering primarily, but not exclusively, human health and the environment.

The PP grew out of the sweeping economic development of the post-war period, with its great impact on the environment and with scientific knowledge proceeding at too slow a pace to be adequately reassuring. Technological advances and mass production had a dark side – they engendered new risks, some of which were also of a potentially catastrophic nature. Indeed, nuclear power had a major role in the spreading of the Principle. It is with specific reference to that risk that Pearce (1980) and Goodin (1980) put forward the first theoretical arguments for restraining firms when they were not able to offer adequate guarantees on the safety of their actions.

The PP can also be invoked to repel limitations not justified by reliable enough prospects of future harms, but the opposite situation was much more frequent in practice, with respect to most risks the PP implied curbing free market forces, despite the lack of certainty that future harms would be avoided.

In fact, in the period following World War II several advanced countries felt that 'one should not wait for conclusive evidence of a risk before putting control measures in place designed to protect the environment or consumers' (Gollier and Treich 2003: 77) and tried to endow themselves with a new guiding principle. This was precisely the PP, which should not be regarded as a new version of rational behaviour in the presence of generic risks. The risks it was to be applied to were new and, to some extent, different – they implied the possibility of irreversible damages and catastrophic events, the probability of which could not be reliably estimated on the basis of scientific knowledge.

Risks like these have multiplied in recent years, covering also new fields, i.e. political terrorism. This is probably the reason why the PP, despite its many problems and vagueness, has been successfully received in many countries.

The first appearance of the PP at an international level dates back to well before the Rio Conference, where the most well-known definition of the Principle was put forward. Generally reference is made to the 1982 United Nations World Charter for Nature, where it was clearly stated that when potential adverse effects are not fully understood the activities should not proceed.[4] Other references to a PP-like principle are present in the Ministerial Declaration of the Second International Conference on the Protection of the North Sea, held in London in 1987[5] and in the Closing Ministerial declaration from the UN Economic Conference for Europe in 1990.[6]

Then came what is regarded as the official definition of the PP – the statement included in Principle 15 of the 1992 Rio Declaration on Environment and Development, 'where there are threats of serious or irreversible damage, lack of full scientific certainty shall not be used as a reason for postponing cost effective measure to prevent environmental degradation'.[7]

Freestone and Hey (1996) argue that after the Rio declaration the PP has been part of almost any treaty, law or official document related to the protection of the environment and human health, both at national and international level. On the other hand, Sunstein (2003: 3) states that 'the PP has become, or at least is becoming, a binding part of customary international law'.

The PP was accorded a particularly favourable reception in the EU, mainly because it was believed to represent an instrument of great utility in the pursuit of sustainable development (Löfstedt 2004: 10). German-like versions of the PP were more and more frequently referred to in European environmental legislation, culminating with the inclusion of the principle in the 1992 Fifth Environmental

Action Program and in the EU Treaty, where it is stated that EU environmental policy 'shall be based on the precautionary principle'.[8] In February 2002 the PP was explicitly adopted by the EU together with implementing guidelines.[9]

The importance attached to the PP in Europe should not blind us to the fact that it was used also in other advanced countries – in the USA, federal courts have repeatedly made use of some notion of precaution, advocating various forms of regulation on its basis (Sunstein 2003: 3).

The precautionary principle: strong, weak or rational?

Despite its success the PP is not free from problems – both its theoretical basis and its practical applications are the objects of severe criticism by scholars belonging to different disciplines and political analysts. To be fair, the Principle is formulated in different ways[10] and, more serious, it is not comprehensive enough to provide reliable guidance in a broad range of situations. To put it shortly, it is more an evocative expression than a precise behavioural rule.

The origin of the problem is unique – the difficulty of striking a balance between rational calculations of costs and benefits on the one hand, and safety and protection against the most serious risks, on the other. Indeed the many definitions emphasize either the risks or the costs, rarely treating them together. Cost-effectiveness is mentioned in the Rio definition to the disappointment of many environmentalists, whose favourite definition of the PP does not make room for cost considerations.[11] To make the range of positions even wider, in some cases the risks to which the PP should be applied are poorly defined, forgetting that a distinguishing feature is irreducible uncertainty. We shall return to this point in the next section. As a result of all this we lack satisfactory analysis, consistent with the requirements of rationality.

To put some order in such a messy field it has been suggested that a distinction should be made between a strong and a weak version of the PP. Unfortunately, neither version is fully satisfactory, mainly because they both fail to take seriously the issue of what rationality implies in the presence of uncertainty and irreversibility.

The distinguishing element of the strong version is the reversed burden of proof (Morris 2000, Sunstein 2003, and Löfstedt 2004) – in practice, no action should be taken unless the actor, usually a firm, has demonstrated beyond any reasonable doubt that no harm will result. A margin of safety should be guaranteed in any decision, 'better safe than sorry', as Sunstein (2003: 9) puts it.[12]

However, the logical consequence of imposing a condition (certainty that no harms will follow) that, in the given conditions (lack of full certainty) can never be fulfilled, is to block almost any activity. In particular, human beings should refrain from using new technologies (no new technology is completely safe), giving up the benefits that such technology may bring about. As Wildavsky (2000) has stated, the search for trials without errors that the strong PP seems to encourage, may lead economic progress to a complete standstill.

Interpreted in this way the PP implies that 'regulation is required whenever there is a possible risk to health, safety or the environment even if the supporting evidence is speculative and even if the economic costs of regulations are high' Sunstein (2003: 13). This formulation of the principle blatantly disregards the actual costs of precaution. It violates rationality also because it does not make use of all available information. Not considering costs and benefits one could end up in choosing an action (block the activity, in our case) that generates less welfare than a viable alternative and is more harmful than expected.[13] It is also possible that the principle leads to inconsistent choices or may prevent any decision at all, as Sunstein (2003: 2) has pointed out. Finally, it is impossible, on the basis of such an interpretation, to have clear guidance on the problem of how to allocate limited risk-reducing resources among competing risks. There are, therefore, very good reasons for criticizing the strong version of the PP. Unfortunately, its many critics do not have an entirely convincing alternative proposal.

The weak PP basically states that lack of full certainty is not a justification for preventing an action that might be harmful. On the other hand regulation can be justified even if we cannot establish a definite connection between, for example, low-level exposure to certain carcinogens and adverse effects on human health (Morris 2000: 8). The 1987 Ministerial Declaration on the North Sea, recalled above, is taken as a good example of the weak PP, because the onus is on the regulator to show harms that might result and the appropriateness of *ex ante* regulation. It would be rather disappointing to interpret the weak PP in terms of placing the burden of proving harm on the regulator, for we would reach an equally unrealistic conclusion as in the case of the strong version – since it is impossible to achieve certainty on harmful effects, any action shall be tolerated.

A more convincing interpretation of the weak version is that regulation is admissible also when negative effects are uncertain. Unfortunately, it is not clear on the basis of which elements such a decision should be taken. Therefore this interpretation does not specify how to tackle the crucial issue. The conclusion to be drawn seems to be that everything is possible – uncertainty is neither necessary nor sufficient for regulation or *laissez faire*.

To be fair, many believe that the void left by the weak PP should be filled by cost–benefit analysis (CBA). Indeed one cannot avoid some type of rational calculations without mistaking in one direction or another. But we need much more than a passing reference to costs and benefits. We should, first of all, clarify whether and in what respect the PP differs from CBA. In fact any action (including those recommended by the strong version of the PP) could be supported by CBA. But there is a deeper and more serious problem – how should rational calculations and CBA be performed under uncertainty and irreversibility? Sometimes it seems that those who send us back to CBA forget this crucial point. This is where we should start.

Regulation and the precautionary principle

Before going into the problem of how to make the PP consistent with rational calculations, some considerations are in order as to the implications of the Principle for the regulation of markets. It is fair to argue that, had it not been for the impact the PP has on the free market, the debates surrounding it would have not been so harsh – at both the theoretical and policy-making levels.

A large number of its opponents look at the PP as an enemy of free markets and as a serious obstacle to the enhancement of the general welfare these are believed to deliver. On the other hand, many supporters of the PP in its strong version hold the view that it is an excellent tool for curbing the excesses of free markets and the private profit motive.

Disregarding purely ideological disputes there is no doubt that the PP would lose all appeal were it not able to ensure, at least in principle, a higher level of social welfare (properly defined) than free markets. However, in the absence of a fully fledged rational calculation, one cannot be sure that this is what the PP leads to.

As argued by Löfstedt (2004), some important changes have been recently introduced by the EU[14] in the interpretation of the PP, and the role that costs should play in it has been explicitly acknowledged. However, the strong version, with its severe regulation implications, is still dominant in practical applications. This has raised the suspicion that the PP provides a shield for bad practices that have the final effect of acting as protectionist policies. Recently, and on more than one occasion,[15] the USA has charged the EU with such behaviour. Someone goes further and believes that the PP may be used by sectional groups – and in particular environmentalists – to ban all that they do not like.

Sunstein believes that proof of an opportunistic application of the principle is to be found in the fact that different countries seem to resort to it in a non-consistent way, adopting a severe protectionist attitude with respect to some risks and completely forgetting about other risks that are by no means less harmful (Sunstein 2003: 12).

The odds are high that undeserving considerations like those Sunstein refers to play a major role in the actual process of political and bureaucratic decisions. Lobbying activities and rent seeking are, after all, tangible phenomena. However, in the absence of a rational approach we cannot say which solution would best enhance social welfare rather than vested interests. Therefore the response to the regulation-free trade dilemma is closely linked to the definition of a rational interpretation of the PP. Once this problem is solved we will be able to establish whether the oddity Sunstein points to is actually due to opportunism. In fact, given the costs and benefits involved, it may turn out that precaution is rational in one case and not so rational in another, apparently more risky, case.

We should therefore go into the problem of how to reconcile the PP with rationality. Despite many statements to the contrary, we believe that the PP can be grounded in rational analysis even though it is not admissible rational behaviour under uncertainty and irreversibility.

Rationality and uncertainty

As we said above, lack of certainty and the possibility of very serious damages are the distinguishing features of the problems to which the PP is applicable. Reading some of the more radical criticisms against the PP one may be forgiven for doubting whether such features have been properly weighted. The crucial problem is to define rational behaviour when the results of actions are uncertain and may engender extremely negative events, also of a catastrophic nature, through irreversible effects, often accumulated over very long periods of time. Let us start considering uncertainty at the individual level. As is well known, decision theory distinguishes four situations: *certainty*, *Knightian risk*, *Knightian uncertainty* or *ambiguity* and *complete ignorance*.

Certainty is a situation in which the decision-maker has a unique and fully reliable probability distribution where only one event has a probability of one and all the others zero. In other words, a given event will surely occur and this knowledge resolves the uncertainty. In this situation it is not difficult to provide solid decision-theory foundation also when the choice involves irreversible consequences on the environment by applying general economic theorems.

The opposite situation is complete ignorance. It is considered complete ignorance when a situation in which either a probability distribution assigns equal probabilities to all the states of the world or there is a set of probability distributions for events and all the probability distributions are equally reliable or unreliable. With complete ignorance the optimality criterion postulates that the decision-maker chooses the action that gives the best among the worst consequences (maxmin rule).[16]

Some scholars believe that the PP applies to situations like this (Majone 2002, and Sunstein 2003) and criticize the maxmin principle on the basis of the consideration that it makes use of only a limited amount of information   that related to prospective losses rather than probabilities. This criticism is not convincing for two reasons: because complete ignorance is characterized, as we said, by equal probabilities for all the events and because the more appropriate framework for the PP is uncertainty, which differs from complete ignorance, and also from risk as we shall presently see.

Knightian risk or risk is a condition in which there is a unique, additive and fully reliable probability distribution on the set of events. Decision theory under risk describes how an individual makes and/or should make a decision between a set of alternatives, when the consequences of each action are tied to events about which the individual is uncertain, that is, she does not know what will occur. The decision-maker formalizes the problem setting alternatives (technically, acts), states of the world and consequences. The individual acts on the basis of a well-defined utility function, which represents her preferences, and evaluates both the consequences and their likelihood. The rational decision-maker's goal is to maximize expected utility in the case in which probabilities are given in advance (von Neumann and Morgenstern 1944) or derived from preferences (Savage 1954). Both theories and their mixed version (Anscombe and Aumann 1963) weigh consequences with a single probability measure, objective and subjective respectively, of the set of states of the world, deriving a linear preference functional. As a consequence, expected utility can be represented as the mathematical expectation of a real function of the set of consequences with respect to a single probability distribution and acts can be ranked with respect to their expected utility.

The decision-maker's description of the states of the world is exhaustive and she has an expected utility function linear in probabilities. In the standard representation of expected utility, the decision-maker's risk attitude is embodied in her utility function. In fact, the decision-maker's risk attitude involves curvature properties of the utility function, and the decision-maker is risk averse (loving) if her utility function is concave (convex).[17]

For our purposes the interesting case is Knightian uncertainty or ambiguity. The distinction between different types of uncertainty is crucial for the analysis of risk associated with any economic activity. Uncertainty means that acts have consequences that are unknown at the time of the decision, whereas risk points to the possibility of an unfavourable occurrence. Global warming is a clear example of uncertain event. There is uncertainty about the link among pollution, gaseous emissions and global mean temperature; moreover there is uncertainty about the relationship between global mean temperature and climate. Floods, storms and droughts are risky events that global warming could induce.

In our interpretation this is the typical situation to which the PP should apply. It covers cases like species extinction, global warming, mad cow disease, avian flu and many others which are of concern to contemporary societies. All these situations are subject to scientific uncertainty. As Treich (2001: 337) puts it, uncertainty of this kind may be thought of as a situation where a panel of experts have different beliefs on the true probability distribution of various events. To understand rational behaviour in this context and the role that the PP can play in it we have to introduce the notion of ambiguity.

Ambiguity: a formal analysis

Ambiguity is a situation in which the decision-maker faces either a non-additive probability distribution or a convex set of additive probability distributions, none of which is fully reliable or completely unreliable, for the set of events. A large body of literature[18] has highlighted systematic discrepancies between theoretically correct behaviour and actual ones in cases in which information is perceived as 'scanty, unreliable, ambiguous' (Ellsberg 1961: 661), and thus the decision-maker cannot rely on a single probabilistic judgement.

Consider a decision problem in which the states of the world included in the model are not exhaustive. The decision-maker faces an 'unfamiliar' world, in the sense that she is aware she does not have a full description of all its states.[19] She can represent her beliefs by a non-necessarily-additive measure or by a set of additive probability distributions for the set of events. When the states of the world do not exhaust the actual ones, and the omitted states are not explicitly introduced, the model underlying the decision is called misspecified. Two closely related approaches have been proposed to bring ambiguity and ambiguity attitude into an 'expected' utility framework. Schmeidler (1989) and Gilboa (1987), following the Anscombe-Aumann and Savage approaches, respectively, axiomatize a generalization of expected utility, which provides a derivation of utility and non-necessarily-additive probability by means of the Choquet integral (Choquet 1954). Gilboa and Schmeidler (1989) extend standard expected utility, representing preferences through a utility function and a set of additive probabilities, instead of a single probability, on the set of events.

Let $\Omega = \{w_1,...,w_n\}$ be a non-empty finite set of states of the world and let $\Sigma = 2^{\Omega}$ be the set of all events. A function $v: \Sigma \rightarrow \Re$ is a non-necessarily-additive probability measure or a capacity if it assigns a 0 value to the impossible event $\varnothing$ and value 1 to the universal event Ω, i.e. the measure is normalized, and for all A, $B \in \Sigma$ such that $A \supset B$, $v(A) \geq v(B)$, i.e. the measure is monotone. A capacity is convex (concave) if for all A, $B \in 2^{\Omega}$, $v(A \cup B) \geq (\leq) v(A) + v(B) - v(A \cap B)$. It is superadditive (subadditive) if for all A, $B \in \Sigma$ such that $v(A \cap B) = \varnothing$, $v(A \cup B) \geq (\leq) v(A) + v(B)$. Notice that a capacity v is superadditive if and only if it is convex, and is subadditive if and only if it is concave. Moreover, if a capacity is both concave and convex, $v(A \cup B) = v(A) + v(B)$, i.e. it is a (additive) probability measure. However, since v is in general a non-additive measure, integration of a real-valued function $f: \Omega \rightarrow \Re$ with respect to v is impossible in the Lebesgue sense and the proper integral for a capacity is the Choquet integral:

$$\int_{\Omega} f dv = \int_{0}^{\infty} v(\{w \mid f(w) \geq t\}) dt + \int_{-\infty}^{0} \left[v(\{w \mid f(w) \geq t\}) - 1 \right] dt \qquad (12.1)$$

The Choquet integral is a generalization of the Lebesgue integral and it can be interpreted as a mathematical expectation with respect to a capacity.

The decision-maker expresses ambiguity aversion (love) if she ranks unfavourable (favourable) states as more likely to occur than favourable (unfavourable) ones. It is easy to see that convexity (concavity) of capacities leads to uncertainty aversion (love). For simplicity's sake, consider the finite n-state version of the Choquet integral:

$$\int f dv = \sum_{k=1}^{n} f(w_k)) \left[v\left(\bigcup_{j=1}^{k} (w_j) \right) - v\left(\bigcup_{j=1}^{k-1} (w_j) \right) \right] \qquad (12.2)$$

where outcomes are ranked as $f(w_1) \geq ... \geq f(w_n)$ and $v(w_0) = 0$ is assumed. In the Choquet integral, less favourable states are over-weighed (under-weighed) based on priors, provided that the capacity is convex (concave). Therefore convex (concave) capacities can be seen as representing decision-makers' pessimism (optimism).

Ambiguity may be represented by a set of possible priors instead of a unique one in the underlying state space, that is 'each subject does not know enough about the problem to rule out a number of possible distributions' (Ellsberg 1961: 657). In this case the decision-maker attaches a set of multiple additive probability measures $\wp$ on $\Omega = \{w_1,...,w_n\}$ and her preferences are compatible with either the *maxmin* or the *maxmax* expected utility decision rules. Gilboa and Schmeidler (1989) proved that if the decision-maker is ambiguity-averse, she maximizes the minimal expected utility with respect to each probability p in the prior set, thus

$$\int_{\Omega} f d\wp = \min_{p \in \wp} \int f dp.$$

On the contrary, if she is ambiguity-loving, she maximizes the maximal expected utility with respect to the set $\wp$, thus

$$\int fd\wp = \max_{p\in\wp} \int fdp.$$

It is worth noting that the representation of ambiguity by means of the Choquet integral (or by the closely-related *maxmin* or *maxmax* models) makes it possible to distinguish ambiguity attitude from marginal utility movements (i.e. decision-maker's risk attitude in standard models).

The economic implications of irreversibility

Besides ambiguity, irreversibility is the other distinguishing feature of situations where the PP is applicable. In the Rio Declaration and in several EU official documents, but not in other definitions of the PP, there is a more or less explicit reference to it. To be sure, many phenomena related to human health and the environment possess this characteristic.

Modification of natural environments induced by human beings may be technically irreversible, or involve very large costs of restoration to an original state in terms of either resources or time required. In fact, environmental assets are such that, once altered, they cannot be brought back to their original state, at least for a long time. Developments like these have become more important in relatively recent times.

Human beings have always exploited and managed the natural environment adroitly. Before the Neolithic Revolution, human ancestors were not just hunter-gatherers but proto-farmers. Ancestors are widely believed to have practised a primitive form of farming combined with hunting and gathering.[20] Around 40,000 years ago, during the Upper Paleolithic Period, Homo Sapiens learned to make better and more varied tools that allowed him to modify the environment. The mammoths disappeared, wild horses were marshalled and dragooned and the Neanderthals were displaced and then extinguished. The first cave paintings in Spain and France testify to the existence of such a society. Proto-farming with hunting and gathering were a successful model, but the increase of the human population induced the downfall of proto-farming and the coming of the Neolithic Revolution, around 10,000 years ago. Ancestors became farmers and adapted to the agricultural age. This can be considered the turning point of the relationship between human beings and the environment. Since then, human beings have destroyed and modified the natural environment and, after the Industrial Revolution, the exploitation of the ecosystem has proceeded at an increasing pace. World population jumped from eight million at the end of the last Ice Age, to 300 million by the time of Christ, reaching six billion today and an estimated 12 billion by the middle of the twenty-first century.

Since the entire world's most fertile land is already cultivated, human beings are converting wild land such as rainforests, tropical wetland, and primitive forests for livestock and agriculture, among other developments. As a consequence four biological species extinguish every day, wild areas disappear at an increasing rate,[21] and climate changes occur. A key aspect distinguishes Homo Sapiens's activity from that of ancestors, the scale of environment modifications. Investing decisions involve large patches of wild land and entire ecosystems and, to a large extent, man-driven changes cannot be reversed in a short period of time. Under these conditions, irreversibility of environmental modifications has to be explicitly considered and regarded as an output of economic activity.

Loss of biological species is a clear example of technical irreversibility,[22] and when natural restorative processes are permitted, costs are very high (the decision to dismantle a dam is an example of costly reversibility). As a consequence, exploitation and depletion of natural assets can be acceptable if essential resources such as oil and coal are involved, but any economic activity may be rejected if it induces permanent alteration or a definitive destruction of essential resources, such as biodiversity, ecosystems or other unique natural assets.[23]

Economists are familiar with irreversibility, having come to grips with it especially in relation to investment activities. In the standard economic theory of investment, irreversibility may be treated either as a sunk cost or by introducing a non-negative rate of investment as a constraint. Sunk costs arise because investment expenditures are industry or firm specific and cannot be recovered. For example, nuclear power plants involve sunk costs because they can only be used to provide electricity, in the same way expenditures for the development of a new medical drug are sunk costs because they are too specific. Constraints of non-negative rates of investment are involved in the exploitation of oil reserves and coalfields or in many R & D programmes. The myopic policy defined by the marginal productivity rule under diminishing returns cannot be applied to constrained development projects. Moreover the optimal path to development with a constraint of irreversibility cannot be achieved by taking the solution to the unconstrained problem and deleting non-feasible paths.[24]

Irreversibility breaks the temporal symmetry between the past and the future. The intuitive concept of irreversibility as a technological or physical constraint can be generalized to include irreversibility as a sunk cost. Uncertainty, as we have seen, means that the consequences of economic decisions cannot be fully determined *ex ante* and all the uncontrolled variables of the decision process are random variables, which depend only on the possible state of nature that will occur in the future.[25]

The interaction between uncertainty, irreversibility of man-driven changes and the opportunity of postponing investment decisions leads us to the concept of option value. The cost of being wrong in either direction is high and there are large potential gains from enhancing flexibility through investments in prevention. It is of economic value to keep future options intact, by means of early prevention efforts. The fact that knowledge (due to scientific developments or to learning by practising) improves over time may give further justification to such behaviour.

Environmental assets (goods and resources) may be regarded (at least in part) as irreplaceable assets, the preservation of which has an option value since it leaves open options in the sphere of consumption (as in the case of a park) or production (as in the case of new drugs derived from medicinal plants), and sometimes both (as with drinking and irrigation water). Option values that include both plain option value and quasi-option value of environmental assets can be considered as precautionary costs of human decisions exposed to uncertainty and irreversibility.

Quasi-option values: a measure of precaution

Among the category of option values we consider the family of quasi-option values as a possible measure of the PP. Roughly speaking, in the environmental literature quasi-option values capture the extra benefits related to the value of information about future possible states of the world, conditional on conservation or preservation of the environment.

In their seminal articles, Arrow and Fisher (1974) and Henry (1974a and 1974b) independently pointed out that under uncertainty, when a given decision could (at least partially) have irreversible effects and learning is possible before future decisions have to be made, it is generally valuable to keep open an option, even if the decision-maker is risk neutral and her marginal utility is constant. They call quasi-option value the extra value attached to the preservation of an option in order to stress the crucial role played by irreversibility and learning and show its independence from risk attitude.

Arrow and Fisher (1974) argue that whenever uncertainty is assumed, 'even where it is not appropriate to postulate risk aversion in evaluating an activity, something of the feel of risk aversion is produced by a restriction on reversibility of decision' (Arrow and Fisher 1974: 318). Henry (1974b) shows that replacing the initial random problem by an associated riskless problem, i.e. an equivalent certainty case, the decision-maker could obtain a non-optimal solution, even if she is risk neutral and the payoff function is quadratic.[26]

Quasi-option value (QOV) is equal to the maximum difference between R^*, the expected revenue of the random problem, and R, the expected revenue of the riskless problem, that is QOV = max $[R^* - R, 0]$. As already said, the quasi-option value represents the conditional value of information, conditional to the reversible action.

It is worth noting that an irreversible investment opportunity is equivalent to a financial perpetual call option on common stock,[27] where the investment expenditure is the exercise price and the project value, that is the expected payoff from investing, is a share of the underlying asset. Dixit and Pindyck derive 'the value of the extra freedom, namely the option to postpone the decision' (Dixit and Pindyck 1994: 97), from the difference between the expected net present values of the random problem and the associated riskless one. Given complete or at least sufficiently complete markets, the value of a project and the value of the option to invest are determined by constructing a replicating portfolio or finding out some perfectly correlated assets and using option-pricing theory.[28] That is, the value of the option to invest is based on the construction of a risk-free portfolio in which the asset is traded (long or short position) or by finding out another asset or a combination of some assets, whose prices are perfectly correlated with the price of the output of the investment project, if that asset is not traded.[29]

Differently from Arrow and Fisher, and Henry, who assume an additive probability distribution over events and derive the expected value associated to each possible decision, under ambiguity, events have a non-additive probability of occurring.[30]

Real option-pricing theory considers that the decision-maker faces various forms of risk, such as uncertainty over future product prices, operating costs, future interest rates, cost and timing of the investment itself. Uncertainty is represented by a set of states of nature, one of which will be revealed as true and option pricing will determine the optimal exercise rule of an investment.

Given competitive markets, no transaction costs and asset prices represented by diffusion processes, it is assumed a unique probability distribution $\Psi \rightarrow [0,1]$ on the measurable space (Ω, Σ), such that the market value of any asset is the expectation of its discounted payments. The asset, which represents the stochastic changes in the project worth, may be considered a random variable $\beta: \Omega \rightarrow R$ of its expected discounted payments and its unique market value equals

$$\int_{\Omega} \beta d\psi$$

As a result, there is only one opportunity value or quasi-option value for each irreversible investment project.

By ambiguity, the optimistic decision maker[31] has a concave capacity $v : \Sigma \rightarrow [0,1]$ on the measurable space (Ω, Σ) and the valuation of the asset will not be the Lebesgue integral of its expected discounted payments (linear pricing rule) but will be obtained by the Choquet integral of the asset's expected discounted payments (non-linear pricing rule).[32] Under ambiguity, asset market prices reveal a capacity instead of a probability distribution, as in the standard theory. As a consequence, the expected value of an asset β is the Choquet integral of its discounted payments with respect to ν, i.e.

$$\int_{\Omega} \beta dv.$$

The ambiguity-loving decision-maker (optimist) might be considered as a financial dealer who has both long and short positions on the asset β, respectively

$$\int_{\Omega} -\beta dv \text{ and } \int_{\Omega} \beta dv.$$

By the subadditivity of the Choquet integral:

$$\int_{\Omega} \beta dv + \int_{\Omega} -\beta dv \int_{\Omega} (\beta - \beta) dv \text{ or } \int_{\Omega} \beta dv + \int_{\Omega} -\beta dv \geq 0 \text{ or } \int_{\Omega} \beta dv \geq -\int_{\Omega} -\beta dv \tag{12.3}$$

the dealer makes a profit, which is a representation of the bid and ask spread of the asset β.

It is suggested that the bid and ask prices of the underlying asset β can be considered as the worst and the best expected payoffs of an irreversible investment project, respectively. The optimistic decision-maker considers the ask price of asset β as the lowest price (*upper bound*) at which she will wish to sell, consistent with her priors. On the contrary, the optimistic decision-maker considers the bid price of asset β as the highest price (*lower bound*) at which she is willing to buy, compatible with her beliefs.

These two asset values crucially depend on ambiguity and the lesser the faith in the likelihood[33] of the events the wider the interval. Given the relationship between the lower and upper Choquet integral with respect to the subadditive capacity v and the bid and ask price of the asset β, it is possible to compute the lower and upper bounds of the investment opportunity value, by considering the diffusion processes of the bid and ask prices (Basili 2001).

This analysis allows us to put the PP on a firmer ground and to suggest that quasi-option values, properly interpreted, may be a good measure of precaution.

Precaution and rationality: a suggested interpretation

A rational interpretation of the PP should start from a careful consideration of the role played by uncertainty and irreversibility. Rationality requires making use of all available information, but when uncertainty prevails the available information is basically of the type Ellsberg pointed to with his paradox. Under such conditions subjectivity is all too important and rationality is compatible with a broad range of decisions. As a consequence the PP can be seen as a criterion for selecting one of them. Interpreted in this way the PP is neither coincident with rationality nor in conflict with it. Rather it complements rationality as a normative criterion.

To gain a better understanding of the problem we distinguish between two different sources of subjectivity. The first is due to the variety of individual preferences that makes for the differences in the ranking of the outcomes. Linked as it is to utility functions, this source of subjectivity is of the more familiar type. This aspect of subjectivity plays an important role in the interpretation of the PP advocated by other authors (Gollier 2001 and Gollier and Treich 2003).

Following this approach the PP typically consists in selecting actions that yield a lower level of consumption in the present in order to protect oneself against uncertainty and irreversibility. Typically the PP would imply reduced consumption. Therefore general measures of restraint may suit some people's preferences and not others. The efficiency of general measures is also to be gauged in this respect. A good measure of precaution thus interpreted is plain option value, which depends on the decision-maker's attitude towards risk and it is equal to her maximum possible consumer surplus.

The second source of subjectivity is directly tied to uncertainty and refers to the different weights people attach to the various probability distributions. In other words, it arises from the different attitudes that rational individuals may have towards ambiguity. This is the source of subjectivity upon which our interpretation of the PP is built.

We suggest that the PP implies pessimistic behaviour, i.e. acting on the basis of a large weight given to the worst distribution of probability one can be aware of on the basis of the best available information. Moreover, the quasi-option value can be a good measure of precaution so defined and may help us to understand what is its 'cost'.

In the preceding section we made a distinction between pessimistic and optimistic attitudes. Attaching a positive value to quasi-options is a sign of cautious behaviour and of confidence that scientific progress and accumulation of knowledge make postponing decisions worthwhile. However, this element, which also highlights that precaution requires a dynamic approach,[34] is not sufficient for our interpretation of the PP based on ambiguity aversion. Indeed, an optimist might also have positive quasi-option values. On the contrary, we believe that precaution is to take a pessimist as reference point. In other words, we have to refer to an ambiguity adverse decision-maker and the measure of precaution is the quasi-option value determined on the basis of the weights she attaches to the worst probability distribution.

Attitude towards ambiguity is, therefore, crucial while individual preferences recede in the background. What counts is whether decisions are taken on the basis of what we may call the worst expectations not their effect on present consumption. In our view, keeping attitude towards ambiguity separate from utility functions helps to make it clear what precaution is really about. In a nutshell, precaution implies that dangers are taken as seriously as possible into account or we could also say that 'early warnings' are given utmost attention.[35] Despite this, catastrophes are nonetheless possible in the future and a reason is that individual preferences may lead to a not-too-cautious behaviour in the present. It seems to us that it is useful to distinguish between the role of too easy an attitude towards ambiguity (to which the PP strictly applies) and the role of individual preferences biased in favour of present consumption and welfare. Such distinction may also be helpful with respect to the policy measures to be adopted in a democratic environment to reduce the overall risk of future catastrophes.

For what it is worth, this interpretation is nothing but a first step in the direction of making the PP a useful guide to policy decisions aimed at improving social welfare. Many problems are still to be solved at the level of individual rationality but the thorniest issues refer to the society level.

The first problem is whether the PP would be adopted by the typical institutions which make social choices – the market and electoral democracy. There are very good reasons for a double negative answer. Gollier and Treich (2003) have argued that markets cannot guarantee precautionary behaviour. We strongly agree with this conclusion even though our definition of the PP is different from theirs.

Also electoral democracy seems to be an inadequate social choice mechanism from the point of view of precaution. One has only to consider that both pessimists and optimists have equal weight while only the former should count. Moreover the unequal distribution of costs and benefits and inequality in the exposures to future risks[36] may compound the risk of future catastrophes. In this respect the worst situation could be the one in which the pessimists are slightly hurt while the optimists suffer a lot. A democratic process might lead to a complete disregard of future catastrophes under such circumstances.

It is likely that a better method for making social choices is deliberative democracy, as suggested by some authors (Sunstein 2002). But the issue is too difficult and we leave it here.

Another important but neglected problem is the actual implementation of the precautionary behaviour at society level. The issue is not whether precaution will be chosen but how to implement it once chosen in some way. Our concern in the next section is specifically with enforcement problems, which are not of lesser importance given that people differ in their preferences, in exposures to risk and in attitudes to uncertainty.

Precaution in a principal–agent model

The specific problem we consider is a typical Principal–Agent problem, where the Principal conforms to the PP but has to rely on an Agent who pursues different ends. Indeed, the agency problem is the conflict which arises when the consequences of the actions do not affect the Agents entitled to decide about these actions – in other words, when the catastrophic event is an externality. To analyze this problem we set up a model which enables ambiguity, catastrophic events and agency to be treated in a single framework. There are many questions that are relevant here. We have chosen to concentrate on a couple of questions: how could an ambiguity adverse Principal motivate the Agent to act in the most favourable way for precaution? Which are the implied costs? In particular, whether a precautionary Principal has to pay the Agent more. Our model aims at casting some light on these issues, which are largely neglected despite their importance in a thorough assessment of the PP.

We assume that the Principal's utility depends on her profit and the latter depends, at least partially, on the Agent's effort.[37] For simplicity's sake, only two types of effort on the part of the Agent are assumed – low and high. The Agent's effort cannot be observed by the Principal, nor can it be inferred from the amount of profits. Hence it is assumed that the Principal's utility is stochastically related to the Agent's effort by a conditional density function. Under these circumstances the Principal has to design a compensation scheme that gives the Agent the incentive to choose the effort level that reflects the Principal's preference.

The Principal conforms to our definition of precaution. In fact she is ambiguity-averse (pessimist), with respect to the relationship between quality of effort and profit, and she has more than one additive conditional density function on contingent events. The Principal feels more confident on obtaining a high profit if the Agent selects a high effort, but she is unable to attach a unique probability to each event induced by the Agent's actions, as in the Ellesberg Paradox.

In this framework we represent ambiguity by E-capacities (Ellsberg capacities).[38] E-capacities are a representation of beliefs of the individual that considers both her probability assessments for events and the reliability (*degree of confidence*) of her probability assessments.[39]

The Principal evaluates her expected utility conditioned on the Agent's effort by combining her expected utility with respect to the most reliable probability distribution and her worst possible expected utility, each of them weighted by her degree of confidence (convex combination).[40]

The Principal maximizes her utility, which is the utility of the profit less the Agent's wage payments. More specifically, she is an E-capacity maximizer with a degree of confidence $\rho \in [0,1]$. If the information partition does not contain only single element sets and the degree of confidence ρ equals 1, there will be ambiguity about events, but the Principal feels her probability assessment is correct. If the degree of confidence ρ equals 0, the Principal will attach a set of probability distributions to events, none of which will be considered fully reliable (complete ambiguity).

Let $u(\phi) = \phi$ be the Principal utility (risk neutrality), with $\phi \in [\phi^\circ, \phi^*]$, respectively the low and high profit. Let e be the Agent's effort level, such that e could be e° (low effort) or e^* (high effort). Since the effort is not observable, the relationship between profit and the Agent's effort level is described by conditional density function $f(\phi \,|\, e)$, with $f(\phi \,|\, e) \geq 0$ for all e and $\phi \in [\phi^\circ, \phi^*]$, all of which are information consistent. It is assumed that the cumulative distribution function $F(\phi \,|\, e^*) \leq F(\phi \,|\, e^\circ)$, for all $\phi \in [\phi^\circ, \phi^*]$, with strict inequality for some f, this implies that the expected profit of the Principal given e^* is larger than e°.[41]

The Agent is a risk-averse utility maximizer with a separable utility function $u(s,e) = v(s) - \gamma(e)$, where $v(s)$ is the utility of monetary wage s and $\gamma(e)$ represents effort disutility in money, such that $\gamma(e^*) > \gamma(\gamma^\circ)$. The Agent's utility increases with s and decreases with e, at a decreasing rates; moreover $u(s,e^\circ) > u(s, e^*)$ for all s.

There is a conflict between the target of the Principal and the purpose of the Agent. Given unobservable effort and ambiguity aversion, the Principal's optimal contract solves the following problem:

$$\text{Max}_{s(\phi)} \left\{ \rho \int_{\phi^\circ}^{\phi^*} (\phi - s(\phi)) f(\phi \,|\, e) d\phi + (1-\rho) \, \min_{s(\phi), f(\phi|e)} \int_{\phi^\circ}^{\phi^*} (\phi - s(\phi)) f(\phi \,|\, e) d\phi \right\} \quad (12.4)$$

such that:

$$(i) \int_{\phi^\circ}^{\phi^*} v(s(\phi)) f(\phi \,|\, e) d\phi - \gamma(e) \geq \overline{u}$$

$$(ii) \, \text{Max}_{\overline{e}} \int_{\phi^\circ}^{\phi^*} v(s(\phi)) f(\phi| \overline{e}) d\phi - \gamma(\overline{e})$$

The condition (i) is a *participation constraint*, that exhibits the Agent expected utility at least equals to his reservation utility level $\overline{u}$, and the condition (ii) is an *incentive constraint*, that assures the Agent's optimal effort level *e*, under the compensation scheme $s(\phi)$.

Since the contract specifies effort level *e*, choosing ϕ to maximize (see Equation 12.1), it is assumed that the Principal has to minimize the expected value of Agent's wage, that is:

$$\text{Max}_{s(\phi)} \left\{ \rho \int_{\phi^\circ}^{\phi^*} -s(\phi) f(\phi \mid e) d\phi + (1-\rho) \min_{s(\phi), f(\phi \mid e)} \int_{\phi^\circ}^{\phi^*} -s(\phi) f(\phi \mid e) d\phi \right\} \tag{12.5}$$

or:

$$\text{Min}_{s(\phi)} \left\{ \rho \int_{\phi^\circ}^{\phi^*} s(\phi) f(\phi \mid e) d\phi + (1-\rho) \max_{s(\phi), f(\phi \mid e)} \int_{\phi^\circ}^{\phi^*} s(\phi) f(\phi \mid e) d\phi \right\} \tag{12.6}$$

such that

$$(i) \int_{\phi^\circ}^{\phi^*} v(s(\phi)) f(\phi \mid e) d\phi - \gamma(e) \geq \overline{u}$$

$$(ii) \text{ Max}_{\overline{e}} \int_{\phi^\circ}^{\phi^*} v(s(\phi)) f(\phi \mid \overline{e}) d\phi - \gamma(\overline{e})$$

Let us consider the case in which the Principal wants to induce the effort level *e**. The constraint (*ii*) can be written as:

$$(iii) \int_{\psi^\circ}^{\phi^*} v(s(\phi)) f(\phi \mid e^*) d\phi - \gamma(e^*) \geq \int_{\phi^\circ}^{\phi^*} v(s(\phi)) f(\phi \mid e^\circ) d\phi - \gamma(e^\circ) \tag{12.7}$$

Consider the problem in Equation 12.6 and assuming that the co-state variables are strictly positive,[42] $s(\phi)$ must to satisfy the first order condition:

$$\rho(-1) f(\phi \mid e^*) + (1-\rho)(-1) f \wedge (\phi \mid e^*) +$$
$$+ \lambda v'(s(\phi)) f(\phi \mid e^*) + \mu v'(s(\phi))[f(\phi \mid e^*) - f(\phi \mid e^\circ)] = 0$$

Where $f \wedge (\phi \mid e^*)$ is the minimum conditional density function with respect to *e** in the information consistent set.[43] Dividing by $f(\phi \mid e) v'(s(\phi))$, the first order condition becomes:

$$\rho\left(-\frac{1}{v'(s(\phi))}\right)+(1+\rho)\left(-\frac{1}{v'(s(\phi))}\frac{f^\wedge(\phi\,|\,e^*)}{f(\phi\,|\,e^*)}\right)+\lambda+\mu\left[1-\frac{f(\phi\,|\,e^\circ)}{f(\phi\,|\,e^*)}\right]=0 \quad (12.8)$$

or:

$$\frac{1}{v'(s(\phi))}\left[\rho+(1-\rho)\frac{f^\wedge(\phi\,|\,e^*)}{f(\phi\,|\,e^*)}\right]=\lambda+\mu\left[1-\frac{f(\phi\,|\,e^\circ)}{f(\phi\,|\,e^*)}\right] \quad (12.9)$$

As a consequence, the wage varies with ρ and it can decrease or increase when ρ increases.

Consider the case in which $\rho=1$, then:

$$\frac{1}{v'(s(\phi))}=\lambda+\mu\left[1-\frac{f(\phi\,|\,e^\circ)}{f(\phi\,|\,e^*)}\right] \quad (12.10)$$

When $\rho=0$, then:

$$\frac{1}{v'(s(\phi))}\frac{f^\wedge(\phi\,|\,e^*)}{f(\phi\,|\,e^*)}=\lambda+\mu\left[1-\frac{f(\phi\,|\,e^\circ)}{f(\phi\,|\,e^*)}\right]$$

or:

$$\frac{1}{v'(s(\phi))}=\frac{f(\phi\,|\,e^*)}{f^\wedge(\phi\,|\,e^*)}\left\{\lambda+\mu\left[1-\frac{f(\phi\,|\,e^\circ)}{f(\phi\,|\,e^*)}\right]\right\} \quad (12.11)$$

The above results show that the optimal wage depends on the Principal's ambiguity aversion. In order to grasp the meaning of this result one should bear in mind that, on the basis of our assumptions, the higher effort e^* is optimal also when the Principal ignores ambiguity or has a less pessimistic attitude. Therefore, the change in the wage function does not have the goal of inducing the effort e^* whereas the lower effort e° would be chosen with less pessimistic probabilities or disregarding ambiguity.

Due to ambiguity, it may very well happen that the more pessimistic probabilities alter the expected utilities attached by the Principal to different ϕ. This in turn implies that in order to maximize her utility the Principal will associate higher or lower wage to the various observed results.

Comparing Equations 12.11 and 12.10 it comes out that when the Principal is ambiguity averse ($\rho=0$), the optimal wage is lower (respectively higher) than the compensation paid when the Principal ignores ambiguity if $f^\wedge(\phi\,|\,e^*)>f(\phi\,|\,e^*)$ (respectively $f^\wedge(\phi\,|\,e^*)<f(\phi\,|\,e^*)$). Roughly speaking, under ambiguity aversion the Principal will pay less for 'bad outcomes', which are more likely given $f^\wedge(\phi\,|\,e^*)$ than given $f(\phi\,|\,e^*)$. Instead, she will pay more for 'good outcomes', which are more likely given $f(\phi\,|\,e^*)$ than $f^\wedge(\phi\,|\,e^*)$.

This means that ambiguity aversion does not necessarily imply that the Principal has to pay more to motivate the Agent; therefore it does not systematically cause a higher amount of agency costs because the incentive scheme is not monotonic even if there are only two outcomes. What is crucial is how the probability of good and bad outcomes changes when evaluated on the basis of the worst distribution.

Concluding remarks

The PP addresses a question of utmost importance in modern societies: how do we behave when there is a threat of serious damages but we know too little about the probability of their occurrence?

The answers so far given to this question and the corresponding interpretations of the PP are in most cases completely unsatisfactory. This is so because two crucial and awkward issues have been dodged: how the PP relates to individual rationality, and how some collective problems (including inequalities of different types) interfere with its application at society level.

In this chapter we have gone into some aspects of these two problems. In particular, as far as individual rationality is concerned, we have argued that uncertainty and irreversibility are essential features of the analytical framework to be adopted. This has allowed us to go beyond the too simplistic juxtaposition of strong and weak interpretations of the principle. We have put particular emphasis on ambiguity aversion which seems to capture a basic feature of the PP, i.e. that decisions should be based on the less favourable probability distribution of future negative events that present knowledge may justify. Indeed, we suggest that the PP is fulfilled when the decision is that which would be made by an ambiguity-adverse agent. This is the way in which we suggest to reconcile the PP with rationality. Individual preferences are less important in our definition of the PP, though they are important in determining the risk of catastrophes. For the reason given in this chapter we believe that it is useful to draw a clear distinction between attitude to ambiguity on the one hand, and individual preferences, on the other, making the former the realm of the PP. We have also shown how quasi-option value can provide a good measure of precaution thus interpreted.

As to the problems that the PP poses at society level – the other big question – we have recalled how difficult it is to reconcile the PP both with the market and the voting mechanism but we have more fully analyzed a specific implementation problem: how a neutral Agent should be compensated by an ambiguity-adverse Principal to elicit the effort which is the best guarantee against future catastrophic events. As our model has shown, this compensation scheme need not be more costly than one which would be adopted by a Principal who does not follow the PP. But these are only preliminary results. Much remains to be done, to give the PP stronger bases and, possibly, a wider appeal.

Appendix

Let g be an act, such that $g: \Omega \to C$, and let C be the set of finite consequences. Let $\{E_1,\dots,E_n\}$ be a partition of Ω with probabilities $p(E_i)$, such that $\sum_{i=1}^{n} p(E_i) = 1$, that is a partition of *unambiguous events*. Given an additive probability distribution π on Ω, let $\Pi(p)$ be the set of *information consistent* additive probabilities, such that

$$\prod(p) := \left\{ \pi \in \Delta(\Omega) \middle| \sum_{\omega \in E_i} \pi(\omega) = p(E_i) \right\}$$

with $i = 1,2,\dots, n$ and for all $A \in \Omega$ let $\beta_i(A): \Omega \to \{0, 1\}$, such that $\beta_i(A) \to \{1$ if $E_i \subseteq A$; 0 otherwise$\}$ be the function characterizing events including at least one unambiguous event (Eichberger and Kelsey 1999: 118).

Due to ambiguity aversion, the Principal has to consider all the set of conditional probability distributions compatible with her incomplete information on the basis of her degree of confidence $\rho \in [0,1]$. Consequently, the *E-capacity* $\upsilon(\pi, \rho)$ is:

$$\upsilon(A \mid \pi, \rho) = \sum_{i=1}^{n} [\rho \pi(A \cap E_i) + (1-\rho)p(E_i)\beta_i(A) \forall A \in \Omega.$$

Notes

1 Marcello Basili, Dipartimento di Economia Politica, Facoltà di Economia R. Goodwin, Università di Siena, Piazza San Francesco 7, 53100 Siena Italy, email basili@unisi.it

2 Maurizio Franzini, Dipartimento di Economia Pubblica, Università di Roma La Sapienza, Via Castro Laurenziano 9, Roma, Italy, email maurizio.franzini@uniroma1.it

3 For example, it was mentioned in the 1974 law on the acid rains phenomenon (Boehmer-Christiansen 1994).

4 There are, however, good reasons to argue that it first appeared in April 1980 when, concerned about the protection of the ozone layer, the European Community Council suggested the reduction of the emissions of CFC gases, which at that time were not yet considered responsible for the phenomenon.

5 The precise formulation was, 'accepting that in order to protect the North Sea from possibly damaging effects of the most dangerous substances, a precautionary principle is necessary which may require action to control inputs of such substances even before a causal link has been established by absolutely clear scientific evidence' (Sunstein 2003: 9).

6 The statement was, 'In order to achieve sustainable development, policies must be based on the precautionary principle … . Where there are threats of serious and irreversible damage, lack of full scientific uncertainty should not be use as a reason for postponing measures to prevent environmental degradation' (Sunstein 2003: 4). It is to be noticed that this definition is not much different from the Rio Declaration, the only difference, in fact not a minor one, being the lack of reference to the cost-effectiveness of the precautionary measures.

7 The Declaration was issued at the United Nation Conference on Environment and Development held in Rio de Janeiro in June 2002.

8 This quotation is to be found in the European Union Treaty, Article 130R (1993) currently Article 174.

9 For a detailed account of the development and the application of the PP in the EU see Majone (2002) and Löfstedt (2004).

10 According to Sandin 1999 (quoted by Löfstedt 2004: 10) there are at least 19 definitions of the PP. Majone (2002: 93) reminds us also that for the original German principle there are no fewer than 11 interpretations.

11 In 1998, environmentalists met at Wingspread in Wisconsin, where they issued the following Declaration, 'When an activity raises threats of harm to human health or the environment, precautionary measures should be taken even if some cause and effects relationships are not established scientifically. In this context the proponent of the activity rather than the public should bear the burden of proof' (Sunstein 2003: 4). This is the official meaning of the PP according to most environmentalists.

12 See also European Commission (2001).

13 The critique levelled by Manson against the strong PP, which Morris (2000: 8) refers to, can be understood as an example of this possibility.

14 In the already mentioned 2000 Communication, the European Commission stressed that the PP has to do with risk management, 'Application of the precautionary principle is part of risk management, where scientific uncertainty precluded a full assessment of the risk and when decision-makers consider that the chosen level of environmental protection of human animal and plant health may be in jeopardy'.

15 Frequently cited episodes range from the EU ban on hormones in beef to genetically modified organisms (Löfstedt 2004: 14, and Majone 2002: 95).

16 Details are in Wald (1950) and Arrow and Hurwicz (1972).

17 If the decision-maker is risk averse she prefers to get the expected value of a gamble rather than the gamble. On the other hand, if the decision-maker is risk loving, she prefers a gamble to its expected value.

18 For a survey, see Camerer (1999).

19 For instance she has a partition of the set of events that is just a rough representation of the actual ones, in the sense that she might believe that there are other 'finer' partitions that she is just not able to see.

20 Australian aborigines do not cultivate land but they are 'firestick farmers' who light bush fires to manage the environment and control vegetation and the creatures that feed on it.

21 Wild land larger than Austria is deforested every year.

22 Recently, it was pointed out that transgenic DNA introgressed into traditional maize landraces in Oaxaca, Mexico (Quist and Chapela 2001). If this contamination were to prove extensive it would be impossible to remove fragments of genetically modified DNA from the genome of traditional plants and the infiltration will last forever.

23 It is assumed that technological progress induces substitution between natural and synthetic resources, but it is impossible to produce synthetic substitutes if whaling, pollution and chemical insecticides extinguish whale and polliniferous insects.

24 See for details Fisher *et al.* (1972).

25 Production of a genetically modified organism (GMO) is an example of uncertain event. There is ambiguity about the link between growing GMO, loss of biodiversity and contamination or infestation of natural plants; moreover there is ambiguity about the relationship between GMO and human health.

26 If 'the criterion function is quadratic, the planning problem for the case of uncertainty can be reduced to the problem for the case of certainty simply replacing, in computation of the optimal first period action, the certainty future values of variables by their unconditional expectations. In this sense, the unconditional expected values of these variables may be regarded as a set of sufficient statistics for the entire joint probability distribution, or alternatively as a set of certainty equivalence' (Simon 1956: 74). Malinvaud (1969) generalizes the applicability of the certainty equivalent method to risky situations in which the payoff function is not quadratic but the functions involved are twice differentiable. However, this approach is inapplicable with irreversibility, which introduces discontinuity in the derivatives of either functions or payoff.

27 A disinvestment opportunity (partial reversibility) is equivalent to a put option and the act to disinvest is equivalent to exercise such an option.

28 If the spanning assumption does not hold, it is possible to value the investment project and the decision to invest by dynamic programming with an exogenous discount rate (Pindyck 1991: 1116).

29 Real option approaches are applied especially to real-estate investments and development decisions – pharmaceutical, aerospace and consumer electronics industries (Merton 1998, and Triantis 2000).

30 If the decision-maker ignores ambiguity, she replays random variables with their Choquet expected values. As a result, benefits under uncertainty are at most equal to benefits under certainty and the method based on Choquet Certainty Equivalent also fails to solve decision problems characterized by ambiguity and irreversibility.

31 If the decision-maker were pessimistic the capacity would be convex, but other things would be equal.

32 If a non-linear pricing rule holds, there might be an interval of prices within which the agent neither buys nor sells short the asset, that is she shows *inertia* (e.g. Dow and Werlang 1992, Simonsen and Werlang 1991, and Basili and Fontini 2001).

33 The faith in likelihood of events represents the weight of evidence, which can be measured by $[1 - \nu(s_i) - \nu(s_i^c)]$ for all $s_i \in \Sigma$. Obviously, if there is a unique and additive probability measure of S, the capacity will be equal to its dual, the upper and lower Choquet integrals will collapse to the standard Lebesgue integral and a unique investment opportunity value will be obtained. In this case the bid and ask spread can be considered as transaction costs, asymmetric information, etc.

34 In the light of this consideration it is surprising that the PP has been the object of criticisms precisely because it is considered too static a criterion, leading to once and for all decisions. This may be the consequence either of bad applications of the principle or of faulty interpretations of it. Rubin (2000: 120) asserts, 'As we saw earlier, the precautionary principle puts a premium on the hopes and fears of the present moment in its risk, averse efforts to protect a given status quo. At the same time, its propensity to act on the basis of incomplete knowledge, discounts greatly the usefulness of acquired knowledge. In essence, then, it presents us with a relatively static view of human possibilities. While it purports to be making protective decisions with an eye to the long run, it really privileges our current hopes, fears, abilities and knowledge'.

35 The importance of 'early warnings' is stressed in the volume by Harremoës *et al.* (2002). To behave as an ambiguous adverse agent is, in our view, the best (or, probably, the only) manner for giving proper consideration to those pieces of information which are 'early warnings'.

36 See Chapter 4 by Faucheux and O'Connor.

37 Our model has several features in common with the one developed in Mas-Colell *et al.* (1995).

38 E-capacities (Ellsberg capacities) are a 'parameterized version of a capacity based on an additive probability distribution that makes it possible to include known probabilities for a partition of unambiguous events' (Eichberger and Kelsey 1999:133). E-capacities were introduced by Ellsberg (1961) and were axiomatized by Eichberger and Kelsey (1999) to accommodate the observed Ellsberg Paradox with the decision theory.

39 See the Appendix.

40 The Choquet integral of an E-capacity 'is a weighted average of the expected utility with regard to an additive probability distribution and the worst expected outcome obtained in the unambiguous events [and] this Choquet integral is identical to a representation of preferences over actions suggested in Ellsberg' (Eichberger and Kelsey 1999: 133).

41 $F(\phi \mid e^*) \leq F(\phi \mid e^o)$ implies first order stochastic dominance.

42 The co-state variables equal to zero are either impossible or induce the violation of the constraints.

43 If the information consistent set only includes singleton there is no ambiguity and the degree of confidence does not matter.

References

Anscombe F.J., and R. Aumann, (1963) 'A definition of subjective probability', *Annals of Mathematical Statistics*, 34, 199–205.

Arrow, K.J. and Hurwicz L. (1972) 'An optimal criterion for decision making under ignorance', in C.F. Carter and J.L. Ford (eds), *Uncertainty and Expectations in Economics*, Oxford: Basil Blackwell.

Arrow, K.J. and A. Fisher (1974) 'Environmental preservation, uncertainty and irreversibility', *Quarterly Journal of Economics*, 89, 312–19.

Basili, M. (2001) 'Knightian uncertainty in financial markets: an assessment', *Economic Notes*, 1: 1–26

Basili, M. and Fontini, F. (2001) 'No-trade in financial markets with uncertainty', *Proceedings of the Second International Symposium on Imprecise Probabilities and Their Applications*, ISIPTA 2001: 27–31.

Boehmer-Christiansen, S. (1994) 'Politics and environmental management', *Journal of Environmental Planning and Management*, 37: 69–85.

Camerer, C. (1999) 'Ambiguity aversion and non-additive probability: experimental evidence, model and application', in L. Luini, (ed.), *Uncertain Decisions: Bridging theory and experiments*, Boston, MA, Dordrecht and London: Kluwer Academic.

Choquet, G. (1954) 'Theory of capacity', *Annales de l'Institute Fourier*, 5: 131–295.

Dow, J. and Werlang S.R.C. (1992) 'Uncertainty aversion, risk aversion, and the optimal choice of portfolio', *Econometrica*, 60: 197–204.

Eichberger, J. and D. Kelsey (1999) 'E-capacity and the Ellsberg paradox', *Theory and Decision*, 46: 107–40

Ellsberg, D. (1961) 'Risk, ambiguity and the Savage axioms', *Quarterly Journal of Economics*, 75: 643–69.

European Commission (2001) *Strategy for a Future Chemicals Policy*, Brussels: European Commission.

Fisher, A.C., Krutilla, J.V. and Cicchetti, C.J. (1972) 'The economics of environmental preservation: a theoretical and empirical analysis', *American Economic Review*, 57: 605–19.

Freestone, D. and Hey, E. (1996) 'Origins and development of the precautionary principle', in D. Freestone and E. Hey (eds), *The Precautionary Principle and International Law: The Challenge of Implementation*, The Hague: Kluwer Law International.

Gilboa, I. (1987) 'Expected utility theory with purely subjective non-additive probabilities', *Journal of Mathematical Economics*, 16: 65–88.

Gilboa, I. and Schmeidler D. (1989) 'Maximin expected utility with non-unique prior', in *Journal of Mathematical Economics*, 18: 141–53.

Gollier, C. (2001) 'Precautionary principle. The economic perspective', *Economic Policy*, 16: 302–27

Gollier, C. and N. Treich (2003) 'Decision-making under scientific uncertainty: the economics of the precautionary principle', *Journal of Risk and Uncertainty*, 27: 77–103.

Goodin, R.E. (1980) 'No moral nukes', in *Ethics*, 90: 417–49

Harremoës P., Gee. D. MacGarvin, M., Stirling, A., Keys, J., Wynne, B. and Guedes Vaz (2002) *The Precautionary Principle in the 20th Century. Late Lessons from Early Warnings*, London: Earthscan.

Henry, C. (1974a) 'Option values in the economics of irreplaceable assets', *Review of Economic Studies*, 41: 89–104.

Henry, C. (1974b) 'Investment decision under uncertainty: the irreversible effect', *American Economic Review*, 64: 1006–12.

Löfstedt, R.E. (2004) 'The swing of the regulatory pendulum in Europe: from precautionary principle to (regulatory) impact analysis', *Journal of Risk and Uncertainty*, 28: 237–60.

Majone, G. (2002) 'What price safety? The precautionary principle and its policy implications', *Journal of Common Market Studies*, 40: 89–109.

Malinvaud E. (1969) 'First order certainty equivalence', *Econometrica*, 37: 706–18.

Mas-Collel, A., Whinston, M.D. and Green, J.R. (1995) *Microeconomic Theory*, New York: Oxford University Press.

Mazur, A. (1996) 'Why do we worry about trace poisons?', http://fplc.edu/RISK/vol7/winter/mazur.htm.

Merton, R.C. (1998) 'Application of option-pricing theory: twenty-five years later', *American Economic Review*, 88: 323–49.

Morris, J. (2000) 'Defining the precautionary principle', in J. Morris (ed.), *Rethinking risk and the precautionary principle*, Oxford: Butterworth-Heinemann.

Pearce, D.W. (1980) 'The preconditions for achieving consensus in the context of technological risk', in M. Dierkes, S. Edwards and R. Coppock (eds), *Technological Risk: Its Perception and Handling in the European Community*, Cambridge, MA: Oelgeschlager, Gunn and Hain Publishers.

Pindyck, R.S. (1991) 'Irreversibility, uncertainty, and investment', *Journal of Economic Literature*, 29: 1110–48.

Quist, D. and Chapela I.H. (2001) 'Transgenic DNA introgressed into traditional maize landraces in Oaxaca, Mexico', *Nature*, 414: 541–3.

Rubin, C.T. (2000) 'Asteroid collisions and precautionary thinking', in J. Morris (ed.), *Rethinking Risk and Precautionary Principle*, Oxford: Butterworth-Heinemann.

Sandin, P. (1999) 'Dimensions of the precautionary principle', *Human and Ecological Risk Assessment*, 6: 889–907.

Savage, L.J. (1954) *The Foundation of Statistics*, New York: John Wiley and Sons. (1972) revised and enlarged edition, Dover: New York.

Schmeidler, D. (1989) 'Subjective probability and expected utility without additivity', *Econometrica*, 57: 571–87.

Simon, H.A. (1956) 'Dynamic programming under uncertainty with a quadratic function', *Econometrica*, 24: 74–81.

Simonsen, M.H. and Werlang, S.R.C. (1991) 'Subadditive probabilities and portfolio inertia', *Revista de Econometrica*, 11: 1–19.

Sunstein, C.R. (2002) *Risk and Reason. Safety, Law, and the Environment*, Cambridge: Cambridge University Press.

Sunstein, C.R. (2003) 'Beyond the precautionary principle', *John M. Olin & Economics Working Paper* No. 149, University of Chicago.

Treich, N. (2001) 'What is the economic meaning of the precautionary principle?', *The Geneva Papers on Risk and Insurance* 26: 334–45.

Triantis, A. J. (2000) 'Real options and corporate risk management', *Journal of Applied Corporate Finance*, 15: 64–73.

Von Neumann, J. and Morgenstern, O. (1944) *Theory of Games and Economic Behavior*, Princeton, NJ: Princeton University Press.

Wald, A. (1950) *Statistical Theory Decisions*, Wiley: New York.

Wildavsky, A. (2000) 'Trial and error versus trial without error', in J. Morris (ed.), *Rethinking Risk and the Precautionary Principle*, Oxford: Butterworth-Heinemann.

Index